# IMPROVE
# YOUR ENGLISH

# IMPROVE YOUR ENGLISH

## THE ESSENTIAL GUIDE TO ENGLISH GRAMMAR, PUNCTUATION AND SPELLING

J E Metcalfe and C Astle

**RIGHT WAY**

Constable & Robinson Ltd
55–56 Russell Square
London
WC1B 4HP
www.constablerobinson.com

First published by Right Way, an imprint of Constable & Robinson, 2013

Originally published in the title *Correct English* in 1995,
material having been drawn from *The Right Way to Improve Your English*,
*How Good is Your English?* and *The Right Way to Spell*.

A copy of the British Library Cataloguing in Publication Data
is available from the British Library

ISBN: 978-0-7160-2345-6

Printed and bound in the EU

1 3 5 7 9 10 8 6 4 2

# CONTENTS

**The English Language**     1

## PART 1: GRAMMAR AND PUNCTUATION

**Introduction**     11

**Grammar and Punctuation Checklist**     14

| | | |
|---|---|---|
| **1.** | Parts of Speech | 17 |
| **2.** | Verbs | 33 |
| **3.** | Pronouns | 51 |
| **4.** | The Sentence and the Paragraph | 67 |
| **5.** | Punctuation | 83 |
| **6.** | Common Mistakes | 127 |
| **7.** | Oddities of the Language | 161 |

## PART 2: SPELLING AND VOCABULARY

**Introduction**     179

| | | |
|---|---|---|
| **8.** | Word Formation | 183 |
| **9.** | Spelling Rules and Conventions | 253 |
| **10.** | Notes on Selected Words | 275 |

**Index**     312

# THE ENGLISH LANGUAGE

The supremacy of English as a world language is a relic of the age when Great Britain was an important world power. The inhabitants of the huge chunks of territory which in old atlases were coloured pink enjoyed the benefits of learning English from explorers, travellers, missionaries and settlers. It is rather remarkable that today, despite minor idiomatic and spelling differences, American custom, an infinity of verbal differences, and diverse political constitutions, there is general consistency in written English throughout the world.

Speech, of course, is far, far older than writing, and the development of the written language from the spoken in different parts of the world is an absorbing subject. The symbols of language, formed to represent objects, actions or syllables of speech, developed, in time, into *characters* which could be combined to form *words*. The first language to be written was Sumerian, which began as simple pictures and which can be traced as far back as 3100 BC.

The Canaanites are said to have developed the first *alphabet* in the middle of the second millennium BC. The convenience of this method of writing led to its adoption by other Semitic peoples and the ancient Greeks, and, while each nation developed its own, the scripts were all based on Canaanite characters. Today there are Hebrew, Greek, Cyrillic, Arabic and Latin alphabets, besides the bewilderingly vast range of characters of the Far East (China and Japan). The Latin or Roman alphabet, now the most widely used in the world, is a derivative of archaic Greek script. The word *alphabet* is so named from the first two letters of the Greek alphabet, *alpha* and *beta*, which in turn were named after the first two signs of the Phoenician alphabet *aleph* and *beth*. Also derived from the Greek alphabet is Cyrillic script, used in Russia, Bulgaria and some Balkan states, originally by members of the Orthodox Church, and called after St Cyril who died in AD 869.

With Julius Caesar's incursions into Britain in 55 and 54 BC, the native Britons perhaps picked up a few Latin expressions and words but, unlike the invaders, they knew nothing about writing. What happened, then, to the only "real" British languages which existed before the Romans came? These languages, themselves derived from even older forms of speech, were the original Celtic tongues, which, most remarkably, had little effect on the development of English. Today they survive in Gaelic, Irish, Welsh, Manx and Cornish, but not in English, despite the fact that English is a mixture of several languages.

It was probably not until the beginning of the real Roman occupation, about a hundred years after Julius Caesar, that the Roman alphabet was introduced into Britain. For a few centuries writing was practised only by monks and other scholars, being chiefly for ecclesiastical and legal documents and in Latin. We read so much today that it is difficult to imagine a time when hardly anybody did any reading. For centuries people passed their time in other ways; perhaps they conversed far more than they do now, and stories would be told by travelling storytellers and bards. Even kings and other leaders had to employ scribes. Monks busied themselves in writing original works or copying others in beautiful manuscript, but "ordinary" people did not need to read them, even if they could.

The development of English took place over a very long time, during which most of the people in Britain were quite content with the spoken language, based on the speech of the sixth-century Anglo-Saxon invaders. Latin persisted, later invaders from

Scandinavia brought much of their language, and the Norman Conquest of 1066 brought French. By the thirteenth century three languages were in use – Latin for scholars, ecclesiastics, philosophers and lawyers, French for the aristocracy, and English for the rest.

The schools began teaching English about 1300 and English was at last permissible in the law courts in 1362. Gradually the various languages mingled, and Geoffrey Chaucer's *Canterbury Tales*, for example, probably written after 1373, was written in an attractive mixture of English and French. Chaucer has been accused of using too many French words as an affectation, but French was certainly more elegant, more melodious, than the written and spoken English of the time. Chaucer was not alone in trying to improve the language, and the following passage, written in 1385, not only shows the awareness of sensitive people to the imperfections of English but is an example of the extraordinary written language of the period:

"As it is knowe how meny maner peple beeth in this lond; there beeth also so many dyvers longages and tongs. Notheless Walsche men and Scots that beeth nought medled with other nations, holdeth wel nyh hir firste longage and speche; . . . but the Flemynges that woneth in the west side of Wales, having left her strange spech, and speketh sexonliche now. Also Englishe men, they had from the bygynnynge thre maner speche: northerns, sowtherne, and middel speche in the middel of the londe, as they come of three maner of peple of Germania: notheless by commyxtion and mellynge first with Danes, and afterwards with Normans, in meny the contrary longage is apayred [corrupted]. . . . All the longage of the Northumbers, and specialliche at York, is so scharp, flitting and frotynge, and unschape, that we southerne men may that langage unethe understonde."

*The Canterbury Tales* shows that in Chaucer's time (c. 1345–1400) Southern English consisted of Anglo-Saxon and Old French. The philosophers and scientists introduced a number of Greek and Arabic words, while the musicians and artists gave us some Italian and Dutch. Later, explorers and their men brought words from the East, from India, China and Malaya.

The English language is thus a hotch-potch of other languages, and the gradual changes have divided its history into three chronological periods known as Old English, Middle English and Modern English. The Old English period is considered to have ended about 1150 and the Middle English period about 1500, since when Modern English has been enriched by countless influences and additions from many other languages to become the English of today.

The "rules" of Modern English have evolved from the speakers of the language through custom, usage and logic, even if at times the logic appears to be curious. There has been an urge, especially important in law, to distinguish between shades of meaning. There has been a wish to avoid tiresome queries and explanations between two persons in conversation. There has been anxiety to express much in little. There has been, above all, the unconscious human desire for orderliness, for that certain kind of discipline which has embraced the other desirable qualities of communication in our language – writing and reading.

The innovation which did more than anything to encourage the use of writing, and *eventually* to encourage more people to learn to read, was the invention of printing in the middle of the fifteenth century. Latin was still the language of the learned, and most of the early printed books were in Latin. Then, with the influx of other languages, came the development of written English with its confused vagaries of grammar and spelling. Before the introduction of printing, one or two monks in their manuscripts had attempted spelling reforms, but when the printers came on the scene they had authors at their mercy. Between 1480 and 1660 they had become accustomed to their own conventions, and ideas of "correct" and "incorrect" spelling were not considered. William Caxton and other early printers tended to adopt the Middle English word patterns of the scribes without, however, any standardisation.

The gradual spread of literacy from the sixteenth century, accompanied by a surge in the publication of printed matter, led a number of scholars to appreciate that inconsistency was an embarrassment.

As the English-speaking world became more organised, as communications developed, as more people became educated, as trade intensified, as ability to read and write became essential, as competition grew, as people's outlooks broadened, as travel became practicable, it became evident that discipline and consistency in the language were not only desirable but necessary. Writers realised that there must be no doubt about meaning, and elimination of doubt could be made possible by observing a certain consistency.

Inconsistency, of course, is still with us, and it can baffle many people. Others, accustomed to British English, appear to resent, even occasionally be enraged by, American spelling, pronunciation, usage, phraseology, idiom and meanings. Such emotion is unjustified, for the Americans have had over three hundred years to develop their own kind of English. When we consider the history of America – at least the history since the arrival of the Europeans – and the mixture of the races that have made it, we should be flattered that they have adopted *our* language and no other nation's.

The English introduced into Virginia in 1607 and into Massachusetts in 1620 was the English of the seventeenth century, and naturally the subsequent evolution followed by the language in America differed somewhat from the evolution followed in Britain. It is surprising that after four centuries the two kinds of English have so much in common, for it is only in the last hundred and fifty years that the speed of communication has tended to neutralise the differences between the two. With the global increase of American influence, some parts of the world have adopted American English simply because they have known no other.

On the subject of inconsistency, it may be entertaining to quote from a work by John Hart. Published in 1569, the work bore the long title *An Orthographie conteyning the due order and reason, howe to paint thimage of mannes voice, most like to the life or nature*. Hart wrote:

> "But in the moderne and present maner of writing (aswell of certaine other languages as of our English) there is such confusion and disorder, as it may be accounted rather a kinde of ciphring, or such a darke kinde of writing, as the best and readiest wit that ever hath bene, could, or that is or shalbe, can or may, by the only gift of reason, attaine to the ready and perfite reading thereof, without a long and tedious labour, for that it is unfit and wrong shapen for the proportion of the voice."

As well as a "kinde of writing" and "perfite" reading most of us, too, have to do a great deal of talking. But speech is different from writing; it is so ephemeral that some minor errors of construction are often overlooked, and many conversations, if put into cold print, would shock by their apparent immaturity of language. Besides the minor errors of construction there are often other common errors such as "Between you and I" and "He ought to, didn't he?"

English pronunciation varies not only between the different English-speaking countries but also – most of all, in fact – between the different regions of the United Kingdom, and, within reason, you can pronounce words as you please as long as your pronunciation is acceptable.

Unlike pronunciation the grammar of a language is not very flexible, and differs little from one generation to another. Idioms and usage are more flexible, changing not only from age to age but also from county to county. The vocabulary of a language, however, is undergoing constant change. Words change in meaning, words in different parts of a country acquire different meanings, and new words are introduced from year to year.

What, then, is good English? The shortest answer to this question is probably "English which is grammatical and is spelt correctly." It is by no means the complete answer, however, for a prose passage can be grammatically and orthographically correct but stultified by such faults as weakness in the choice and order of words, using many more words than are necessary, going a long way round to say something (circumlocution), using well-worn and overworked groups of words (clichés), ambiguity, imprecision, "commercial English", all forms of padding, and that strange obscurity which turns a rat-catcher into a rodent operative.

The prose writer should also be sparing in the use of foreign words and phrases. A foreign word or phrase may be used if there is no exactly suitable word or phrase in English, or, occasionally, if it effects an economy in writing. But the use of too many alien expressions may offend the reader who does not know what they mean. Care should be taken, too, with quotations. Time spent in checking the exact words of a quoted author should not be grudged. Shakespeare's line from *The Merchant of Venice*, "All that glisters is not gold," is often misquoted as "All is not gold that glitters," and one year the misquotation even appeared in a literary year book.

The grammar and vocabulary of the English language can form a most engrossing study, and it is hoped that your interest in them will be stimulated by this book.

As Ralph Waldo Emerson, in *Letters and Social Aims,* truly said: "Language is a city, to the building of which every human being brought a stone."

PART 1

# GRAMMAR
# AND PUNCTUATION

# INTRODUCTION

Grammar is the basis of a language, the framework on which ideas are hung, and the loftiest imagery of thought can fall flat if ungrammatically expressed. It exists in any language long before the language comes to be written, for grammar and punctuation are largely based on logic which in turn is based on fundamental linguistic premises.

Broadly, English grammar is based on the grammars of the languages from which English is derived. The earliest source was the old Anglo-Saxon, or Germanic, so called from the Angli, a Germanic tribe which settled in Britain in the fifth and sixth centuries, and it is strange that the original languages of these islands survive only in the Celtic and Cymric tongues, such as Gaelic and Welsh.

Scholars added Latin, and in the eleventh century the Danes brought Scandinavian. The Normans introduced a great deal of French to the language; Greek and Arabic words were introduced by philosophers and scientists, musicians and artists gave us some Italian and Dutch. Later Indian, Chinese and Malayan words were brought by Eastern explorers.

Since 1500 there have been changes in literary and conversational style, changes in usage, changes in the meanings of words, changes in spelling, and changes in the order of words ("syntax"), but grammar has hardly changed at all. The fundamental rules now observed and to be respected, in fact, are the rules observed by the Elizabethan writers.

In discussing English grammar we assume it to be mainly the grammar of prose. In great poetry and in good verse, however, it is remarkable how, in spite of scansion, rhyme, and the order of words and phrases, little or no grammatical fault can be found, and refuge is taken in "poetic licence" infrequently. Poetry is not meant to be strictly analysed but, if it is, it is usually found to consist of a series of grammatically-constructed sentences.

We may not be aspiring poets but we all have to do a certain amount of writing today, writing that is not intended for publication, and these notes are for the guidance of those who know they are hazy about English and want to improve, those who think they are writing good English but would be surprised at their numerous mistakes, and those who are interested in the English language for its own sake.

A person who is brought up to love books and respect authorship will naturally take an interest in the way things are written, will gradually come to recognise good writing, and will try to instil the essential qualities into his own writing, no matter what sort of writing he may be doing.

If we were to make a list of well-known writers – novelists, journalists, essayists and others – in whose work little grammatical fault could be found, the list would be pleasingly long. But even those who normally write grammatically and tolerably well sometimes make mistakes. The most respected writers can nod occasionally. Many people write too hastily, and their work, especially in the fields of learning, science, industry and business, is such that few people in their ordinary business take time to revise anything they have written. Dictation is not conducive to good writing, and should be restricted to the preparation of a first draft which must be painstakingly amended before the final version is produced.

Many university graduates with excellent degrees tend to believe that grammar, punctuation, spelling and syntax do not matter. Indeed, empires have been built by those who do not know their adverbs from their adjectives or their "principles" from their "principals". But "good English" distinguishes the professional from the amateur, and most of us cannot afford to write "its" for "it's" or to use a colon where a comma is needed. Messages may be too easily misunderstood if we get the fundamentals wrong.

# GRAMMAR AND PUNCTUATION CHECKLIST

1.  PARTS OF SPEECH                                                    17
    **Adjectives**                                                    21
        *Articles, 22.*
    **Adverbs**                                                       22
    **Conjunctions**                                                  23
        *"But", 26; Conjunctive phrases, 26; "Since", "for",*
        *"as", 28; Starting sentences, 24.*
    **Interjections**                                                 32
    **Nouns**                                                         18
        *Plurals, 19; Possessives, 19.*
    **Prepositions**                                                  29
        *Other uses of prepositions, 31; The placing of prepositions, 30.*
    **Pronouns**                                                      23
    **Verbs**                                                         20

2.  VERBS                                                             33
    **The conditional**                                               42
    **The imperative**                                                44
    **The infinitive**                                                33
        *Omission of "to" from the infinitive, 35; The split infinitive, 34.*
    **Participles**                                                   36
        *Verbs ending in "t" or "d", 37.*
    **Past-tense construction**                                       36
    **Present-tense construction**                                    35
    **"Shall" and "will"**                                            39
    **The subjunctive**                                               43
    **Transitive and intransitive verbs**                            45
        *"Lay" and "lie", 45.*
    **The verb "to be"**                                              48
        *"Am I not?", 49; The complement, 48; Ellipsis with "to be"*
        *and "to have", 49; Singular and plural, 48.*

3.  PRONOUNS                                                          51
    **Demonstrative pronouns**                                        52
        *"All", 56; "Either and neither", 54; "None", 54; "Some", 56.*
    **Indefinite pronouns**                                           64
        *"Every", 64; "It", 65.*
    **Interrogative pronouns**                                        61
        *"What", 62.*

Personal pronouns 51
Possessive pronouns 62
Relative pronouns 57
*"Which" and "that", 58; "Who" and "whom", 57; "Whose", 58.*

4.  THE SENTENCE AND THE PARAGRAPH 67
Sentences 67
*The object of a sentence, 70; Subject and predicate, 69;
Subjective and objective pronouns, 71.*
Compound sentences 71
*"Also", 77; Connecting the parts of a sentence, 73; "Only", 76;
Parenthesis, 74; Syntax, 75.*
Paragraphs 77
*Arrangement of ideas, 79; Misuses of the language, 80;*
Numerals 75

5.  PUNCTUATION 83
The apostrophe 120
*Omitted letters, 122; Possession, 121.*
Brackets 118
*Square brackets, 119.*
Capital letters 124
*Small capitals, 125.*
The colon 97
*The colon as a link, 97; The colon with quotations, 98.*
The comma 85
*Commas in enumeration, 87; Enumeration of adjectives, 93;
Misuse of the comma, 91; The comma with numerals, 93;
Parenthetical use of commas, 89; The comma with quotations, 93.*
The dash 115
*The dash as a link, 118; The dash as a pause, 116;
The dash in parenthesis, 116.*
The exclamation mark 101
*Misuse of the exclamation mark, 102.*
The full stop 83
*The full stop with abbreviations, 84.*
The hyphen 110
*Compound words, 110; The hyphen as a grouping agent, 111;
The effect of omitting the hyphen, 113; Words with prefixes, 112.*
Italics 126
Marks of omission 123

**Other means of adjectival grouping**     114

**The question mark**     99

*Misuse of the question mark, 100.*

**Quotation marks**     103

*Quotation marks with full stops and commas, 106;
Interrupted quotations, 109; Misuse of quotation marks, 104;
Quotation marks with other punctuation marks, 108;
Quotation marks with paragraphs, 110; Single and double
quotation marks, 104.*

**The semicolon**     94

*The semicolon in grouping, 95; Misuse of the semicolon, 95;
The semicolon in verse, 94.*

**6. COMMON MISTAKES**     127

*Adjectives as adverbs (the use of), 134; "All right", 149; "An" (the
misuse of), 142; Articles (omission of), 141; "At about", 142;
"Attain", 145; "Averse from", 149; "Between each", 131; "But,
however", 147; "Centred", 160; "Chart" and "Charter", 138;
"Christmas", 149; "Circumstances", 141; "Compare", 143;
Conditionals (redundant), 135; Confused words, 149; "Different
from", 145; "Disinterested" and "uninterested", 160; "Due to",
138; "Either" and "neither", 133; "Every" and "each", 129;
"Extended tour", 146; "Include" and "including", 137; "Lay" and
"lie", 145; "Learn" for "teach", 147; "Loan" and "lend", 147;
"Moot point", 149; "Ought to", 145; "Parallel with", 143;
Participles (unattached), 150; Past participles (redundant), 150;
"Perpendicular" and "vertical", 143; "Persuade" and "convince",
160; "Promise", 144; "Reason", 140; "Right here", 148; Sentences
(unformed), 136; Singular and plural (confusion of), 132; Subject
and object, 127; "That" (the misuse of), 148; "Those kind", 141;
"Times greater than", 146; "Try and", 145; "Used to", 144;
"Verbal agreement", 160; Verbs with prepositions, 142; "Who" and
"whom", 128; "Whose", 129; Words (unrelated), 159.*

**7. ODDITIES OF THE LANGUAGE**     161

*Adjectives (switched), 166; "And/or", 168; "As from", 167; "As to",
"as regards", "with regard to", 163; "To build", 170; Clichés, 161;
Commercial English, 162; Ellipsis in comparisons, 166; "The
former" and "the latter", 164; Great Britain, 175; Intruders, 175;
Latin abbreviations, 168; "Little" and "a little", 169; "Lost to",
167; "Messrs", 172; Plurals (problems of), 170; Possessive problems,
170; "Scotch", "Scottish", "Scots", 172; Scottish usage, 173.*

# 1

# PARTS OF SPEECH

To write and speak correct English you have to get right back to fundamentals and understand why certain things are right and other things are wrong.

You may be surprised to find how much more there is about parts of speech than you realised in your schooldays and discover fascination of something that is usually taken for granted.

Nearly every word in the English language can be classified into its kind, the different kinds of words being known as "parts of speech"; the classifications having become crystallised through centuries of linguistic discipline. The following are the parts of speech: nouns, verbs, adjectives, adverbs, pronouns, conjunctions, prepositions, and interjections.

As will be seen later, the various parts of speech are not always firmly fixed and unfortunately the classifications are not perfect. Most words are easy to classify – that is, you know at a glance which part of speech a word belongs to – but some words can belong to two or more parts of speech. It frequently happens that a word cannot readily be classified at all; for example, it can form part of a phrase that, of little or no meaning in itself, has become understandable only through the common usage of years or centuries. Such use of a word or phrase, constituting an *idiom*, is said to be idiomatic.

Of all eight parts of speech, the most tantalising are pronouns. Although there is no question about the principal pronouns, it must be admitted that this classification has somewhat hazy boundaries and there can be much vagueness about words which lie near the frontiers.

Before proceeding, however, let us, as an interesting exercise, consider a sentence and try to classify each of its words.

"It frequently happens that a word cannot readily be classified at all."

*It:* pronoun, but the use here is idiomatic.
*Frequently:* adverb.
*Happens:* verb.
*That:* relative pronoun, but the use here is idiomatic.
*A:* adjective; indefinite article. (See page 22.)
*Word:* noun.
*Cannot . . . be classified:* verb (actually a combination of verbs, or "compound verb").
*Readily:* adverb.
*At all:* idiomatic.

Thus in this one sentence, chosen at random, it is not possible to classify firmly *every* word into an appropriate part of speech, but for a true understanding of the language parts of speech must be studied.

In the following descriptions of parts of speech it will often be necessary to wander from the main stream of discussion to examine the curiosities of individual words.

## NOUNS

Nouns are just *things*, animate or inanimate, real or imaginary, visible or invisible. English has the advantage that inanimate things are of neuter gender: that is, they are not masculine or feminine as they are, for example, in French.

*Proper nouns* are names of people, places, oceans, ships, racehorses, streets, and so forth. A proper noun (except in the case of a few peculiar surnames) always starts with a capital letter.

## PLURALS

Most plurals in English consist of the singular form with the addition of *s* or *es*, with or without some modification. There are, however, several other ways of indicating plurality and for details see Part 2, page 257.

Of the plurals of nouns and names which themselves end with *s*, many people have hazy ideas. Such nouns are *lens*, *iris*, and *gas*, and such proper nouns (names) are *Jones*, *Francis*, and *Jenkins*. To make such words plural, simply add *-es*. "The Jenkinses went out to dinner" is perfectly correct.

Exceptions are *means* and *news*. We talk about "this means" and "these means", but *news* is always regarded as singular.

## POSSESSIVES

Ownership, or a "belonging to", is signified by a possessive, which usually, in the case of a single possessor, is denoted by the "apostrophe *s*".

The singular cases are those like "The horse's mouth", and "One week's time". If a proper noun ends in *s* the rule is still applied, for example, "Mark Jones's car".

Where ownership or the "belonging to" is shared by two or more nouns, the joint possession is usually indicated by "*s* apostrophe", as in "The girls' school".

Collective nouns are treated as singular, and the apostrophe comes before the *s*. Examples are: "The children's toys", and "The men's work". See pages 120–122 for more examples.

There is an implied possession in "One week's time", the phrase meaning the length of time belonging to one week. Similarly we can have "Tomorrow's weather" and "In two weeks' time" or "A hundred years' time". But remember that the apostrophe must not be used if you omit the word "time" and simply say something like "In two weeks I shall be twenty-one."

Mistakes are often made when people's homes are being written about. When you say, "I went to the Johnstones'," you mean you went to the home not of Mr Johnstone or Mrs Johnstone but of both Johnstones, so that "the Johnstones' " is just an abbreviation of "the Johnstones' home". It is equally simple if your friends' name ends in *s*, in which case you write: "I went to the Joneses'," or "I went to the Inglises'."

In spite of the simplicity of this kind of possessive, mistakes appear in print almost every day, mistakes that are evidence of cloudy thinking.

An interesting use of the possessive is in references to the names of firms. If you want to write to tell someone where you bought your curtains you can say: "I bought my curtains at Smith's" or ". . . at Smiths'," meaning, of course, Smith's or Smiths' shop. If the firm is run by one man called Smith it is correct to write "Smith's", but if the firm is big enough to be controlled by a few of the Smith family then "Smiths' " is correct. If you do not know how many Smiths there are, or how big the firm is, you are on the safe side if you write "Smith's".

Some firms and organisations call themselves by the possessive form, for example, "Sainsbury's", and others – "Morrisons", for example – drop the apostrophe.

## VERBS

Verbs are the words that indicate *action*, a doing of something. Thus, in the simple sentences, "I go", "He had", "She will come", the verbs are **go**, **had** and **will come**.

When it is desired to talk or write about a verb in its general sense, it is usual to add the preposition **to**, and the form **to eat** (and so forth) is termed the *infinitive*.

In one way verbs are the most important of the parts of speech, for, as you will see in Chapter 4, every true sentence must contain a verb. There is so much to know about verbs and their use, in fact, that they will form the subject of a special chapter (Chapter 2).

## ADJECTIVES

Adjectives are words that qualify nouns. They describe what kinds of things they are, or which things they are. Common adjectives are *big*, *pretty*, *sour*, *young*, *best*.

Adjectives include personal titles, such as *Mr*, *Mrs*, *Miss*, *Ms*, *Sir* and *Lord*, where the name immediately follows. In "The Duke of . . .", on the other hand, *Duke* is a noun.

Adjectives include those of possession: *my*, *your*, *his*, *her*, *our*, *their*. For the sake of emphasis, the possessive adjective is sometimes followed by *own*, as in "my own hat", when *own* also becomes an adjective.

These words can also be grouped under the classification of "possessive pronouns", but as they are selective, in saying *whose* things are meant, the words are also adjectives. The allied forms *mine*, *yours*, *theirs*, however, which cannot precede a noun, and which imply "my hat", "your . . .", or "their . . .", are definitely pronouns.

Adjectives include such vague expressions as *numerous*, *many*, *innumerable*, *few*, *no* (meaning not any), where the expression directly precedes the noun.

There are exceptional cases, of course, where the adjective follows the noun, but such cases are usually found only in special literary constructions, in poetical language, and in oratory. The beginning of Milton's *Lycidas* is but one example:

> "Yet once more, O ye laurels, and once more
> Ye myrtles brown, with ivy never sere,
> I come to pluck your berries harsh and crude,
> And with forced fingers rude
> Shatter your leaves before the mellowing year."

Adjectives include colours, numerals, and nationalities. There is often some difficulty in deciding whether to use a capital *F* in such everyday things as "French chalk", "French window", and "French polish". It is often considered that, as the French origin has got lost in the vortex of common English usage, a small *f* will do. But as the word **French** deserves a capital in its own right, it is as well to use it always.

## ARTICLES

Adjectives include the articles: *a* and *an* are called the "indefinite articles", while the adjective *the*, for obvious reasons, is called the "definite article".

There has been a tendency to write and speak of "an hotel", as if the *h* were silent, but if you want to write and speak good English do not be afraid of "a hotel".

Think of all the nouns you can starting with a sounded ("aspirate") *h*. Do you prefix them with *an*? Of course not. Where the *h* is silent, as in *honour*, *hour*, the article *an* is correct.

Another tendency is to write "an unique article", instead of "a unique article", which most people actually say. This, too, is incomprehensible, for nobody would write about "an unicorn".

The omission of the definite article *the* at the beginning of a sentence, clause or phrase occasionally occurs in newspapers and periodicals, but do not be misled by this custom into thinking it is good English.

## ADVERBS

Adverbs qualify verbs as adjectives qualify nouns. Thus, while a verb tells you about the doing of something, an adverb tells you how it is done. Most adverbs consist of adjectives followed by the suffix *-ly* (see page 251), as in *quickly*, *cleverly*, *cautiously*, *willingly*.

Not all adverbs end in *-ly*. *How* itself is an adverb. So is *well*, as in "He does it well". *Fast* and *hard* are two common examples, and these, incidentally, are words which can be both adverbs and adjectives.

In the short imperative sentence, "Run fast", *fast* is an adverb. ("Imperative" implies a command, an order.) And yet, if we say "We had a fast run", *fast* is an adjective. It is similar with *hard* which is an adverb in "Hit him hard" but an adjective in "I took a hard knock".

The adverb *hardly* has a different meaning from the adverb *hard*. *Hardly* means "scarcely", "nearly", "not quite", and is probably connected with the archaic (old-fashioned) *hard* meaning "near". "He lives hard by the church" used to be common usage.

There are some words which are classified as adverbs largely because they are nearer to adverbs than they are to any other part of speech. Examples of such "adverbs" are *where*, *there*, *whatever* and *however*. In so far as these words qualify verbs – as in "You put it there", and "I did it, however" – they are adverbs, but the point is a technical one and we need spend no more time on it.

Adverbs can also qualify adjectives as in "You are extremely kind"; "It is a ridiculously simple problem". They can even qualify other adverbs: "He did it remarkably quickly"; "How well you draw!"

Adverbs can qualify participles, as in "I am greatly pleased".

## PRONOUNS

So much can be written about pronouns that, like verbs, they demand a chapter to themselves, and our study of them will be found in Chapter 3.

## CONJUNCTIONS

A *clause* is a complete statement, forming part of a sentence, which contains a verb; it may, in fact, be a short sentence. A *phrase*, on the other hand, does not include a verb (see page 71).

Very often a sentence is composed of two or more shorter sentences or clauses which must be joined in some way. Consider the following.

"The night was dark *and* it was cold."

"The night was cold *but* there was no fire."

"Nero played *while* Rome burned."

Each clause in each of these sentences is self-sufficient. It could be written on its own. Yet to avoid jerkiness in construction and ensure a smoother flow the different pairs of clauses are linked by the words *and*, *but* and *while*. These words are conjunctions.

Conjunctions, besides linking parts of a sentence, also express something in themselves.

In our first example, the second clause, after *and*, simply continues the emotion evoked by the darkness of the night. The conjunction *but*, however, signifies a contrast between the two clauses of the second sentence. The same effect could be produced by saying: "*Although* the night was cold there was no fire." There is a more detailed discussion of *but* later in this chapter.

A skilfully-applied conjunction, then, not only serves its primary purpose of joining parts of a sentence together, but also pays a contribution – sometimes quite an important contribution – to the general sense of the sentence. This subject will be dealt with more fully in Chapter 4. Meanwhile it may be useful to list the more common conjunctions which are: *and*, *but* (or *yet*), *while*, *although* (or *though*), *because* (or *as*, *for*, *since*), *or*, *if*. The words in brackets in the list are usually, but not necessarily, alternative forms.

## STARTING SENTENCES

In spite of schoolday admonitions against starting a sentence with *And* or *But*, there is nothing pernicious in the practice provided it is kept under proper control. There is very good precedent, in fact, in the Old Testament, where innumerable verses start with either of these two words.

When a sentence starts with *But*, a contrast with the preceding sentence is implied.

*And* and *But*, however, are the only conjunctions with which you can start a simple sentence. (A simple sentence is a sentence without a secondary sentence or clause.)

Try starting a simple sentence with any of the other conjunctions in the above list. You will find it is incomplete without another statement to follow or precede it.

"While John was weeding the garden."

"Although it was raining."

"Since (As, Because) it was Wednesday."

"Or you can have this one."

"If I were you." *(Not* "If I was you." See page 43, "The Subjunctive".)

Without the conjunction at the beginning, each of these sentences makes sense; but with the conjunction, it is left hanging in the air.

Thus, apart from *and* and *but*, all conjunctions require at least two clauses to be linked together. Sometimes you may come across *Or* used at the beginning of a sentence, but on inspection you will probably find that the preceding sentence has finished too early.

Do not be confused if you find *Though* or *Although* used at the beginning of a sentence and *apparently* without a supporting sentence, as in:

"Though sick, he was able to work."

This really means: "He was able to work though he was sick."

In the first sentence, the words "he was" are *understood*. "Understood" parts of a sentence are very common in the English language, but the trouble is that some people lose track of what is "understood".

## CONJUNCTIVE PHRASES

Besides words of conjunction, there are also conjunctive phrases, such as "despite the fact that", "owing to the fact that", "for the reason that", and "in addition to which". These are somewhat clumsy, and come under the heading of "circumlocution". Usually there is no reason why such phrases should not be replaced by single words. Thus, in the examples given, the first could be replaced by **although**, the second and third by **as** or **because**, and the fourth by **and**.

## "BUT"

In the use of **but** as a conjunction it is essential that the two connected statements are in contrast to one another. I have given as an example: "The night was cold but there was no fire."

That is right; but often you see **but** used wrongly, where there is no contrast or where the contrast is already expressed. Consider the sentence:

"He did not die, but he recovered and lived to a ripe old age."

If he did not die he must have recovered, so that there is no contrast after **but**. The word is therefore misused. If, however, we simply replace **but** by **and**, the sentence is clumsy. It would be better to reconstruct the sentence and say: "He did not die; he recovered and lived to a ripe old age."

A similar case is:

"In vain I tried, but I failed."

If I tried in vain it is obvious that I failed; therefore, either **in vain** must be dropped or **but** must be replaced by **and**. You can fall into a trap here if you are not careful.

**But** can also be used to indicate a contrast between opposing *words* – for example, between two adjectives, two nouns, or two verbs.

Correct examples are:

"It is not hot but cold."

"It is not a dog but a cat."

"He is not coming but going."

This is the trap. Although these examples are right the following examples are wrong, because *but* neutralises factors which are already opposed:

"It is not hot but it is cold."

"It is not a dog but it is a cat."

"He is not coming but he is going."

If you want to repeat "it is" in each case, the *but* should be replaced by a semicolon. The former construction, however, is preferable.

## "But" As "Except"

The use of *but* to mean *except* is common. Consider the sentence: "Nobody knows but me." Is this right or wrong?

We must first decide whether *but* is intended as a preposition or a conjunction. If a preposition is intended (see page 29), then the objective *me* is correct (see page 71).

If, however, a conjunction is intended, the sentence is probably a shortening of "Nobody knows, but I know," and in this, even though the sentence does not strictly make sense, *I* is right.

If our assumption is correct, that the sentence is abbreviated, then *I* is subjective. There are other cases, nevertheless, where no assumption need be made as there is no doubt about the matter.

"The boy stood on the burning deck

Whence all but he had fled."

The phrase "all but he" is the subject preceding the verb "had fled", and the use of *he* is correct. Think how discordant the line would sound if Felicia Hemans had written (in *Casablanca*) "Whence all but him had fled."

Thus, when we know definitely whether we are dealing with subject or object, there is no doubt about the "case" following *but*.

27

For example: subjective case – "Everyone but I went home"; objective case – "They gave some to everyone but me."

But *where doubt exists* – and it often does – it is an idiomatic custom to assume that *but* (meaning *except*) is a preposition and therefore followed by the objective case.

A rather odd use of *but* which might be mentioned here is in such constructions as: "Who knows but that the old man was the culprit after all?" In such sentences *that* is sometimes replaced by *what*, but as the whole construction is idiomatic it does not matter much.

This kind of language is permissible if used sparingly in conversation. It is apt to get out of control when used by the woolly-minded, and we hear confused absurdities like: "Who knows but what the old man was not the culprit after all?"

## "SINCE", "FOR", "AS"

The three words *since*, *for* and *as* can mean the same as (or are *synonymous* with) *because*, and it is in this connection that they are used as conjunctions. In the following sentence all four are of equal value:

"I went home because/since/for/as it was obvious I was needed."

These three words, however, have other functions, too.

Probably the commonest application of *since* is as a preposition, as in: "He has not been home since Christmas." *For*, too, is commonest as a preposition.

In "Commonest *as* a preposition", what is this use of *as*? Here, it means "according to the manner of". In this use it frankly cannot be designated as being a member of any particular part of speech, any more than it can be classified in such sentences as:

"It shone as brightly as the sun."

"He is as happy as a king."

In the next chapter you will come across the *subjunctive* mood of a verb, and you are using the subjunctive in saying things like: "I felt as if I were dreaming."

The word *as* can also mean *like* in the sense of being "similar to". "He is as a child" means the same as "He is like a child". It is used as *also*, or *too*, in the phrase "as well", where the word *well* is equally meaningless. "I am coming as well."

An extension of this idiom is provided by such constructions as: "Jim is coming as well as Jack", where "as well as" means "in addition to".

Truly, *as* is a tantalising little word, but a word of great utility.

## PREPOSITIONS

A preposition is a word which expresses the relationship of one word with another, usually (but not always) of a noun, a pronoun, or a participle (see page 36).

In the phrase "in the house", *in* is a preposition used to express the relationship of a noun with something else. Other examples of prepositions with nouns are: "*near* the stream", "*with* a will", "*by* hook or *by* crook".

Examples of prepositions with pronouns are: "*to* you", "*from* me", "*with* them".

Examples of prepositions with present participles are: "*without* going", "*by* living", "*beyond* walking".

Here is a list of other prepositions:

| | | | |
|---|---|---|---|
| of | off | below | across |
| for | up | above | beside |
| outside | down | beneath | toward(s) |
| outwith | before | around | along |
| (Scottish) | after | past | among(st) |
| inside | under | till (until) | amid(st) |
| on | over | abreast (of) | unto |

No doubt you will be able to think of many more.

It used to be thought ungrammatical to end a sentence (or a clause in a sentence) with a preposition. The foundation of this incorrect belief may have been the apparent meaning of the word "*preposition*" itself, signifying "*before position*".

The word, however, is unfortunate, and to interpret it literally would be tantamount to adjusting the language to suit its meaning – for, after all, the language is older than the term "preposition".

## THE PLACING OF PREPOSITIONS

The placing of a preposition depends to some extent on the type of writing or speech in which it is to be used. It is possible in informal English to move the preposition to the end of the sentence. "There is the boy I gave the toffee to" sounds freer, less pedantic, than "There is the boy to whom I gave the toffee."

What is suitable for a casual remark, however, may not be suitable, for example, for a statesman's speech. Consider the following:

"The fate of this great nation, of whom it might be said that at no time in two thousand years has she attempted to shirk her responsibilities, is today hanging by a slender thread. There are countries to whom she has offered the hand of friendship. There are countries to whom she has gladly given every help in time of war. These things shall surely not go unregarded. The world is ever growing smaller, and the tremendous continents between which the mighty seas roll unceasingly are drawing ever closer together. It behoves us all, therefore, to stand together in brotherhood, so that, when the time comes, we shall not be wanting for support. But with what are our friends to support us? Never fear. They have the spiritual resources of centuries."

There are several prepositions in that passage, not one of which falls at the end of a sentence or the end of a clause. The only sentence that might be improved by a shunting of the preposition is that containing **with**: "But what are our friends to support us with?"

Ending a sentence (or a clause in a sentence) with a preposition may not sound elegant, and you may wish to reconstruct it: that is, you can rearrange the sentence in such a way that the use of a preposition is avoided.

If the sense of a sentence or clause, however, demands that a preposition be placed at the end, and the result is harmonious, then put the preposition there.

In *phrasal verbs* such as "look after" or "blow up" the preposition/adverb remains after the verb, so the formal type of construction is not possible. "The children I was looking after," could not be rewritten ". . . after whom I was looking"; nor could "which bridge did they blow up?" be rearranged.

## OTHER USES OF PREPOSITIONS

Frequently a preposition can be used alone, without a noun, pronoun, or participle, but in all such cases the supporting word is understood. In the following examples the understood words are in brackets:

"I saw three ships come sailing by (the shore)."

"There is a man outside (the door)."

"I am going in (the house)."

"The doctor has gone up (the stairs)."

A little reflection will suggest innumerable examples of this type.

Occasionally a preposition is used as an adjective, as in "*up* train", "*down* train", "*inside* berth", "*outside* seat", "*under* dog", and "*past* president".

When using the preposition *to*, remember that you can go *to* places, but never "go places", unless the place is "home" or "abroad". Thus, you can say "I am going home", but if you want to say "my home" you must say "I am going to my home" and not "I am going my home."

You can say "I am going abroad", but not "I am going India." People often say "I wrote him" (which is wrong), when they mean "I wrote to him."

Where a verb is preceded by *to*, the "infinitive" of the verb is formed (see page 35).

## INTERJECTIONS

Another part of speech to be considered is the *interjection* or *exclamation*.

An exclamation such as "Ah!" or an exclamatory phrase such as "What nonsense!" plays no part in the construction of a sentence. It is a voluntary or involuntary remark, and as an exclamation it takes the exclamation mark (!), which will be considered in Chapter 5 when the subject of punctuation is reached.

According to literature of a bygone age, and to pseudohistorical novels, our ancestors were in the habit of saying "Zounds!", "By Jove!" and "Gadzooks!". The commonest exclamations of the present day are perhaps "Oh dear!", "Good heavens!", "Great!", "Marvellous!", "Splendid!", "Oh!", "Ugh!", "Damn!", and the various expletives.

Quite often, "Alas!" is used parenthetically; that is, it can be put into a sentence in such a way that a break is formed. It can be an oratorical aid, as in: "The party's prospects – alas! – have been ruined by the irresponsible action of a few hotheads."

There is a curious exclamatory use of "Why!". "Why! He's done it again" is an example. Perhaps it is because of the sound of the word that so satisfactorily expresses surprise, or the shape of the mouth in saying it.

# 2

# VERBS

Verbs are the parts of speech which denote action, or "the doing of something". Thus, in the simple sentences, "I go", "He had", "She will come", "I shall leave", the verbs are *go*, *had*, *will come* and *shall leave*.

The meaning of tenses – past, present and future – is well enough known. In the above short sentences, *go* is in the present tense, *had* in the past tense, and both *will come* and *shall leave* are in the future tense. This chapter deals with a few features about verbs which are not so well known, or about which there may be doubt.

In one way, verbs are the most important of the parts of speech, for, as you will see in Chapter 4, a verb is an essential part of a true sentence.

While there are three *tenses* of verbs – past, present and future – there are four verb *moods* (or "modes"). These are the infinitive, the conditional, the subjunctive and the imperative.

## THE INFINITIVE

A verb written or said by itself, when applied to nothing in particular, is unlimited, or infinite, in scope, and thus we have the term *infinitive*.

"I work", "You work", "He works", "They work", are all particular applications of the act of working; but "to work" is the general function, unlimited in scope, and thus the infinitive mood of the verb. The use of the infinitive is necessary to complete certain kinds of statement, as in the following: "I am going to work", "He means to eat his breakfast", and "They hope to catch the train".

In talking or writing about verbs in general it is usual to give them infinitive forms. Thus we refer to the verbs *to eat*, *to live*, *to sleep*, *to open*. In languages other than English the preposition *to* is implied; thus, in French, the infinitive forms of the four verbs above are *manger* (to eat), *vivre* (to live), *dormir* (to sleep), and *ouvrir* (to open).

## THE SPLIT INFINITIVE

The inclusion, or implication, of the little word *to* in the infinitives of other languages may be the origin of the dictum that in English it is shocking to "split" the infinitive – that is, to insert a word or words between *to* and its verb. Here are some examples of split infinitives:

"He started *to slowly walk* down the road."

"I want *to further examine* your proposals."

"He was forced *to unconsciously shield* his eyes from the glare."

"It would be better to ignore the letter than *to belatedly and clumsily proffer* your apologies."

One thing that strikes us about these sentences is their awkwardness. None of them *sounds* right. Here they are without the split infinitives:

"He started to walk slowly down the road."

"I want to examine your proposals further."

"He was unconsciously forced to shield his eyes from the glare."

"It would be better to ignore the letter than belatedly and clumsily proffer your apologies." (This sentence has been improved simply by the removal of *to*.)

Yet it is not entirely on grounds of euphony (smoothness or agreeability of sound) that infinitive-splitting is condemned. The most likely reason, as we have seen, is the fact that in most Western languages the infinitive form of a verb, being one word only, cannot be split.

Our own language is English, however, and it seems unreasonable that the rules of English grammar should be rigidly based on the rules of older or foreign grammars.

Many good newspapers have a rule against the split infinitive, and "copy" containing a split infinitive is usually altered. But there are times when it is more melodious and less artificial to split an infinitive than to stick slavishly to the rule. Consider the following three sentences:

"We regret it is impossible to legally authorise the termination of the lease."

"We regret it is impossible to authorise legally the termination of the lease."

"We regret it is impossible legally to authorise the termination of the lease."

I think you will agree that the first is the smoothest and the third the roughest. The third, moreover, is ambiguous, since the adverb *legally* could be related to *is impossible*; that is, the sentence could mean "We regret it is legally impossible. . . ."

The conclusions about the split infinitive, then, seem to be these: avoid it if you can; if you find that avoiding it makes the sentence sound unnatural or ambiguous, split it; but preferably remodel the sentence rather than split the infinitive.

## OMISSION OF "TO" FROM THE INFINITIVE

There are legitimate cases where, in the use of an infinitive, the word *to* is understood but not expressed – that is, it is implied. An example is: "Help me carry the shopping."

The omission of *to* before *carry* is a very common example of "ellipsis" (a shortening), especially in conjunction with the verb *to help* and there is nothing wrong with this kind of sentence.

## PRESENT-TENSE CONSTRUCTION

English is a language in which there are two present-tense constructions. The present continuous implies an action happening now:

"I am working."

"It is snowing."

"What's the baby doing? He's tearing up a £20 note." It is also used for an action happening about this time but not necessarily at the moment of speaking:

"I am reading a play by Shaw."

"She is teaching French and learning Spanish."

The simple present tense is used mainly to express habitual actions:

"He smokes."

"Dogs bark."

"Cats drink milk."

"He writes" might mean anything. "He writes novels" signifies a current but not necessarily continuous habit of the person discussed. But "He is writing" means that he is writing at this moment, or at this particular time.

## PAST-TENSE CONSTRUCTION

There are two corresponding constructions in the past tense – "I wrote" and "I was writing". For "I was writing" some other languages have an equivalent which the French call the "past-imperfect". The imperfect is a very suitable term, for the construction is more vague, less definite, than the equivalent of "I wrote".

## PARTICIPLES

Participles are those forms of a verb ending (for example) in *-ing* and *-ed*. Thus, in "I am waiting", **waiting** is the *present participle* of the verb "to wait", and in "I have waited" **waited** is the *past participle*.

Present participles invariably end in *-ing*. Past participles, on the other hand, have various endings, as in **known**, **been**, **gone**, **come**, *lost*, but the commonest ending is *-ed*. A participle is often used as a *verbal adjective*, as in "the rising sun" and "the lost property".

The past participle *lost* is an example of a -t ending. Other *-t* endings are in *learnt*, *dreamt*, and *leapt*. It is true that these past participles are often interchanged with the simple past tense of the verbs – *learned*, *dreamed* and *leaped* – but you may prefer to keep the *-t* endings for the past participles. Thus, you say, "I dreamed" and "I have dreamt", the *-ed* ending, after all, being common to most other verbs in their past-tense constuctions.

An unusual case of a dual form is provided by *past* and *passed*. Both are past participles of the verb "to pass", but while *past* is used with the verb "to be" *passed* is used with the verb "to have". The sentences "I am past middle age" and "I have passed middle age" are both correct.

For a great many verbs the past tense is the same as the past participle, examples being: "I passed", "I have passed", "I loved", "I have loved", "He dug", "He has dug", "They read", "They have read".

Be on your guard, however, with the following verbs – the so-called "strong" verbs – in which the dominant vowel is *i*:

| Infinitive | Past tense | Past participle |
| --- | --- | --- |
| to drink | drank | have (has) drunk |
| to sink | sank | have (has) sunk |
| to swim | swam | have (has) swum |
| to sing | sang | have (has) sung |
| to begin | began | have (has) begun |

Far too often you hear the *a* vowel used instead of the *u* vowel and the *u* instead of the *a*.

## VERBS ENDING IN "T" OR "D"
Verbs which can cause doubt include those ending in *t* or *d*, for example, *bet*, *let*, *hit*, *sit*, *bid*, *forbid*, *pad*, *rid* and *bud*.

The past-tense and part-participle forms of these verbs are maddeningly inconsistent, and the only guide to "correctness" is accepted usage.

With regard to *bet*, it is usual to say "I bet him five pounds" in a particular application, or "I have bet on a horse." Yet, when speaking of betting in a general sense, we say such things as "They betted all day long." These forms sound more pleasant than "I betted him five pounds" and "They bet all day long." If the second sentence is in the present tense, of course, it is the only way of saying it.

The past tense and past participle of *let*, on the other hand, are always *let*. It would never occur to anyone to say anything other than "I let my house" or "I have let my house", just as no one would think of saying "I hitted him" or "I have hitted him."

The past tense and past participle of *bid*, in the auction-room sense, are both *bid*, as in "I bid him ten pounds" or "I have bid him ten pounds." In the other sense of *bid* and *forbid*, however, the past tense is *bade* and *forbade* and the past participle *bidden* and *forbidden*, as illustrated in the two sentences: "His mother bade him come home" and "Smoking on the London Underground has been forbidden."

*Pad*, unlike *bid*, always changes into *padded*. "The cat padded about the room while I padded the cushions." In the past, *rid* behaved similarly, as in the sentence: "The cat has ridded the barn of mice" and "The weed-killer ridded the path of weeds." However, today we generally say "The cat has rid the barn of mice" and "The weed-killer rid the path of weeds", as well as "I was well rid of him." The past tense and past participle of bud, nevertheless, are always *budded*.

The past tense and past participle of *sit* can be *sat* or *seated*. Usage is strange, for the following examples of accepted English show no apparent rule or regularity:

"They all sat."

"I sat down."

"We have sat here long enough."

"I sat on the chair."

"I seated (sat) my baby on the stool."

"Are you all seated?"

"Pray be seated."

We often hear (for example) of a "deep-seated complaint". Strictly, the adverb **deeply** should be used, but common licence permits otherwise. The past participle **seated** is contained in the compound adjective, and **deep-sat** would sound odd.

## "SHALL" AND "WILL"

There used to be much confusion over **shall** and **will**. Even people whose grammar was almost faultless in other respects fell down in the use of these words. Generally, the fault was to use **will** for **shall** rather than the reverse.

The rules were:

For plain future tense (that is, mere statement of intention), the first person (**I** or **we**) took **shall**. For example, "I shall go home" if I was simply affirming my intention of going home in the future.

For plain future tense, the second person (**you**) and the third person (**he**, **she**, **they**, or a pronoun) took **will**. For example, "You will go home."

"I will", or "We will", on the other hand, was not used for a plain statement of intention, but only when there was a choice or volition (exercise of the will). "I will go home" meant that I had the choice of going or not going, that I really wanted to go home, that I had considered the possibility of not going home but discarded the idea.

Nowadays, however, it is accepted that when using the first person **will** and **shall** may be interchanged:

"I shall (will) be 21 on Tuesday."

"This time tomorrow I shall (will) be in France."

"Of course I shall (will) write to you."

When using other persons (*you*, *he*, *they*) *will* is still usually used unless a threat or a promise is implied:

"You shall pay for this!"

"They shall get the reward!"

If a future action is indefinite, or only casually hinted at, or used vaguely in an idiomatic manner, *shall* is customary as in the following examples:

"When the nation has no more use for him, he shall be cast into the wilderness."

"John shall always be the first to arrive." (But the *definite* future would be: "John will be the first to arrive tomorrow.")

"Perhaps some time there shall be world peace."

"Virtue shall not go unrewarded."

"Nation shall rise against nation."

In a great many such sentences as these the use of *will* instead of *shall* goes unnoticed, and there are innumerable borderline cases where either word would be justified.

The words *should* and *would* are the conditional forms (see page 42) of *shall* and *will* and the same rules given above used to apply to them.

Thus, if I said "I would go home", it meant that, given the *choice* of staying or going home, I should prefer to go home. To say, "I would like to go home" or "I would prefer to go home" was considered wrong; "I should like/prefer to go home" was the correct construction. Today, however, both sentences are accepted.

Another use of *would* is in such constructions as the following:

"I *would* call and find nobody in."

"We *would* decide to go for a picnic when it's raining."

In such cases *would* is usually emphasised, the implication being that it is the subject's misfortune to have made a wrong choice.

*Should*, of course, can also and very commonly mean "ought to" or "am [is, are] obliged to".

We often use the word *that* after clauses incorporating such verbs as *demand*, *be anxious* and *intend*. Future tense in most cases of this kind is expressed by *shall*, as in the following:

"The chairman demands that every member shall be in his place by seven o'clock."

"We are anxious that this special occasion shall be extended to all applicants."

"The Government intends that all such persons shall benefit by this order." (This would be better expressed as: "The Government intends all such persons to benefit. . . .")

*That*-clauses taking *will* are those incorporating, for example, *hope*, *fear* and *anticipate*, where the outcome is indefinite. Examples are:

"It is hoped that many members of the company will be present."

"If he went out in this storm I fear that he would get lost." (This is an example of the conditional.)

"It is a difficult climb, and we do not anticipate that he will reach the summit."

Again, of course, the pronoun *I* naturally takes *shall*, as in "I hope that I shall pass my examination."

In some cases the word *that* can be omitted, but in the omission you should be sparing. Thus, although the second and third of these examples could be read quite smoothly without *that*, the first would sound incomplete (see page 58).

It is not usual to adopt *shall* or *will* in a construction with *expect*. Normal constructions are, for example, the following:

"England expects every man to do his duty."

"I expect it to be fine tomorrow."

"They expect to be well treated."

If we wish to use *shall* or *will*, however, we should remember that the verb *expect* takes *shall* only if the expectation is strict or peremptory. **Shall** would thus be applied only in the first of these examples:

"England expects that every man shall do his duty."

"I expect that it will be fine tomorrow."

"They expect that they will be well treated."

## THE CONDITIONAL

"The conditional" referred to in preceding pages is not a tense but a mood, and whereas in French, for example, there is a special form of verb for the conditional, in English it is expressed by the addition of **should**, **would** or **could** to the verb.

Simple examples are:

"If you came home you would be welcomed."

"If I said such a thing I should be ashamed."

"He could do the job if he had the tools."

Thus, very often (but not always), the conditional is accompanied by an **if**-clause, stating the condition. In the three sentences just given, the conditions are:

"**If** you came home . . ."

"**If** I said such a thing . . ."

"**If** he had the tools . . ."

It will have been noticed that, when used conditionally, **if** takes the past tense – **came** (not **come**), **said** (not **say**), **had** (not **has**).

The thing to avoid is the clumsy construction with a *redundant conditional* and past participle.

Often you hear this kind of thing:

"I should have thought that it would have been necessary to inform the people."

If the speaker says, correctly, "It would have been necessary to inform the people", that is one thing. If he says, also correctly, "I should have thought", that is another thing.

But the compound statement requires only one conditional and one past participle to give the meaning. The speaker's opinion could be correctly expressed in one of two ways, either: "I should have thought that it was necessary to inform the people"; or "I think it would have been necessary to inform the people." (The second sentence sounds better with **that** omitted.)

## THE SUBJUNCTIVE

The subjunctive is a mood which, in English, is almost obsolete, but is still perfectly legitimate when used in the right place. In French it is still very much alive, like the conditional.

The subjunctive is the form of a verb used for something that might have been imagined but did not actually occur; for a hypothesis, but not for a fact. In modern practice the effect of its use is confined to the verb **to be**. The subjunctive **were** can be used with **if** when dealing with a hypothetical or imaginery situation.

A common example of this is "If I were you . . ." **I** could never be **you**; therefore the use of the subjunctive **were** is legitimate.

In most **if**-sentences or clauses the subjunctive can safely be used as long as the sentence is not concerned with fact or with likely possibility. Thus, another correct example of its use is: "If I were given wings I should fly away."

In a bygone age we could have used constructions like (for instance) "If his theory be correct . . ." (instead of "is correct"). His theory might be correct. We may even know it is correct, and choose to start our sentence in an oratorical way. Hence it may *not* be mere assumption, or hypothesis, that his theory is correct, and it would be preferable by modern standards to use **is**.

In general, the only subjunctive now used with **if** is **were** and not **be**, except perhaps in poetry and fanciful oratory. One construction, with an understood **if** omitted, has lasted since Gay's *The Beggar's Opera* (1727):

"How happy could I be with either,
Were t'other dear charmer away!"

The subjunctive **were** is used in a hypothetical or actual situation if the **if** is omitted.

This type of sentence is in common use today; for example: "Were I to go home I might find it" instead of "If I should go home . . ."

A recognised modern use of **be** is in such constructions as:

"The committee decided that the man be asked to resign."

"There was a suggestion that the press not be told."

"Whether this be the case or not, I shall refuse to lend her money."

A further surviving use of the subjunctive is with "I wish . . .", as in: "I wish the examination were over."

Use a subjunctive **be** with **though** or **although** but refrain from using it if the result sounds artificial or stilted. It is best to use the subjunctive mood sparingly, and only if you are sure you are using it correctly.

## THE IMPERATIVE

The word *imperative* denotes urgency, anxiety, as in: "It is absolutely imperative that we catch the night train." It denies the existence of any choice or alternative.

From there it is easy to see how the imperative mood arose. Commands and orders are given in the imperative mood of a verb. "Come here!" "Go away!" "Hurry!" "Wait!" "Don't worry!" "Stop!" All these are examples of the imperative. Usually an imperative word or clause is followed by an exclamation mark, this being one of the few cases where an exclamation mark is justified.

Other examples of the imperative are:

"Let's go!"

"Out of my way!" ("Get" is understood.)

"Don't let's be worried by these rumours."

"Let the earth be filled with the fruits of Thy goodness." (An imperative sentence of some length may not need the exclamation mark.)

"Cry 'Havoc!', and let slip the dogs of war."

## TRANSITIVE AND INTRANSITIVE VERBS

"I hammer the nail."

"I sleep in peace."

What is the difference between the two verbs **hammer** and **sleep**?

Briefly, the difference is that you can hammer something, but you cannot sleep something. **Sleep**, as a verb, is sufficient in itself.

The word "transitive", like all those other "trans-" words, is derived from the Latin prefix meaning "across", "over", "beyond" or "through", and a transitive verb is one which directly connects the *subject* of a sentence with its *object*. If the subject can do something with the verb to the object, the verb is transitive.

Transitive verbs that suggest themselves are "hit", "eat", "read", "spend", "take", "repair", "write", "organise" and "simplify". Most transitive verbs can at times be used without an object.

An intransitive verb, as has been noted, can exist by itself, without an object. Thus the simple sentence "I live" makes sense as it stands. An intransitive verb can, however, connect the object with the subject through a preposition or through a phrase. "I live" can be expanded into "I live in my house" (through the preposition *in*) or into "I live very close to a stream" (through the phrase **very close to**).

### "LAY" AND "LIE"

Discussion of transitive and intransitive verbs gives a golden opportunity to discuss the often ill-treated verbs **to lay** and **to lie**.

**To lay** is transitive. That is, you can lay something down. You can lay a book on a table, and a hen can lay an egg.

*To lie* is intransitive – not only in the sense of telling an untruth, but also in the sense of "to recline", which is our concern here.

*Lie* is sufficient in itself, as in the following:

"I lie on the bed."

"The dog lies on the floor."

"She went to lie down."

These are all correct examples of the use of the verb *to lie*.

Most people are fairly well conversant with the difference between *lay* and *lie,* but some people very often use *lay* when they mean *lie*. They say, for instance:

"I was laying down when the doctor called."

"My grandmother went for a lay-down."

The origin of this error – the use of *lay* instead of *lie* – is no doubt due to the fact that the past tense of *lie* is *lay*, as in:

"I lay on the bed."

"The dog lay on the floor."

"She went to lie down" is still correct, for the past tense of the sentence is conveyed by the verb *went*.

The past tense of *lay*, on the other hand, is *laid*, as in:

"I laid the book on the table."

"The hen laid an egg."

So far, so good. But the difficulties to some people seem to increase when past participles are involved.

The following are correct examples of the use of the past participles:

### To lay:

"I have laid the book on the table."

"The hen has laid an egg."

### To lie:

"I have lain on the bed."

"The dog has lain on the floor."

It is important to remember that *lain* is *never* used with the verb *to lay*, and *laid* is *never* used with the verb *to lie*.

People get themselves more and more confused, even in print, when they start dealing with the compound verbs *overlay*, *underlay*, *overlie* and *underlie*. Frequently sentences like the following are heard or read:

"The sandstones are overlaid by the shales."

"The case was underlaid by the secret that they were twins."

"Having overlain the primer by the first undercoating, allow to dry thoroughly."

"The author then became convinced that the low-grade ore overlaid the old workings."

The first three sentences are examples of the wrong past participle, and the fourth sentence (by a scientist) is an example of the use of the wrong word for the past tense.

If in doubt about the correct form, first ask yourself your meaning. The meanings of the above sentences are:

"The shales overlie the sandstones."

"The secret that they were twins underlay the case."

"Having laid the first undercoating over the primer, allow it to dry thoroughly."

". . . the low-grade ore lay over the old workings." Now, you know that the past participle of lay is laid and the past participle of lie is lain. Then the first three sentences, corrected, should be:

"The sandstones are overlain by the shales."

"The case was underlain by the secret that they were twins."

"Having overlaid the primer . . ."

And you know that the past tense of lie is lay, so that the fourth sentence should be:

"The author then became convinced that the low-grade ore overlay the old workings."

# THE VERB "TO BE"

There are a few anomalies (irregularities), and some special features, to be observed about the verb *to be*.

## THE COMPLEMENT

Where the verb *to be* is accompanied by a pronoun forming the object of a sentence or clause – the "complement" of the verb – the pronoun must be subjective. (Subject and object are to be discussed in Chapter 4.) Examples of the wrong and right use of the complement are:

| *Wrong* | *Right* |
|---|---|
| "This is him [her]." | "This is he [she]." |
| "It was me." | "It was I." |
| "I am him [her]." | "I am he [she]." |
| "The people you saw were us." | "The people you saw were we." |
| "Those are them." | "Those are they." |

The fact that this rule is often broken in conversation is no excuse for breaking it in writing, unless dialogue is being quoted.

## SINGULAR AND PLURAL

The subject of a sentence may differ *in number* from its object; that is, one may be singular when the other is plural.

The verb, then, takes the number of the subject, as in:

"My wages *are* one thing to be considered."

"One thing to be considered *is* my wages."

"These pages *are* the part to be omitted."

"The part to be omitted *is* these pages."

Collective nouns like "crew", "family", and "team" can take a singular or plural verb. "Our team is the best" implies a single group or unit. "Our team are wearing their new T-shirts" means a number of individuals.

A *compound* subject is a subject *compounded* of two or more words of which, for our present purposes, one is singular and the other plural, as in "One of these things."

The verb *to be* in this case takes the singular form. A correct example is: "One of these eggs *is* bad." Occasionally, however, you hear the wrong construction: "One of these eggs *are* bad."

## "AM I NOT?"

We can say, perfectly correctly, "I'm not", but the abbreviation for "Am I not?" is usually "Aren't I?" in British English. It is not strictly correct and is a colloquialism avoided in American English. We can say "Haven't I?", "Aren't we?", "Hasn't he?" and "Isn't she?" But when we want to abbreviate "Am I not?" we realise we cannot do it easily. Perhaps there is something to be said for the usage, often heard amongst Scots, of "Amn't I?", at least it is perfectly grammatical.

## ELLIPSIS WITH "TO BE" AND "TO HAVE"

*Ellipsis* means "a shortening", and although in grammar it takes several forms, here, we are concerned only with its effects on the verbs *to be* and *to have*.

Instead of saying, "He was leading and I was following", we could say "He was leading and I following." The omission of the second *was* constitutes an example of ellipsis, as it is "understood" to be covered by the first *was*.

So much is clear, and such ellipsis forms part of everyday writing and speech.

It is often thought that where one of the subjects is singular and the other plural, each verb must take its appropriate case, as in: "They were leading and I was following." There is nothing wrong with this, but in short sentences, where the two subjects are close together – in this case, *They* and *I* – it is permissible to omit the second verb. The sentence would then become: "They were leading and I following."

Other permissible examples are:

"You are fifty and I sixty."

"He has an umbrella and I a raincoat."

In these examples, the two subjects are comparable; each statement would still make sense if the subjects were interchanged. But if the subjects are not comparable, ellipsis of this kind is not permissible.

For instance, consider the sentence: "The road was long and they hungry."

With the subjects interchanged the sentence does not make sense: obviously the road could not be hungry, and the subjects are therefore not comparable. The sentence should read, then: "The road was long and they were hungry."

Where the two subjects are some distance removed from each other the practice should not be used. Think of the clumsiness of the following: "They were leading, and I, who had just come out of hospital and was feeling weak, following."

By the time the reader has reached the word *weak* he has mentally lost touch with the start of the sentence and the subject *I*. There is clearly something lacking; and all that is necessary is the insertion of *was* before *following*.

# 3

# PRONOUNS

Of all the parts of speech pronouns are perhaps the most loosely used. Strictly, a pronoun is a word taking the place of a noun which has already been referred to or is understood, but many words which, for the sake of convenience are called pronouns, do not easily fall into this definition.

Pronouns are sometimes classified, accepted classifications being, for example, personal pronouns, demonstrative pronouns, relative pronouns and interrogative pronouns. Some pronouns can belong to more than one kind, and this is one reason why classifications should not be studied too rigidly. The classifications are convenient for description, however, and will be followed here, but as long as you know a pronoun when you hear or see one it matters little what sort of pronoun it is.

## PERSONAL PRONOUNS

Personal pronouns – the easiest to recognise – can take the place of proper names or of articled nouns like ***the man***.

Subjective and objective forms of the personal pronouns are the following:

| Subject | Object | Subject | Object |
|---------|--------|---------|--------|
| I | Me | We | Us |
| He | Him | You | You |
| She | Her | They | Them |

The differences between *subject* and *object* are explained in Chapter 4 and examples of common mistakes receive special attention later in the book.

An idiomatic use of *you*, similar in application to the French "*on*", is its substitution for *one* or *anyone*. As this use of *you* sounds less pedantic than *one*, it has become accepted English.

*One* is fairly formal:

"One shouldn't believe everything one reads in the papers."

"One has to show one's pass at the gate."

Care must be taken not to use both *you* and *one* in the same sentence or in the same passage. One of the drawbacks of *you* is that once one starts applying the idiom one cannot change over to *one* until a decent interval has elapsed.

## DEMONSTRATIVE PRONOUNS

Demonstrative pronouns, as is fairly obvious, have the duty of demonstrating, as in the following sentences:

"*This* is my apple."

"*That* is her peach."

"*These* are your pears."

"*Those* are his plums."

The personal pronoun *they* can also be demonstrative, as in

"*They* are the people I like."

In each of the above sentences the demonstrative pronoun (printed in *bold italics*) is the subject. The objective forms of the words, however, (except for *they*) are the same, as in:

"I want *this*."

"You want *that*."

"He wants *these*."

"She wants *those*."

In the case of *they*, the objective form is the same as the subjective form only if the verb is the verb "to be". Thus, "Those are *they*" is correct, and "Those are *them*" is wrong.

The use of *them* as object is correct for all other verbs, as in "I have *them*" and "You ate *them*."

***Them*** cannot be used as subject, and commonly heard sentences such as "Them are the ones I like" or even "Them is . . . ." are not correct.

When we use demonstrative pronouns our reader or listener must know what we are referring to. Apart from the simple examples already given, further examples, of a type very widely used, are the following:

"This drawing supersedes ***that*** dated August 19th . . ."

"Employees to whom it applies are ***those*** with relevant experience."

Besides ***this***, ***that***, ***these*** and ***those***, however, there are other pronouns which deserve to be included in the demonstrative class. These are: ***none***, ***all***, ***neither***, ***either***, ***some***, ***any***.

Except for ***none***, demonstrative pronouns can be used as adjectives before nouns, as secondary adjectives before adjectives and nouns, and as adjectives in the form of articles. The subjective and objective forms are the same, examples being:

"I adore those roses."

"These foolish things remind me of you."

"Look at this picture."

"That happy man hasn't a care in the world.

The use of demonstrative pronouns as adjectives with the word ***one*** – as in "this one" and, very colloquially, "these ones" – is unjustified, as the word "ones" is quite superfluous. Incidentally, the use of "one" in this sense makes it a pronoun.

Consider the sentence: "These apples are good, but those are better." ***These*** is an adjective describing the apples. ***Those*** can be either a demonstrative pronoun demonstrating which apples are referred to, or an abbreviation of "those apples", but, as the result is the same whichever way you look at it, it does not matter.

What ***does*** matter, however, is how you refer to kinds of things. You must never say "those kind" of anything. Say "those kinds", if you like, or "these kinds" or "this kind" or "that kind". But to say "those kind" is to apply a plural adjective to a singular noun.

## "NONE"

The word *none* sometimes presents difficulties in the choice of the appropriate verb form. Should we say "None is" or "None are", "None come" or "None comes"?

If we have been taught that *none* (which literally means "not one") is always singular, then "None is" and "None comes" are correct. But the word can have a plural application, in which case "None are" and "None come" may be correct.

My advice in deciding whether to say "None is" or "None are" is to consider the context, consider the sense, consider the sound, and then make up your mind. You need not be ashamed of saying "None are" if the sense of the sentence supports it and it *sounds* right, as in "None are coming tonight."

## "EITHER" AND "NEITHER"

"Either solution is correct" comes easily to most people. But often we read sentences like "Neither Dickens nor Thackeray were panderers to the public taste" instead of "Neither Dickens nor Thackeray was a panderer to the public taste."

*Either* and *neither* are very logical words, and the rule of application is simple. You know already, of course, that *either* is used with *or* and *neither* is used with *nor*, but *neither* seems to cause the more confusion in the public mind.

If both the things under discussion are singular, *neither* takes the singular number of its following verb, as in: "Neither Roger nor John has enough experience to take on the job."

You can say "neither are" only if both things spoken about are plural, as in: "Neither men nor women are eligible" and "Neither birds nor fish are mammals." More is said about *either* and *neither* on page 133, Chapter 6.

Difficulty arises when one of the things you are dealing with takes the singular form of the verb and the other the plural. What should be said in the following cases?

"Neither you nor I was [were] there."

"Although it was a vine harvest, neither grapes nor wine were [was] much in abundance."

Though the general rule is that *neither . . . nor* takes a singular verb, when the subjects are different persons or things, plural verbs are normal. As there is no real solution to this difficulty, perhaps the wise course is to evade the dilemma by a different construction and say:

"Neither of us was there" or "You and I weren't there."

"Although it was a vine harvest, there were not many grapes and there was little wine."

In general *neither . . . nor* and *either . . . or* must refer to only two people or things but this rule is often broken and you will hear *neither* applied to more than two things, or sets of things, as in: "Neither men nor women nor children were allowed to leave. *Either* and *neither* can also, of course, be used with other parts of speech besides nouns, but they are then no longer pronouns.

| | |
|---|---|
| *With verb* | "He can either come or go." |
| | "I could neither laugh nor cry." |
| *With adverb* | "Do it either willingly or unwillingly." |
| | "She wrapped it up neither neatly nor carefully." |
| *With adjective* | "I will have either red or blue paint." |
| | "She was neither beautiful nor ugly." |
| *With preposition* | "It is a long way either to or from school." |
| | "He looked neither on nor under the table." |

## "ALL"

Though the useful little word *all* is also an adjective, it is included here among the pronouns by virtue of its use in such constructions as:

"He left all to his son."

"Of the hundred candidates, all passed."

As an adjective of number, *all* takes a plural, as in "all men" or "all the men", and as in Orwell's classic dictum: "All animals are equal, but some animals are more equal than others."

*All* can be singular in a limited sense, as in "I ate all the jam", where jam is something that can be divided, or in "Do you want all the table?" In these cases, however, *all* probably means "all the parts of", so that it might be regarded as a plural after all.

"After all." What does that mean? This is one of the innumerable idioms of our language, although it is interesting to note that the French similarly say "Après tout." In effect, it is simply an abbreviation of "After all the evidence has been considered", or "After all is said and done".

Often you come across "all of" instead of just "all". The word *of* is unnecessary, except in "all of it" and "all of them".

## "SOME"

We often use constructions like: "Some man or other said . . ." and "He gave it to some child in the street."

The word *some* here signifies that we do not know which man or which child was involved. If we said "The man . . ." or ". . .to the child", our listener or reader would know at once which man or which child was meant.

To say "A man . . ." or ". . . to a child" could mean that the listener might or might not know the man or the child. But the use of *some* in this sense shows definitely that the speaker is ignorant of the identities. The same application is found in *somebody* and *someone*.

*Some* is also used as an adjective of indefinite number, examples being "You can trust some people", "I dislike some colours".

It can also mean "a portion" as opposed to "all", as in "some of them", "some of it". But here *of* is necessary in all cases. Thus, while we say "all the time" and "all the meat" the corresponding constructions with *some* are "some of the time" and "some of the meat".

There is also an idiomatic, colloquial, exclamatory use of *some*. In World War II, when Hitler spoke of wringing Britain's neck like that of a chicken, Churchill remarked: "Some chicken; some neck!"

## RELATIVE PRONOUNS

"This is the boy *who* gave it to me."

"The pen, *which* I laid on the desk, is missing."

"You cannot bite the hand *that* feeds you."

"The parents, *whose* children were in school, gathered outside the gates."

"I carefully examined the book, the covers *of which* appeared unmarked."

"The person *who* was on the stairs was a visitor."

"The person *whom* I saw on the stairs was a visitor."

In the above sentences, the words in bold italics are called *relative pronouns*, as each connects a noun to a clause (or statement) to which it is related.

The relative pronouns can be related not only to nouns but also to other pronouns. The following are examples:

"I, who am old . . ."

"Give it to him who needs it most."

"That which is wrong is useless."

"I'll have any that fits."

### "WHO" AND "WHOM"

*Whom* is the objective form of *who*, and both are applied *only* to personal nouns and pronouns. (For "Subject and Object" see page 127.) You must not say such things as "The person who I saw . . ." or "Whom is the next speaker?"

*Who* and *whom* can cause confusion. In its simplest applications, however, the subjective use of *who* is usually clearly understood, as in such sentences as:

"I saw the man who did it."

"The lady who dealt with the enquiry is out of the office."

In these sentences there is no room for confusion of thought, as there often is with the use of *whom* (see page 128).

Occasionally you may see *who* and *whom* applied to animals: "The horse who won the St Leger . . .", "The dog whom I entered at Cruft's . . ." especially if we think of them as individuals. In spite of their being living creatures, nevertheless, animals usually take the relative pronouns *which* and *that*.

## "WHOSE"

The relative personal pronoun of possession is *whose*, the correct application of which is usually understood, as in the following:

"People whose rents have been raised can appeal."

"James, whose father was a poet, decided to study physics."

Some people dislike the use of *whose* with things, but this is quite common:

"He has done it again at the Duchess, in a play whose full title is . . ." instead of: ". . . in a play of which the full title is . . .".

## "WHICH" AND "THAT"

There is no difference between *which* and *that* in their use as relative pronouns. "The stone which the builders refused . . ." can just as well be expressed: "The stone that the builders refused . . .".

As a relative pronoun, *which* usually refers to things, not people:

"The apple, which I gave you, is bad."

*Which* is often used in informing clauses. In defining clauses it is a formal alternative to *that*.

"The apple that I gave you is bad."

Both mean the same, but you may prefer the first simply because it sounds slightly more musical. The choice between **which** and **that**, in fact, is often influenced solely by the arrangement of the vowel sounds and consonants.

"The hat that I wore at the party" may sound better than "The hat which I wore at the party."

In this example, however, and in the previous one, the relative pronoun could be omitted altogether, thus:

"The apple I gave you is bad."

"The hat I wore at the party . . ."

"The car (which/that) I hired broke down."

The relative pronoun can only be omitted in cases where it can be sufficiently "understood".

The omission of the relative pronoun, in cases where the sentence is still left intelligible, is one of those practices in English which can be accepted or rejected only by consideration of the "sound" of the particular passage.

But it *is* important that the sentence be left intelligible by the omission. In the preceding paragraph, for instance, the relative pronoun **which** could not possibly have been omitted.

The relative pronoun to be omitted sometimes carries a supporting verb, and this, too, is likewise discarded. In the following passage the relative pronouns and the supporting verbs which *could* be omitted are in square brackets.

"The conference, [which is] held at Scarborough every summer, is a representative gathering of all the provincial institutes in the country. It is refreshing to see these hundreds of young people, who have all given up their holidays and [who] have journeyed here at their own expense, joining together in a single common cause that has been justly described as 'ennobling'. The healthy tan [which has been] given by the sun, the cool grace [which] their outlook has bred in them, and the individual freedom of thought that distinguishes them from members of rival organisations, make you feel that the future of the human race is assured."

Do not pay any attention to the sense of the passage, which is one of those empty pieces of prose it is easy to write. Whether or not the words in square brackets are included is a matter of personal judgment. On the whole, economy in words is to be encouraged as long as the language is not debased, and frequently such economy results in power and smoothness of rhythm. But if on reading over the passage you are convinced that the inclusion of a *who* or *which* or *that*, with a supporting verb if necessary, would improve the harmony, clarify the meaning, or remove any ambiguity, then you should certainly include it.

Sometimes for the sake of emphasis the word *which*, when used as a relative pronoun, is followed by its related noun. "He was married in 1914, which year he was always to remember for other reasons, too."

The inclusion of the noun *year* after *which* clearly indicates the relationship between "1914" and the rest of the sentence. If you try to read or say the sentence without *year*, it sounds strangely incomplete.

Other examples are:

"Geoffrey Dawson was an editor of *The Times*, which paper had been founded in 1788."

"As the author of *Peter Pan*, which play was to have a phenomenal success, Barrie was unduly modest."

From a discussion of *which* and *that* in their capacity as relative pronouns, it is but a short step to the use of *that* when related to a verb.

In very common use are the phrases "confirm that", "believe that", "learn that", "understand that", "report that", and many others like them. Where the word *that* is understood it can occasionally be omitted, as in: "I believe you have a room vacant."

Sometimes the omission of *that* sounds unbalanced and unformed, but such constructions as the following are often heard and seen:

"Our customers report they are satisfied with our service in every way."

"Will you please confirm the man left of his own accord?"

"We learn the applicant had been a convict."

"Our correspondent understands the majority of the strikers have returned to work."

## INTERROGATIVE PRONOUNS

Interrogative pronouns are those which interrogate, or ask questions.

"Who is that?"

"Which is the right road?"

"What did he say?"

In these sentences, *who*, *which* and *what* are the interrogative pronouns. *Whose*, already mentioned as a personal possessive pronoun, can also be an interrogative pronoun, as in: "Whose are those?"

*Which* and *what*, like the demonstratives, can be used before nouns or before adjectives and nouns, examples being:

"Which road is the right one?"

"What man is that?"

For practical purposes, the two words *in this application* are sometimes interchangeable.

Thus, we could say: "What is the right road?" Usually, however, the question "Which . . . ?" signifies a choice from a definite number, and "What . . . ?" signifies a vague decision from an indefinite number. Illustrations are:

"Of these games, which would you like to play?"

"What would you like to play?"

Except in cases like those given, *what* can never be used for *which*.

## "WHAT"

*What* is one of those many useful words in the English language which have several functions. As we have seen, it is an interrogative pronoun.

*What* is now generally accepted as *that which*. "What I do is my own business." This sounds better than: "That which I do is my own business."

Less gracious examples of this use of *what* are:

"He gave him what is called a knock-out."

"I made what was for me a big mistake."

You hear constructions like these every day. They are not very elegant, and are unnecessarily long. Both statements could be expressed more briefly and in better English.

The question "What?" is short for "What did you say?" A blunt "What?" in polite speech is often looked upon as bad manners, and "Pardon" or "Beg pardon" is usually preferred. Both of which, of course, are short for the much more pleasant "I beg your pardon."

In the sentence "I'll tell you what", the word *what* is the prelude to something that is vaguely understood. Thus, the sentence in full might be "I'll tell you what will happen" or "I'll tell you what we'll do." In this connection, of course, *what* means "that which".

There is also "What for?" meaning "Why?" Here, however, the body of the sentence, although omitted, is understood between the speaker and the addressed. It might be: "What did you hit him for?" or "What did she go for?" These two questions could follow "I hit him" and "She went".

The old idiom "Give him what-for" seems to have grown in use merely by constant repetition between one person and another.

## POSSESSIVE PRONOUNS

Possessive pronouns are of two kinds – those used as adjectives, and those used alone.

Of the first kind, examples are *my*, *thy*, *his*, *her*, *its*, *our*, *your* and *their*. Such words (except *his*) must be followed by nouns or by words or phrases acting as nouns, as in "My goings-out and comings-in." The old-fashioned *thy* is included because (with *thou*) it is still part of the language.

Care must be taken not to put an apostrophe-*s* in the possessive *its*, and the reader is referred to page 65.

The second kind of possessive pronoun comprises *mine*, *thine*, *his*, *hers*, *ours*, *yours* and *theirs*. These words are sometimes called "absolute" possessives as they can stand alone, examples being:

"This hat is mine."

"Those books are theirs."

"Was it hers?"

There is no apostrophe in the *s*-endings of these words, but occasionally you will see an apostrophe so misused. *Either* and *neither*, however, both have possessive forms, and both take the apostrophe (*either's*, *neither's*).

Formerly *mine* and *thine* were used for *my* and *thy* before vowels and the aspirate *h*. The translators of the Bible were capable exponents of it; consider, for example, such poetical prose as this:

"I will lift up mine eyes unto the hills, from whence cometh my help."

"So that thou incline thine ear unto wisdom, and apply thine heart to understanding . . ."

"Rejoice not when thine enemy falleth, and let not thine heart be glad when he stumbleth."

Shakespeare, too, followed the adjectival use of *mine* and *thine*:

"Bid me discourse, I will enchant thine ear . . ."

". . . he furnished me

From mine own library with volumes that

I prize above my dukedom."

"Shall I not take mine ease in mine inn but I shall have my pocket picked?"

# INDEFINITE PRONOUNS

Some pronouns cannot easily be classified as personal, demonstrative, relative, interrogative or possessive.

If a pronoun cannot be put neatly into any of these pigeonholes, and yet is unmistakably a pronoun, it can be labelled an *indefinite* pronoun. This term is also applied to a pronoun if there is doubt or vagueness about the noun for which it is substituted.

Some of the pronouns already discussed are in some ways indefinite pronouns. Examples are *all*, *none*, *some*, *either*, *neither* and *any*, discussed with demonstrative pronouns but which might also be called indefinite.

Apart from these, the indefinite pronouns include the words *enough*, *each* and *other*, which are also adjectives, and *aught*, *naught* and *else*, which cannot be used as adjectives. Indefinite pronouns might also include *every*, and certainly must include *it*.

## "EVERY"

*Every* is here called a pronoun, as it used to be a pronoun rather than an adjective. Originally it was an abbreviation of "ever-each". Shakespeare used it as a simple pronoun and not as an adjective – "Every of your wishes" – and yet today its use is entirely adjectival.

The most important thing to remember about *every* is that it is a singular word. It is most curious that while everyone naturally and correctly says "Put everything in its place" he probably also says "Everyone has to be in their seats by seven o'clock."

The senseless feature of this construction is that, although the singularity of everyone is acknowledged by the use of has, there is the misuse of the personal possessive plural pronoun their.

Lewis Carroll made the Duchess say: "If everybody minded their own business, the world would go round a deal faster than it does." The author of Alice, however, was quoting, and is not to be accused of carelessness in himself.

The difficulty with the words everyone, everybody and nobody is in using an accompanying pronoun to cover both sexes. The correct construction would be: "Everyone has to be in his or her seat . . ." or "If everybody minded his or her own business . . ."

If that sounds clumsy to you, why not use his alone? In various aspects of law and medicine the masculine personal pronouns are understood to apply to both genders. If, then, you dislike the "his or her" construction, you could say: "Everybody should mind his own business." There are sound precedents for this practice in other languages.

## "IT"

A very hardworked little word is *it*. In its normal use it is an impersonal pronoun (as opposed to a personal pronoun): "The door was open when I passed the first time, but when I passed the second time *it* was shut."

Apart from this, however, *it* has many other applications. Often the governing noun is understood, as in "Give it up", when *it* is the problem or the battle.

Nobody can explain the significance of *it* in "It frequently happens . . ." But in "It is a rainy day" *it* means "the day", for it would sound odd to say "The day is a rainy day." We cannot say what *it* is, however, in "It is raining".

*It* defies us there. It almost defies us in such sentences as "Let's rough it" and "It's up to you", but here we know that *it* takes the place of some vague subject or object which is unknown. (Subject and object are discussed in the next chapter.)

*It* also enables us to avoid unrelated participles, for example, study the sentence: "It being assumed that the bridge is finished in time, the first train will cross the river in August." If we were slipshod grammarians we should say, absurdly: "Assuming that the bridge is finished in time, the first train . . ."

To conclude this chapter, it is worth repeating one important piece of instruction about *it*. *It's* is short for "It is", as in "It's sunny". The possessive of *it* is *its*, as in "its colour", "its size".

# 4

# THE SENTENCE
# AND THE PARAGRAPH

If grammar is the basis of language, the sentence is the basis of grammar. A passage of true prose is composed of a series of sentences, each sentence being connected in some way or other with the preceding sentence. The whole series of sentences should show the writer's train of thought in that particular passage. When the writer wants to switch to another train of thought he may, for convenience, and for lucidity, start a fresh paragraph.

## SENTENCES

A sentence should be a *complete* statement. To make sense, it must consist of, at least, a subject and a verb. A string of words between two full stops is thus not necessarily a sentence. "I live", though a simple statement, is a complete statement and a perfectly good sentence. Too often we read incoherent passages like this:

"Jane wanted a dog. A real dog. No matter what kind of dog. Just a dog. A dog that would be her own."

In that collection of words there is only one sentence – "Jane wanted a dog."

Occasionally you may read business letters that start like this: "Referring to your letter of the 16th November." After the full stop the reader is left groping in mid-air, for these words obviously do not make a sentence. After "November" there should be a comma, followed by a proper noun or a pronoun attached to the present participle "referring".

Thus, such a sentence might be the following: "Referring to your letter of the 16th November, I am surprised to learn that the account is still unpaid."

But even when there is an attempt to complete the sentence, the comma is sometimes followed by a noun or pronoun which is not attached, and could not possibly be attached, to the participle. We all read "sentences" like this almost every day of our lives: "Referring to your letter of the 16th November, the horse was sold last Monday." Literally, this means that while the horse was being sold the animal was referring to the letter.

The common misuse of participles, however, is a subject discussed in more detail in Chapter 6.

While on the subject of so-called sentences which are not sentences, here are some actual examples from newspapers.

". . . were the stars at Guildhall Art Gallery yesterday afternoon. Invisible stars except for the early arrivals."

"I wrote on Monday that the Planning Committee had agreed in principle to a plaque costing between £5,000 and £10,000. This in addition to a memorial already in Princesshay."

"Canada seems the right place to hold such a celebration – the Hereford is still comfortably the most popular beef breed of the New World. This though that Scots interloper, the Aberdeen Angus, is steadily improving its position."

One cutting is from a Sunday paper, in which a reviewer describes a Japanese novel "translated into easy but not very elegant English by an American." The reviewer's own English is not very elegant, either, for later in the same review she writes:

"But some people like . . . to think of the Inquisition as a medieval bogy good for a shiver and not the beastly mechanism that creaked its way into the nineteenth century. To whom the book may be recommended."

It is easy to find grammatical faults in trade circulars. This extract from a joinery catalogue is a typical example of the kind of writing that should be avoided in trade publications:

"Delivery can be given immediately from stock of all . . .

illustrated in this catalogue. All External Joinery being supplied primed all round with high-quality red paint."

As it stands, the second part of the passage is not a sentence, but replacement of "being" by "is" would make it correct. Incidentally, the unnecessary use of capitals in "External Joinery" is a typical example of the indiscriminate use of capitals in some trade publications.

## SUBJECT AND PREDICATE

Some of us probably remember how at school we were taught to divide a sentence into "subject and predicate", and this division is quite useful as long as it is understood.

The *subject* of a sentence is the person or thing the statement is about. In our simple sentence, "I live", the pronoun "I" is the subject. Generally, the subject comes before the verb, but sometimes, for the sake of a special effect, the order is reversed. "Came the dawn" is a familiar example of this *inversion*, as it is called, and in this case "the dawn" is the subject.

The *predicate* is the part of the sentence following the subject, and *must* contain the verb. Although the word itself has several meanings, which you can find out from any English dictionary, its derivation, from the Latin *praedicare* (to proclaim) immediately gives its meaning as applied to grammar. It is the predicate which *proclaims* what the sentence is about.

In the sentence, "I live", it is the predicate "live" which gives meaning to the statement and completes the sentence. But this is a very short, if effective, sentence, and more often we use or read sentences which are not only longer but also more complex.

For the moment, however, let us avoid complexity and consider such longer simple sentences as the following.

(*a*) "I live in a house."

(*b*) "He gave a pound."

(c) "The tree grows near the stream."

(d) "She loves books."

Division of these sentences into subject and predicate gives:

| Subject | Predicate |
| --- | --- |
| (a) "I | live [verb] in a house." |
| (b) "He | gave [verb] a pound." |
| (c) "The tree | grows [verb] near the stream." |
| (d) "She | loves [verb] books." |

Further examination of these sentences shows the presence of two kinds of predicate, the difference being determined by the kind of verb. Verbs of the (b) and (d) kind are *transitive* while verbs of the (a) and (c) kind are *intransitive* (see page 45). It is worth remembering, nevertheless, that even though a complex sentence may consist of several sub-sentences, each of the sub-sentences can be divided into subject and predicate.

## THE OBJECT OF A SENTENCE

It may be clear by now what is meant by the term "the *object* of a sentence". The object is the part of a sentence affected by the subject through a transitive verb.

In the simple sentence, "I eat bread", **bread** is the object. In examples (b) and (d) above, the objects are a **pound** and **books**.

It is not essential for every sentence to have an object. "I eat" is a perfectly good sentence on its own, without an object.

An intransitive verb, of course, cannot be followed by an object. Examples of intransitive verbs are **sleep**, **lie**, **stand**, **sit**, **walk**, **swim**, **come**, **go**, **run**, **live** and **fly**. (There is a transitive form of **run** in the sense of running an organisation.) A construction like "Walk a mile" or "Swim the river" does not make its verb transitive, for the subject is not really doing anything *to* the mile or the river.

Some verbs can be either transitive or intransitive. In our example (*c*), where there is no object, **grows** is intransitive. In "The gardener grows cucumbers", the verb is transitive, with **cucumbers** as the object.

The object of a sentence need not follow the transitive verb. In the sentence, "Pale hands I loved", the object is **hands**, for this is another kind of inversion.

## SUBJECTIVE AND OBJECTIVE PRONOUNS

The subjective forms of the personal pronouns are often wrongly used for the object, and you hear misconstructions like:

"He took Mother and I for a ride in the car."

"The manager met my friend and I at the station."

In both sentences **I** should be **me**. People who are not sure of their English sometimes try to get over the difficulty by using **myself**: "Those present at the meeting included the mayor, his wife and myself."

A preposition is always followed by the objective form of a personal pronoun, so that "Between you and me" is correct. The following should make you shudder:

"Between you and I. . ."

"Come and sit beside we girls."

Misuse of the subjective forms of the personal pronouns is one of the commonest mistakes in English. Less common is the misuse of the objective forms, and the misuse of **them** ("Them's the best") is often due to regional peculiarities of dialect.

Remember, however, the peculiarities of the verb **to be** described in Chapter 2 on page 48, and that "It is I" is strangely correct.

## COMPOUND SENTENCES

A *clause* is a short complete sentence forming part of a longer sentence. It must, therefore, contain a subject and a verb. A *phrase* is a group of words *not* containing a verb, and which may or may not form part of a clause or sentence. Far too often the term "phrase" is wrongly used for a clause. (See page 23.)

A compound sentence is composed of two or more clauses suitably connected. Here is an example:

"John went for a walk and met Bob, who was shopping for his mother."

This is composed of the following sentences, each of which is complete in itself: "John went for a walk. John met Bob. Bob was shopping for his mother."

The sentences forming a passage of prose should be neither too short nor too long, unless the writer is aiming at some special effect. In a book of instruction, for example, short sentences may be advisable. Sentences which are too short sound jerky and are irritating to the reader or listener. Sentences which are too long soon cause the reader or listener to clamour for a rest, and the main matter of the sentence may be forgotten.

The ideal length for a sentence is that which makes the reader or listener aware of smoothness of flow, and gives him time to collect his thoughts at suitable intervals. The consistently short sentences in some of the popular newspapers are similar in form to the short sentences found in very young children's reading-books, and writing for adults in this manner is not to be encouraged. At the other extreme are long, involved sentences which could do with much pruning and revision – sentences containing elaborate parentheses and collections of clauses and phrases – and these are not to be encouraged, either.

This is not to imply that all the sentences in a prose passage should be of equal length. That would be dull, even if it could be achieved. The writer's aim should be to convey his meaning not merely by a string of facts and opinions, but as smoothly and rhythmically – as musically, if you like – as he can within his capabilities.

In the judging of suitable lengths for sentences there is nothing like constant practice. When you have written a passage of prose, read it over as though you were hearing it read. Consider each sentence not in itself but as part of the passage. Then adjust it, putting in a conjunction here and a parenthesis there, removing an **and** and inserting a full stop, replacing a comma by a semicolon. Do not be too lazy to write it all over again – remember that striving for perfection is one of the things that distinguish the artist from the craftsman.

It is a good idea, if time allows, to revise your writing after a month's rest. You may then be able to notice defects you never saw before.

## CONNECTING THE PARTS OF A SENTENCE

The separate clauses in a sentence can be connected by *conjunctions*, which, besides linking parts of a sentence, also express something in themselves. The choice of conjunctions depends on the writer's or the speaker's meaning.

For exercise, let us try to rewrite the following group of jerky sentences.

"I left the house. I thought it was half-past eight. It was a wet morning. It was warm. Few people were about. I could not understand this. I caught a bus. The bus was half-empty. The bus took me to the station. My train was usually at the platform. This morning it wasn't. I looked at the station clock. I realised my mistake. I had got up an hour too early."

That passage sounds most depressing as it stands, but its style is not uncommon. We could rewrite it like this:

"I thought it was half-past eight when I left the house one wet but warm morning, and could not understand why so few people were about. I caught a half-empty bus which took me to the station, and although my train was usually at the platform, this morning it wasn't. On looking at the station clock I realised my mistake. I had got up an hour too early."

The second version is easier and more pleasant to read than the series of unconnected statements of the first version. There are fourteen sentences in the passage, which we have rewritten in four sentences.

We have used a few conjunctions – *and*, *although*, *but*. We have used some relative pronouns – *when* and *which*. The fifth and sixth sentences have been replaced by the clause ". . . and could not understand why so few people were about." The use of the present participle "On looking . . ." telescopes two sentences into one.

## PARENTHESIS

A parenthesis is a word, clause, sentence or phrase inserted in a sentence that is grammatically complete without it. A simple example is in the sentence: "The party's prospects – alas! – have been ruined by the irresponsible actions of a few hotheads."

The word "alas!" is the parenthesis. In this example it is separated from the rest of the sentence by two dashes, which themselves are called parentheses. Parenthesis can also be indicated by brackets or by commas. Besides round brackets there are square brackets which also have their use (see page 119).

A whole sentence, or even a whole paragraph, can sometimes with advantage be placed in parentheses in the midst of a passage of prose.

Besides its use for the interpolation of something, however, parenthesis can be a means of linking parts of a sentence, and when skilfully applied it can be effective, thus:

"The state of the country at that time – there had been six major industrial strikes in two years – was parlous. Repeated demands for higher wages, demands which without exception were meekly accepted, had resulted in undisguised inflation. Tax-dodging was on the increase, and the corrupt prospered while the honest struggled along in vain. The economy of the country was at a low ebb, and exports for the year in question (worth £100,000,000 five years before) had dwindled by over 50 per cent."

In that passage there are three examples of parenthesis – that between the dashes ("there had . . . two years"), that between commas ("demands which . . . meekly accepted"), and that between brackets ("worth . . . before").

It should be stressed that a parenthesis should not be so long as to be unwieldy. You will sometimes see atrocious examples, consisting of whole auxiliary passages complete with full stops, semicolons and commas, placed in brackets or between dashes. To avoid such awkwardness, you need only the use of a little care and some rewriting.

SYNTAX

There may be several grammatical ways in English of arranging the clauses, phrases, and words in a sentence to result in the same meaning. The subject of arrangement is known as *syntax*, and ideally the arrangement to choose is that which reads the most smoothly and rhythmically while clearly expressing the sense. In this respect English is fairly flexible.

Although it is not true that almost any sentence can be rearranged, it is easy to pick out sentences that have a number of possibilities. Consider the following.

"The children's party will as usual be held in the church hall on Boxing Day."

"In the church hall on Boxing Day will be held the usual party for children."

"On Boxing Day, in the church hall, the usual party for children will be held."

"The usual Boxing Day children's party will be held in the church hall."

Other arrangements may suggest themselves to you. These sentences are all variations of the same theme, and all give the correct meaning though the last sentence probably sounds the most pleasant.

If alternative forms of order give confusing or ambiguous results, those are the forms to avoid. For instance, could we have said "the usual children's party"? We could, but only at the cost of ambiguity. This construction could imply that the same children were always invited to the party, and so we avoid the ambiguity by saying "the usual party for children" or "the usual Boxing Day children's party."

## "ONLY"

A word frequently used in the wrong place is *only*. Every day you hear such sentences as: "I only arrived here three hours ago." The speaker means that up to the present his stay has been short, and the word *only* refers to *three hours*, so that the sentence should be: "I arrived here only three hours ago."

*Only arrived*, strictly, is a belittlement of the act of arriving, as if arriving was of no importance. In this particular sentence, fortunately, this is clearly not the speaker's meaning, and hence no ambiguity results from the misplacing of *only*. But in other sentences there could easily be ambiguity, as, for example, in the following. The correct constructions are in brackets.

"I only offered five pounds for it and she looked insulted." ("I offered only five pounds . . .")

"Bob only lives in the house." ("Only Bob lives . . .")

"Children will only be admitted if accompanied by adults." ("Children will be admitted only if . . .")

"There will only be a strike in the factory if the men do not get a pay rise." ("There will be a strike in the factory only if. . .")

"I only ran away when he became aggressive." ("I ran away only when . . .")

"I only believe half of what he says." ("I believe only half . . .")

## "ALSO"

A word which can easily be used ambiguously is *also*. Consider the sentence, "They also serve who only stand and wait", from Milton's *On his Blindness*.

*Only* is used correctly, but *also* may be associated with *they* or with *serve*. If it is associated with *they*, there is an implication that other people are serving more actively, but that they who only stand and wait are serving, too.

If *also* is associated with the verb *serve*, the sentence means that while they are standing and waiting they are *also* serving.

In speech, a hint as to the meaning could be given by accentuation, so that if the first meaning was intended stress could be laid on *they*, and if the second meaning was intended stress could be laid on *serve*. We are sure that Milton had the first meaning in mind.

Another example of the ambiguity of *also* is in this passage: "We went to Devon and met my aunt and uncle, who had been to Cornwall. During our holiday we also went to Cornwall, and then to Dorset." *Also* can be associated with *we* or with *Cornwall*.

Now consider the use of *also* in such a sentence as the following: "I gave her an apple, a pear, an orange, and also a peach."

You might think that *also* after *and* is unnecessary. So it is, if the speaker is simply enumerating the fruits he gave. But if the speaker's intention is to emphasise his generosity, and to imply that the recipient has done very well to get the first three fruits, then *also* after *and* may be justified.

At other times *also* is even used in place of *and*, as in: "We bought all kinds of Christmas presents – toys, books, games, also things to wear." *Also* here is not only wrong but clumsy.

## PARAGRAPHS

A passage of prose is divided into *paragraphs*, as we all know, the first sentence of a new paragraph being started on a fresh line and usually "inset" slightly to warn the reader that a new paragraph is about to begin.

Generally, the start of a new paragraph should indicate a deviation, or a break, in the sequence of thoughts and ideas.

The arrangement of sentences in paragraphs is also convenient, gives a more pleasing appearance than a solid block of prose, and tends to make reading easy.

How long should paragraphs be? To this enquiry, no ready answer can be given, for much depends on the kind of prose in question.

In works of instruction or edification it is helpful to keep the paragraphs as short as possible without spoiling the flow of ideas or the appearance of the page, as is the aim of this book.

It is conventional to start a new paragraph at the start of quoted speech, especially in fictional writing, even if the speech consists only of an exclamation like "Ah!"

In non-fictional works paragraphs should not be made too long even if the flow of ideas is continuous. A whole page of unbroken type can look forbidding, and if there is no natural break or deviation it is better to make an artificial one. Two or three paragraphs on a page of manuscript, typescript or print look better than a page of scrappy paragraphs and better than no paragraphs at all.

One of the most effective ways of preventing stodginess is to vary the length of your paragraphs. Impact can be added to a simple point by putting it in a very short paragraph.

What of letters? A typed business letter should consist of relatively short paragraphs, as the recipient will probably have dozens of such letters to read in a day and the sender should try to make his task easy.

The arrangement and tone of a personal letter depend on to whom it is written; thus, you could say the same things to $B$ in a very different way from the manner and arrangement in which you could say them to $A$, even to the extent of making your paragraphs longer or shorter.

## ARRANGEMENT OF IDEAS

An idea is something that occurs to one – a thought, a mental image, a notion, a conception, a supposition, a plan, a view, an intention, or just an opinion. An idea that comes into one's head may be the result of a preceding idea, and may give rise to one following.

In writing, or in speech of some length, ideas should be expressed in some order. That is, do not try to write or say anything just as it comes to your mind. Marshall your ideas, put them in order, and be selective.

In a long impromptu speech it is not as easy to do this as in writing, or in a prepared speech, and some speakers, experienced in the art, are better at arrangement of ideas than others. Statesmen's replies in Parliament, and judicial speeches in court, are often wonderful examples of unprepared speech at its best.

I assume that you are neither a statesmen nor a legal light, and that your speech is confined to ordinary conversation at its various levels. No doubt, however, you often have to write, and in writing you have the chance of planning and revision denied to ready speakers. Use the chance, and make the most of it: marshall your ideas, put them in the logical order (or the most logical), and be selective.

Being selective means that you should not be afraid of throwing out a sentence, a clause, or a phrase, as long as the sense remains and the passage can do without it. Economy in words, in fact, is an essential virtue in good writing, and, like the arrangement of ideas, can only be achieved with practice.

In some kinds of writing you can spread yourself – in a novel, for instance, or in a letter to an intimate friend. In a short story or an essay, on the other hand, you are more restricted, but restricted only in one field. When you are restricted in nine or ten fields it is not easy, for it means that on each topic all inessential writing has to be ruthlessly cut out.

Try to lead the reader from one idea to the next. If there is to be a contrast, or a change of mood, build up to it with all the resources – facts, deductions and theories – at your command. If a conclusion is to be drawn, try to influence the reader to see it as you see it.

This is all very general advice, and to gain appreciation of the niceties of exposition there is nothing like constant reading and practice.

## MISUSES OF THE LANGUAGE

### Circumlocution

Avoid "circumlocutions" – that is, things said in a roundabout way. For example, "most of" is preferable to "the major part of", and "the poor" is preferable to "the lower-income groups". The notice, "Please deposit unwanted articles in the receptacle provided", if written by a language-conscious person would read: "Please throw rubbish into the bin". Interpolated clauses and phrases like "It cannot be denied that" and "in the act of" can take up valuable space.

### Use of Adjectives

Avoid unnecessary adjectives, as in "arid desert", "silvery moon", "slippery ice". You might just as reasonably talk of "wet water". Prose that is ridden with unnecessary adjectives quickly loses the reader.

Nevertheless, you should make full use of helpful or explanatory adjectives. There are numerous adjectives which, skilfully used, can save half a dozen or more words of description.

There is nothing to prevent you, also, from using compound adjectives, unless they are clumsy. For the sake of economy I should permit "face-saving action", "ninety-year-old Mrs Smith", "the newly-married couple", "the public-spirited council". Here "language-conscious person" is used. Shakespeare had his "lily-liver'd loon".

By "clumsy" is meant such laboured constructions as "operation-famous surgeon", "sea-encircled island", "risen-from-the-foam Venus", "greatly-to-be-admired heroine", "universally-acclaimed book". The use of such heavy adjectives is not to be encouraged.

You will notice that compound adjectives are made up of two or more *hyphenated* words. This practice is dealt with more fully in Chapter 5.

## Use of Parenthesis

Make use of smooth parenthetical phrases, clauses and minor sentences in such a way that ideas, statements and explanations can be slipped into major sentences. Smoothness is important; the parenthesis should be so unobtrusive as to be hardly noticeable.

## Digressions

If your writing is confined to a definite amount of space, keep digressions to a minimum. Digressions – not "padding" – may be perfectly justified if you have room for them and they are relevant to your subject. Too often, unfortunately, a writer inserts a digression out of vanity or egoism. Sometimes a digression comes perilously close to padding.

## Padding

Avoid padding absolutely. Of all the sins of speech and writing it is one of the most recognisable, even though it may be quite grammatical. It can take many forms and you have only to pick up a newspaper and read some dreary speech to find it.

Padding is the vice of using strings of words, sentences and paragraphs and saying absolutely nothing, or at any rate nothing of value. It is a very easy vice to acquire, but writers and speakers can only "fool some of the people some of the time".

## NUMERALS

If a sentence starts with a number the number must be written in words, unless the number is a date. Thus:

"Fifty years ago there were fewer cars on the roads."

"Twenty-three sacks of corn were stolen from the warehouse last night."

"1564 was the year of Shakespeare's birth."

If a number is *quoted* in speech it should also be written in words, as in the following examples:

"'Sir,' I said, 'I have to report the arrival of a hundred and twenty-two cases of stores.' "

"When I asked his date of birth he replied, The twenty-ninth of February, nineteen sixty-eight.' "

# 5

# PUNCTUATION

Punctuation literally means *pointing* (Latin, *punctus*, a point), and in grammar it is the name given to the division of statements, or collections of words, into sentences, clauses, phrases, questions, quotations and exclamations.

Speech is punctuated by pauses of different length, by the speaker's tone of voice, by inflection, by emphasis, by facial expression, and, in the case of questions, by the order of words. In writing, however, there is the advantage of a series of *punctuation marks*, marks which are more than mere conventions as, used intelligently, they can give meaning to prose or verse and prevent misunderstanding.

Punctuation can be regarded as guidance to the reader, so the use of capital letters and, in printing, the use of *italics* are included in this section.

The punctuation marks in English consist of the following:

| | |
|---|---|
| Full stop . | Single quotation marks ' ' |
| Comma , | Double quotation marks " " |
| Semicolon ; | Hyphen - |
| Colon : | Dash – |
| Question mark ? | Round brackets ( ) |
| Exclamation mark ! | Square brackets [ ] |

There are also the apostrophe (') and marks of omission (. . .).

## THE FULL STOP
Everybody knows that the full stop is used at the end of a sentence. It should indicate, in fact, that the sentence has come to a *stop*. Yet

too often we come across letters that start like this: "Referring to your letter of the 12th February." This collection of words is not a sentence, and after the full stop the reader is left floundering.

After "February" there should be a comma, followed by the noun or pronoun attached to the present participle "Referring". A correct construction would thus consist of something like this: "Referring to your letter of the 12th February, we regret to say that the work has not yet been done." An *incorrect* construction would be: "Referring to your letter of the 12th February, the work has not yet been done." This means, quite absurdly, that the work has been referring to your letter.

## THE FULL STOP WITH ABBREVIATIONS

As is commonly known, the full stop is sometimes used to denote abbreviations. It is impossible to make hard and fast rules on the use or omission of a full stop in a given abbreviation, so the best recommendation is to avoid ambiguity and be consistent. The modern trend in the UK is now towards an "open" style for abbreviations in which there are few full stops.

It is usual to allow the full stop only to denote those abbreviations which are parts of words, and *not* those abbreviations in which the first and last letters of words are given (contractions). Thus, exponents of this practice allow, for example, *Mr*, *Mrs*, *Col* (Colonel), *Dr*, *Revd*, *St* (Saint or Street), and *Rd* (Road). Typical abbreviations where a full stop is used are *Jan.*, *Sept.*, *Mon.*, *Yorks.*, *Prof.*, *Gen.*, *Capt.*, *approx.* and *Co.*

For initials of capital letters that stand for organisations the full stop is very much the exception rather than the rule. *BBC* is now widely accepted, as are *EU*, *PLO*, *KGB* and so on. The forms *AD* and *BC* are rarely seen with full stops these days and regularly appear in print in small capitals (see page 125). Academic qualifications such as **BA** or **DD** and the designations **MP** or **PC** (Privy Councillor) are usually written without full stops.

Lower case initials tend to keep their full stops, notably *i.e.*, *e.g.*, *a.m.*, *p.m.*, *q.v.* and the like. The abbreviation *plc* (public limited company) has never had full stops. **Per cent** is an abbreviation of **per centum** and so formerly needed the full stop, but nowadays is usually seen without it.

Incidentally, if an abbreviation comes at the end of a sentence there should logically be two full stops – the first for the abbreviation and the second to mark the end of the sentence. In practice, nevertheless, it is conventional to make one full stop do for the two.

## THE COMMA

The comma is a very useful little mark. Less abrupt than the full stop, it can mark the end of a clause or a phrase within a sentence and give a hint that there is something to follow.

While the correct use of the comma is fairly well understood, there is a tendency either to use too many commas or not enough. Here are two examples, one of each failing:

### Too many commas

"It was a fine day, and the sun was hot. As I walked through the meadow, towards the river, I heard the cuckoo, whose call followed me wherever I walked, but who seemed intent on eluding me. For an instant I spied him, perched on top of a tall elm, but when he knew that he was spotted, he flew off again. I reached the water's edge, and took off my shoes and socks."

There is no misuse of commas in this passage, but there is an effect of jerkiness. The passage would be smoother, easier to read, if it was rewritten in this way:

"It was a fine day, and the sun was hot. As I walked through the meadow towards the river I heard the cuckoo, whose call followed me wherever I walked but who seemed intent on eluding me. For an instant I spied him perched on top of a tall elm, but when he knew that he was spotted he flew off again. I reached the water's edge and took off my shoes and socks."

## Not enough commas

"The Member for Moortown in the Commons today in an amendment proposed that the duty on imported sealing-wax be raised by six per cent as from January 1 to conform with the inflated cost of production in Commonwealth countries.

"The Member for Sunville supporting the amendment said that as a director of a sealing-wax company in this country he thought that every effort should be made to stop overseas competition. The President of the Board of Trade in his reply said there was no evidence of any adverse effect on the sealing-wax market of competitive imports, and although he had not been informed of any complaints from the trade he was appointing a special sub-committee to investigate the whole question."

In its mad rush along, this passage is just as irritating as the previous passage which suffered from an excess of commas. The reader is left breathless. The following calmer version shows that only a few commas are necessary:

"The Member for Moortown, in the Commons today, in an amendment, proposed that the duty on imported sealing-wax be raised by six per cent as from January 1, to conform with the inflated cost of production in Commonwealth countries.

"The Member for Sunville, supporting the amendment, said that as a director of a sealing-wax company in this country he thought that every effort should be made to stop overseas competition. The President of the Board of Trade, in his reply, said there was no evidence of any adverse effect on the sealing-wax market of competitive imports, and, although he had not been informed of any complaints from the trade, he was appointing a special sub-committee to investigate the whole question."

Legal documents, of course, are notorious for their lack of commas. This failing is said to have originated in the days of old when scriveners were paid on piecework and the insertion of commas wasted valuable time. There is no doubt that legal documents would be more comprehensible if they were properly punctuated.

## COMMAS IN ENUMERATION

It is modern accepted practice in the UK to omit the last comma before **and** in an enumeration, thus:

"They brought gifts of flowers, fruit, clothing, toys and money to the refugees."

An exception would be made in the case of possible ambiguity or doubt, as in:

"The train will stop at Harrow, Pinner, Northwood, Watford, and Bushey."

"Watford and Bushey" might be interpreted as the name of a single station, just as "Harrow and Wealdstone" is one station.

Another case where the last comma would be justified, even essential, is in: "The motion received the support of the Bishops of Durham, Winchester, Grantham, Bath and Wells, and Newcastle."

Where the enumerated items collectively form the subject of a sentence preceding a verb, the insertion of a comma *after* the last item depends largely upon personal preference.

We can write: "All books, magazines, papers and other publications must be submitted to the censor for examination."

This seems preferable to, and reads more smoothly than, the following: "All books, magazines, papers and other publications, must be submitted to the censor for examination."

In the second example it can be argued that the comma after "publications" is necessary for grouping the items of the subject, but the grouping is given by the first two commas and the word "and".

Now consider the following passage:

"Strong sense of duty, sympathetic regard for the feelings of others, high moral purpose and understanding of different points of view were the qualities for which the leader was loved."

In this passage each item is a group of words. It would probably be spoken with a natural pause after each item. The result would be better, then, with a comma after "purpose" and another comma after "view".

## Confusing Enumerations

Confusing examples of enumerations occur in the daily media, especially where names of dignitaries are accompanied by explanatory phrases. Frequently this kind of reporting appears:

"A civic reception was held at the Town Hall today, when the Lord Mayor, Ald. Henry Skrimpton, the Lady Mayoress, Ald. James Todd, the Sheriff, and Mrs Todd, entertained the members of the Pacific Islands Expedition to lunch. The guests included Col G. Dykes, leader of the expedition, his chief assistant, Major P. Hamm, Dr A. Grayling, the chief scientist and technical adviser, Mr W. Jones, meterological officer, the expedition's botanist, Mr S. Crumm, the supplies officer, Mr H. Lawrence, Mr K. Smollett, treasurer and secretary, and Dr Leonard Foxhall, medical officer."

At a casual reading the list is not easy to understand. Information of this nature is better tabulated, but it is more literary to make a continuous prose passage of the information.

The news item would be more intelligible if use was made of *(a)* brackets or of *(b)* semicolons, thus:

*(a)* "The guests included Col G. Dykes (leader of the expedition), Major P. Hamm (his chief assistant), Dr A. Grayling (the chief scientist and technical adviser), . . ." and so on.

(*b*)"The guests included: Col G. Dykes, leader of the expedition; Major P. Hamm, his chief assistant; Dr A. Grayling, the chief scientist and technical adviser; . . ." and so on.

## PARENTHETICAL USE OF COMMAS

In the original version of the above list of civic guests, some of the commas are used parenthetically. That is (as you will recall from the last chapter), the words in parenthesis could have been omitted without any destruction of the sense, the parenthetical phrases being "leader of the expedition", "Major P. Hamm", "the chief scientist and technical adviser", and so on to "medical officer".

In this particular case, of course, as shown in the revised versions, it would have been more reasonable to stick to a definite order, with each name followed by its bearer's function in the expedition. One revision allows the semicolons, these being stronger than the commas, to control the groupings. The other revision, with brackets, allows the writer to retain a parenthetical construction.

The parenthetical use of commas is common. In the preceding paragraph the phrase "of course" was between parenthetical commas. Other examples (with the parenthetical words in *italics*) are the following:

"The inherent vagaries of mining are too well known, but, *subject to this qualification*, the unofficial prediction of success may be accepted."

"In Congolia, a prolific weed, *the water-hyacinth,* has made its appearance." (Note the correct use of the hyphen. A "water hyacinth" would be a hyacinth made of water.)

"Peter Paul Rubens (1577–1640), *the greatest painter of the Flemish School*, was born at Siegen in Nassau."

It is unnecessary to give any more such examples, but it might be added that clauses starting with relative pronouns, when inserted in sentences, are also parenthetical, as in the following:

"His frightening experience, which nearly cost him his life, left him a nervous wreck."

"Stratford-on-Avon, where Shakespeare was born in 1564, is a picturesque little town."

"The year 1314, when the independence of Scotland was established at Bannockburn, was a milestone in British history."

The parenthetical use of commas, then, should be easily understood. But in using commas in this way the writer must not forget that he is using a parenthesis, and a very common mistake is to omit the second comma. Let us rewrite wrongly two of our examples:

"The inherent vagaries of mining are too well known, but, subject to this qualification the unofficial prediction of success may be accepted."

"In Congolia a prolific weed, the water-hyacinth has made its appearance."

The trouble is that the comma has so many uses, and is so inconspicuous, that it is apt to be overlooked. Now, if we chose to use brackets instead of commas for our passages in parenthesis, we should never dream of omitting the second bracket; so why omit the second comma?

The possibility of confusion when essential commas are omitted can be illustrated by the following examples:

"In 1926 I was told there had been an epidemic."

"In 1926, I was told, there had been an epidemic." The first sentence is ambiguous. Was it 1926 when the writer was told of the epidemic? The correctly-punctuated second sentence makes the meaning perfectly clear.

Sometimes, though more rarely, you even come across an omission of the first comma. Here is an extract from a published definition of an inn:

". . . an establishment held out by the proprietor as offering food, drink, and if required, sleeping accommodation, . . ."

The words "if required" are a parenthesis, and there should be a comma after "and".

If one comma of the parenthesis is omitted, so should the other be omitted, and many parenthetic words and phrases can safely be used without commas. An example is "therefore", as in: "I therefore should be grateful for the return of the map." The use of commas otherwise results in such stilted sentences as: "I, therefore, should be glad if you would advise me by return of the amount of interest from this investment."

Similarly it is considered unacceptably fussy or old-fashioned, in the writing of dates in a prose passage, to give the year parenthetically between commas, as in: "On the 21st June, 1946, and again on the 18th September, 1947, I sailed from Liverpool." The commas can be missed out as in: "On the 5th May 1995 he celebrated his eighteenth birthday with a party." Sometimes the first comma only is inserted, and the omission of the second leaves the parenthesis open, as in: "On the 21st June, 1946 I sailed from Liverpool."

A comma should be used where a number follows the year as in: "In 1995, 18-year-old Daniel passed his driving test."

## MISUSE OF THE COMMA

Many people have a habit of separating a simple subject from its verb by a comma and you often find sentences of this kind: "My uncle and cousin, were going to the farm."

It is difficult to understand this error. Not only is the comma grammatically unjustified – it has no function for grouping or for parenthesis – but in speech there would be no pause before the verb. In the case of the compound subject, on the other hand, where the speaker would be reciting a catalogue of word-groups to make up his subject, there would be a pause before the verb.

Another common error is to misuse a comma in certain cases with a participle. Here are some examples:

"My guest, having gone home, I went to bed."

"Mr Brown, being a little deaf, the speaker raised his voice."

These sentences, as written, are logically wrong. Each is a case of cause-and-effect grouping, the grouping being decided by the comma.

The subject of the first sentence is "I" and the subject of the second sentence is "the speaker". The other parts of the sentences, the groups dependent on the participles "having" and "being", are subordinate. The sentences should be punctuated thus:

"My guest having gone home, I went to bed."

"Mr Brown being a little deaf, the speaker raised his voice."

Now, the following sentences are quite all right:

"My guest, having gone home, arrived to find his house in darkness."

"Mr Brown, being a little deaf, had to strain his ears to catch what the speaker said."

The subjects of the sentences are now "My guest" and "Mr Brown". The phrases "having gone home" and "being a little deaf" are now parenthetical, and are therefore put between pairs of commas.

A notice found in the bedroom of a London hotel stated:

"If you wish to stay beyond the period booked, it is essential, that, you contact reception office, on the evening before the original, departure date. Provided that, the room is still available, we will of course be pleased to help you. If not, we must hold you to the original booking."

There are, of course, far too many commas in this notice, and the word *notify* would be preferable to the word *contact*. A better version of the same notice would be this:

"If you wish to stay beyond the period booked it is essential that you notify the reception office on the evening before the originally-planned departure date. Provided that the room is still available, we shall, of course, be pleased to help you. If the room is not available we must hold you to the original booking."

There is an example of "good" English in this notice. The writer has said "Provided that" instead of the much-misused "Providing that . . ." The present participle *providing* needs an attachment, such as the personal pronoun *I* in the following: "Providing my son with a spade, I asked him to dig the garden."

## ENUMERATION OF ADJECTIVES

If you have doubts about the use of the comma in the enumeration of adjectives, a safe and simple rule is this. If there are only two adjectives, omit the comma, as in "a hot dry day". If there are three or more adjectives in a row, use commas after all except the last, as in "a hot, dry, dusty day". You would write "a sticky sweet mixture" but "a sticky, sweet, warm, mysterious mixture".

With two adjectives you can use *and* if you wish, just as in the previous paragraph – "a safe and simple rule".

## THE COMMA WITH NUMERALS

Although it does not come within the sphere of grammar, the use of a comma with numerals should be mentioned briefly.

It is customary in the English-speaking world to divide a number into its thousands by the comma. Exceptions are dates (for example, 2000 BC and AD 1914) and reference numbers (for example, Model No. 3652).

It is interesting that while we use the comma to divide the thousands and the full stop for the decimal point (85,617.23), European practice is the opposite (85.617,23). Alternatively, Europeans use a space to group the digits in a number with five or more figures (56 423,75).

## THE COMMA WITH QUOTATIONS

The comma can be used to introduce quoted speeches, as in:

"As George passed the queue at the box office he said, 'It's a good thing we booked early.' "

The colon can be used as an alternative, and this is dealt with more fully on page 97.

If a quotation is broken, however, commas must be used, as in the following:

" 'Before you go,' said Susan, 'you must see my holiday photos.' "

## THE SEMICOLON

It is convenient to regard the semicolon as something between the full stop and the comma in value, though it is used much less frequently than either. It has a definite use, however – for instance, when a slight break in a sentence is preferable to a new sentence.

The following are legitimate examples of the use of the semicolon.

"The production from the illicit diggings surpasses by far that from the recognised mines; last year the company exported only £1,500,000 worth of diamonds, while the value of black-market exports is estimated at £10,000,000."

"The proposed extension to Malaysia would involve a capital of some millions of pounds; and we cannot help thinking of the lonely pioneer who eighty years ago arrived there with nothing."

"No one was hurt in the incident; the only real damage was to a few panes of glass."

"Mr Jones believed that the new extension would cut off a significant amount of daylight from his house; his neighbour contended that, because it was not a very tall structure, it would do no such thing."

"He bought the car in Germany; at least that's what he said."

"None of her relatives liked her; her nephew, for example, refused to communicate with her or mention her at all."

### THE SEMICOLON IN VERSE

The semicolon is much used in the writing of verse – and in verse is included everything from the highest level of true poetry to the meanest doggerel. In verse, a semicolon is often used where a full stop would be too abrupt and would tend to destroy the rhythm. Some poets like to use the colon, too, but often simply as a change from the semicolon, from which it differs in value only slightly.

Shakespeare was fond of the semicolon, as you will see from all his plays and poems.

If you open almost any book of verse you will see examples of the use of the semicolon; the writing of verse, in fact, is good discipline in the grouping of words, and the punctuation of true poets is usually beyond reproach.

## THE SEMICOLON IN GROUPING

In the *grouping* of words, the semicolon is used where a stronger means of grouping is desirable than would be provided by the comma. Particularly is this the case in enumerations, where (as we have already seen) commas are not clear enough. An enumeration (or list) may be introduced by a colon, which is slightly stronger than a semicolon and is useful for indicating that the writer is "leading up" to something. For an example of this use of the semicolon you should refer to paragraph (*b*) on page 89.

## MISUSE OF THE SEMICOLON

It is wrong to use a semicolon where a comma should be used in the normal way. One fault which is not uncommon is to use a relative pronoun after such a misused semicolon, as in the following sentences:

"We gave the chieftain a present of tobacco; which he accepted gratefully as if it were a handful of gold."

"Jonathan took his bride to a lonely island in the Outer Hebrides; where, it may be assumed, they were safe from the attentions of the press."

"The Emperor in question was Napoleon Bonaparte; who, it will be conceded, had more than a spark of humanity."

In each of these sentences a comma should be used instead of the semicolon.

In enumerations, semicolons should be used only if commas would cause confusion, but they are often used in passages where commas would do. Here, for instance, is a list of adverse factors which have overtaken an unfortunate company:

"Dividends have been much reduced; the mines are among the deepest in the world; costs are likely to rise, and technical problems are increasing."

There is no justification for the semicolons after the first two adverse factors. If the passage is intended to be read with a pause after each group of words the reader will use his own sense even if there are commas instead of semicolons. In any case, if the writer of the sentence wanted to be consistent he should have used a semicolon after the third item ("costs are likely to rise") instead of a comma.

Here is an extract from a newspaper's leading article:

"Having given his heirs all he dares; having bought the best advice on showing foresight; having taken every legal step to frustrate the tax-inspector, what prospect does the millionaire or the demi-millionaire face?"

The first two semicolons are unnecessary. To be consistent in his malpractice, moreover, the writer should have used a semicolon after "tax-inspector". The use of a comma here groups the final clause ("what prospect does the millionaire or the demi-millionaire face?") only with the last item of the enumeration ("having taken every legal step to frustrate the tax-inspector"), whereas the writer's intention is to group it with all the items.

The semicolon has no right to be in the following:

"Summer temperatures, as one might suppose, reach unbearable heights, and the whole zone is one of utter desolation; no living thing, animal or vegetable existing there."

There should be a comma after "desolation" and another after "vegetable".

## THE COLON

The colon is slightly stronger than the semicolon. In the past, however, the two were used interchangeably, and either was used as an intermediate stop somewhere between the full stop and comma in value. Many of the poets and dramatists had a liking for the colon, and in the Cathedral Psalter (the Prayer Book version of the Psalms) it was adopted as a symbol for the division of each verse into halves for chanting. The translators of the Bible liked both the colon and the semicolon.

The use of the colon as a punctuation mark in the construction of a sentence is to indicate that the part of the sentence which follows is a result of, or a direct corollary to, the preceding part.

Thus, in my opinion, the colon is more justified than the semicolon in such a sentence as:

"Food was scarce in the forest that winter: neither of the woodmen had had any breakfast for three days."

A full stop would have made two scrappy sentences. A semicolon would have given the right rhythm, but would not have emphasised the connection between the two parts. A colon gives the strongest effect: the reader stops sharply on reaching it, and is forced to the reality of the situation by reading the subsequent part of the sentence.

Here is another good example of the justifiable use of the colon in punctuation:

"It is not a just law: in fact, it is unjust in the extreme."

### THE COLON AS A LINK

The colon is also a *connecting* sign, and one very common use of it is not in the grammatical punctuation of a sentence but in connecting the general with the particular. This kind of construction is widespread and legitimate, with a phrase or a word following a sentence through a connecting colon:

"There are six rooms in the house: four upstairs and two downstairs."

"The explanation of his progress was to be found in one word: ambition."

"One of the first subjects to which the new Prime Minister will have to devote his attention is one to which the very structure of the Cabinet suggests a predisposition: European economic cooperation."

Now, in each of these cases a dash (–) would have served quite as well as a colon. There are, in fact, innumerable instances where the link between two items can be provided by either a dash or a colon.

In this book you will often find examples of writing introduced, perhaps, by the words "the following" and a colon, the colon being the link between the general and the particular.

## THE COLON WITH QUOTATIONS

It is sometimes a practice to introduce any quoted material (words in quotation marks) by a colon. Where speech is concerned, however, too many colons can be conspicuous.

"As she stepped into the conservatory she saw a dark shape gliding over the floor. Involuntarily gasping: 'Oh!', she went shivering into the commodious lounge and told her story to her horror-struck husband.

"He muttered: 'Come with me, my dear,' and led her into the library, where from a high shelf he took a dusty brown leather volume, smelling of age and mildew. Pointing to a chair, he said: 'Be seated. Listen to this.'

"For the first time in her life she listened to the dread story of the Fanshawes, and when the dry trembling recital came to an end two hours later she murmured: 'So that's it.' "

The colons before the short speeches break up the prose too much. There is also a tendency to read the prose as if the colons were pauses. Commas could be used in place of the colons, and although not quite so distracting they, too, might induce pauses where pauses were not intended.

In the case of such short speeches it would be best to ignore both colons and commas before the quotation marks and carry straight on, like this:

"Involuntarily gasping 'Oh!', she went shivering into the commodious lounge. . . . He muttered 'Come with me, my dear.' . . . Pointing to a chair, he said 'Be seated. Listen to this.' . . . She murmured 'So that's it.' "

Commas would be used before somewhat longer quotations, and colons before still longer quotations. A single sentence, if not too long, may be preceded by a comma. A long sentence, or a passage of two or more sentences, may be preceded by a colon. Certainly, if a new paragraph is to start with a quotation, it is often introduced by a colon.

## THE QUESTION MARK

The question mark is not greatly maltreated, and on the whole its use is understood.

Unfortunately, however, it is too often omitted from those requests which are politely given in the form of questions, such as, "Will you kindly note that I shall be away from home all next week?"

The writers of business correspondence are especially unconscious of the need for the question mark, especially if a question starts "Will you . . . ?" The following are examples of the requests that are sent out every day:

"Will you please return the plans at your convenience."

"Will you take steps to ensure that there is no recurrence of this trouble."

"Will you please supply the undermentioned goods." "May I . . . ?" is another beginning which, it is often assumed, does not need a question mark:

"May I draw your attention to your non-compliance with the new condition embodied in Clause 32 (c)."

The assumption seems to be that where a question implies a command, an order, a request, there is no doubt about the answer. The writers of such sentences do not for a moment think that the readers may say "No." In spite of that, however, these sentences are grammatically in the form of questions, and therefore the question mark is absolutely necessary.

## MISUSE OF THE QUESTION MARK

There are sentences which, though simple statements, are intended to imply questioning. In speech, the implication may be given by the tone of voice or the lilt, but in writing there is no logical justification for the question mark. Here are four examples:

"I wonder if I could see the manager."

"Surely it is not true."

"Don't tell me you are going away."

"You really haven't found it."

There is a strong temptation to use a question mark after such sentences as these, but any sentence, to justify the question mark, should be framed as a question.

With the exception of the first example, each sentence could be followed by an exclamation mark, as most probably it would be uttered in an exclamatory tone.

There are, moreover, exclamatory sentences which are expressed as questions but which do not take the question mark. "How are the mighty fallen!" is not a question but an oratorical way of saying "How the mighty are fallen!"

Such a construction can be either a question or an exclamation.

Thus, "How often does it happen?" is a direct question. "How often does it happen!" is an exclamation of surprise at the frequency of "it".

There was a peculiar Victorian and Edwardian form of request starting with "Do you . . .", which was not a question at all. These are two examples:

"Do you hold my horse while I look at his hoof."

"Do you take this road while I'll take that, and we'll see who arrives first."

In the first example, "Do you hold" was regarded as the imperative mood of the verb "to hold", and hence there was no hint of a question in this form of construction. "Do you take" was the imperative mood of the verb "to take".

One pitfall to be avoided is the use of a question mark in brackets after a word of phrase which you may consider unjustified. In readers' letters to newspapers this kind of facetiousness is not uncommon:

"The experience (?) of many of our county councillors should surely lead them to the conclusion that on new housing estates the roads should be laid first."

This, like a profusion of exclamation marks, is an unmistakable sign of the inexperienced writer. It amounts to a raising of the eyebrows, a nudge in the ribs. The writer is trying to imply that in his opinion many of the councillors lack experience, and he should boldly say so, even if it means another sentence. How, in speech, can a question mark be placed between two brackets?

## THE EXCLAMATION MARK

With rare exceptions, the use of the exclamation mark must be limited to exclamations, exclamatory sentences and exclamatory phrases.

Another name for exclamation marks is "interjections" (see page 32). Once called a "point of admiration" the exclamation mark should be used with discrimination and care in exclamatory sentences and phrases.

An exclamatory sentence could be something like this: "All my jewels have been stolen!" Such a statement looks too casual without the exclamation mark, as if the speaker did not care very much. Other examples are:

"He surely hasn't come home already!"

"I am saved at last!" "Get out!"

A point to remember is that the exclamatory sentences are usually *quoted* sentences spoken emotionally or under stress. A passage in narrative form would certainly *not* be written like this:

"She entered the room and found that all her jewels had been stolen! Her black-sheep brother surely had not come home already! Then she remembered that her brother had just been elected to the city council, and had decided to reform. Clearly he could not have been the culprit. He was saved at last! She need not tell him to get out!"

Exclamatory phrases are such observations as "Good heavens!", "What a mess!", "Oh! What a beautiful morning!", "Hey! Look out!", "If only I'd known!" and "God forbid!"

The general attitude to the exclamation mark is the attitude of the naïve minister in Barrie's *Farewell, Miss Julie Logan*. The Revd Adam Yestreen is explaining humour to Miss Julie.

"I drew a note of exclamation, and showed her how they were put into books, at the end of sentences, to indicate that the remark was of a humorous character. She got the loan of the pencil and practised making notes of exclamation under my instruction."

## MISUSE OF THE EXCLAMATION MARK

The overuse of the exclamation mark is frowned on as vulgar and, despite what one sees in print, multiple exclamation marks, such as the pair at the end of this sentence, stand for sensationalism and should be banned!!

Many people (especially the more demonstrative among us) seem incapable of writing personal letters without these emblems of emotion. They wrongly think that every sentence meant to be surprising, amusing, peculiar, or in any way out of the ordinary, should be followed by an exclamation mark.

"This is funny," they seem to say, or "This is witty, this is astonishing, this will make your hair curl." But the truth is that the essence of the surprise, the humour, the wit, the unusual, should be in the writing itself, and if these qualities are lacking all the exclamation marks in the whole world will not create them.

It is as if the writer is screaming at his reader to take special notice of his devastating sentence, but the civilised writer should not adopt the tactics of the signwriter or the poster artist.

## QUOTATION MARKS

The term "quotation marks" is far better than the old-fashioned "inverted commas". For one thing, only the first marks (") – before the quotation – are inverted commas, the second marks (") being commas the right way round but stuck up in the air.

For another thing, the term "inverted commas" is top-heavy. And for another (even though this is a book on English), French quotation marks are not commas, inverted or otherwise, but are like this: « ».

Then let us consider what quotation marks are for. Primarily, they are for anything *actually quoted*; this may sound silly, but, as you will see later, it is not as silly as it sounds. Quotation marks are for quoting speech, or for copying something that is written. They are for illustrating the unusualness, doubtfulness, or other peculiarity, real or imagined, of a word or a group of words. They may be used for titles of books, plays, films, articles, poems and periodicals, and for names of ships, paintings, houses, inns and hotels.

## SINGLE AND DOUBLE QUOTATION MARKS

Many people are understandably confused by the apparently indiscriminate use of single quotation marks (' ') and double quotation marks (" ").

The more logical practice is to use single marks for all quotations unless there is one quotation inside another, when the inside quotation receives double marks. This practice gives this kind of result:

'As I walked out of the house I said to him, "We shall never meet again." Yet, had I known it, I was wrong.'

'The title of the book, "Purple Skies", gives no clue as to its contents.'

'The dictatorial policy of "indoctrination" has proved futile.'

However, conventional practice in this direction is illogical. It is more conventional to use double marks for all quoted matter except for quoted quotations, which are given single marks. The practice of using single marks inside double marks is the practice adopted throughout this book.

## MISUSE OF QUOTATION MARKS

It is important to remember that quotation marks enclose passages which are *actually quoted*. Writers who have failed in the observance of this obvious truth include novelists whose pages abound with passages in quotation marks which are not quotations at all.

Let me show what I mean by a simple example:

"Jack Horner said, 'What a good boy am I!' "

The double quotation marks, incidentally, show that the passage is merely an example, and not part of the text of the book.

The speech "What a good boy am I!" consists of Jack's *actual words*, and is thus a quotation. (Notice the correct use of the exclamation mark.)

But if the sentence had been expressed in this way: "Jack said that he was a good boy", the actual words are not given. Hence there is no quotation, and the use of quotation marks would be wrong.

Yet, in effect, many novelists and other kinds of writers would write the second example thus:

"Jack said that 'he had been a good boy'." You will realise that this is entirely wrong.

Jane Austen had an irritating trick of putting in quotation marks passages in which the speaker was referred to as *he* instead of *I*. Look at this, from *Persuasion*, where Sir Walter is addressing a company:

"Sir Walter thought much of Mrs Wallis; she was said to be an excessively pretty woman, beautiful. 'He longed to see her. He hoped she might make some amends for the many very plain faces he was continually passing in the streets. . . . It was evident how little the women were used to the sight of anything tolerable, by the effect which a man of decent appearance produced. . . .' Modest Sir Walter!"

The words in the single quotation marks are obviously not the words Sir Walter used, for the speaker would have used *I* and the present tense of the verbs. As the passage is written, the quotation marks are wrong and unnecessary.

Here is another example from the same novel:

"A knock at the door suspended every thing. 'A knock at the door! and so late! . . .. Mrs Clay decidedly thought it Mr Elliot's knock.' Mrs Clay was right."

Presumably Mrs Clay was speaking; but why did Jane Austen use quotation marks when she was not giving Mrs Clay's actual words?

Towards our own time, even such celebrated novelists as Sir Hugh Walpole have not been guiltless. Consider this, from *The Secret City*:

"He would tell you, if you inquired, that 'he couldn't stand those fellows who looked into every glass they passed.' "

If Walpole had wanted to give the man's speech in quotation marks, it would probably have been like this:

" 'I can't stand those fellows who look into every glass they pass.' "

The alternative form would be as it is printed, but without the quotation marks, thus:

"He would tell you, if you inquired, that he couldn't stand those fellows who looked into every glass they passed."

Here is an extract from an erstwhile advertisement of an oil company:

"Forty-six years ago Blériot flew the Channel and in the prophetic words of Lord Northcliffe at the time 'Britain was no longer an island.' "

The words of Lord Northcliffe were "Britain is no longer an island", and the error of the copywriter is emphasised by the phrase "at the time".

The passage, in fact, is slightly confused. The copywriter probably wanted to use the phrase "prophetic words", and realised that this called for a quotation. "Britain is" would not have sounded right in association with "Blériot flew", and therefore "Britain was" appeared.

Reconstruction would have solved the problem, in some such manner as the following:

"Forty-six years ago Blériot flew the Channel, and, as Lord Northcliffe remarked at the time, Britain was no longer an island."

## QUOTATION MARKS WITH FULL STOPS AND COMMAS

You have probably noticed that in most newspapers, and in some books and magazines, closing quotation marks for quoted speech are placed *after* a full stop or comma if there happens to be one.

This is done purely for appearance, even if the full stop or comma is not part of the quotation. You will probably agree that, in the following, the first example looks neater on the page:

" 'My name is Samuel,' he said."

" 'My name is Samuel', he said."

Logically, however, the comma here is not part of the quotation, and should be outside the closing mark. Usually, in fact, the logical place for a comma *is* outside. An exception can occur in an interrupted speech of which the comma forms a part, as in:

"There are, unfortunately,' she said, 'very few first-class applicants for the post.' "

The comma after "unfortunately" is part of the broken sentence, is therefore part of the quotation, and correctly appears before the intermediate quotation mark.

In the following example the comma is *not* part of the broken sentence, and correctly appears after the intermediate quotation mark:

" 'There are', she said, 'very few first-class applicants.' "

Yet according to convention this would be printed thus:

" 'There are,' she said, 'very few first-class applicants.' "

If we want to follow logic, a full stop can be placed inside or outside, the position depending on the mental sequence. In the following examples, the full stop is rightly placed outside:

"Lady Nugent, as we have seen, could not paint her flamingo, but had to call in 'a nature artist'."

"Lack of sunlight, shortages of fresh fruit and vegetables and the intense cold combine to bring on what is called 'Lapp sickness'."

(This sentence would be better with commas after **vegetables** and **cold.** And **so-called** would be better than **what is called**.)

"Above all, Griffo supplied a novel fount . . .. based on the 'cancelleresca corsiva' of the papal chancery, which humanists had taken over for their informal writing, and later received the name of 'italics'."

Sometimes, the placing of full stops outside quotation marks looks untidy, as in the following examples:

"To Charles XII these occupations of Peter afforded some scornful amusement. 'Let him build towns' are the words accredited to him 'and we will come and take them'."

" 'One ambassador flies out as another flies in'."

"When Dr Johnson averred that Milton's *Lycidas* was *easy, vulgar* and therefore *disgusting,* he intended to say that it was 'effortless, popular, and therefore not in good taste'."

These three examples show why many publishers and printers do not always follow logic and instead sometimes place quotation marks outside full stops and commas.

## QUOTATION MARKS WITH OTHER PUNCTUATION MARKS

When it comes to the use of quotation marks with punctuation marks other than the full stop and the comma, logic seems to be the only guide.

If the punctuation mark is part of the quotation, then it obviously is placed *before* the closing quotation marks; if it is *not* included in the quotation, then it is placed *after* the closing quotation marks.

### The Semicolon

The semicolon, by virtue of its nature, can hardly come at the end of, and inside, a quotation. It therefore appears after the quotation marks, as follows:

"He unfurled the banner bearing the magic word 'Excelsior'; then, at the head of his little band, he marched proudly into the night."

### The Colon

The colon, too, comes after the quotation marks, as in this example:

"The following is the cast of 'Macbeth': . . . ."

### The Question Mark

Depending on the sense of the sentence, the question mark can be inside, outside, or both. Here are three examples, one of each kind of application:

"Are you happy?"

"Did you see 'The Maid of Orleans'?"

"Did she say 'Do you love me?'?"

Marguerite Sheen, in *Twilight on the Floods*, has misplaced a question mark in the following:

"Yet how could he say bluntly: 'I have married the girl you love?' "

This should be:

"Yet how could he say bluntly: 'I have married the girl you love.'?"

## The Exclamation Mark

The exclamation mark, like the question mark, can be in three positions:

" 'Get out of my sight!' he said."

"How horrid of him to call you 'Parasite'!" "How casual of him just to say 'Oh!'!"

## INTERRUPTED QUOTATIONS

Already dealt with are interrupted speeches of this kind:

" 'It's all right,' he gasped with relief, 'there's nobody in.' "

But another kind of interruption in a quotation or an extract is an interpolation, or explanatory note put in by the quoter for the benefit of the reader. Sometimes you see such interpolations enclosed by ordinary brackets, but this method is clearly inadequate as the quotation itself may contain words in such brackets.

One convention in printing is the use of square brackets to distinguish the interpolation from words in ordinary round brackets forming part of the quotation. Here is an example of such practice:

"The Member for South Beasley said: 'The Minister has pointed out that when the Imported Inks (Restriction of Colours) Bill becomes law, it [the Bill] will not seek to prohibit ink-users from selecting their favourite colours when purchasing inks. Can the Minister give us his assurance that when they [inks] are bought, they will be found to be equal in quality and in the fastness of their dyes with the inks at present obtainable?' (Laughter.)"

The square brackets indicate that the words they enclose are not part of the speech of the Member for South Beasley, but are simply inserted to help the reader to define "it" and "they". The quotation or the extract could be broken with quotation marks and dashes. The square-bracketed parts of the above would then appear in this way:

" '. . .. Bill becomes law, it' – the Bill – 'will not seek to prohibit . . . that when they' – inks – 'are bought, they will be found. . .' "

## QUOTATION MARKS WITH PARAGRAPHS

When a quoted passage or speech is divided into paragraphs, it is customary to use quotation marks at the beginning of the passage and at the beginning of each paragraph, but only the last paragraph is given quotation marks at the end.

# THE HYPHEN

The hyphen, a really logical punctuation mark, has two functions. One is to link separate words to make one compound word. The other is to act as a grouping agent. (See also page 114.)

## COMPOUND WORDS

Simple examples of compound words are *orange-box*, *paper-fastener* and *water-carrier*. Without the hyphen these would mean, absurdly, an orange-coloured box, a fastener made of paper, and a carrier made of water. Similarly, when the first part of the compound is a present participle, the hyphen is often essential, as in *changing-room* (instead of a room that is changing), *laughing-gas* and *writing-desk*. Without the hyphen these compounds would be ambiguous.

There is little fear of ambiguity in *copper-mining*, *ducking-stool*, *fruit-picker*, *manhole-cover*, *piano-stool* and *steel-production*, even when the hyphen is absent, but the fact that the items are *single* objects or activities, in my opinion, justifies the hyphen.

There are innumerable cases where the first word acts as an adjective describing the second, when there is no need for the hyphen, examples being *football team*, *herb garden*, *monkey house*, *punctuation mark* and *washing machine*. There is a commendable tendency to drop the hyphen after the combination has been well established, so that we now have, as accepted nouns, *dishwasher*, *earthworks*, *glassblower*, *haystack*, *inkwell*, *lampshade*, *weedkiller* and a thousand others.

## THE HYPHEN AS A GROUPING AGENT

As a grouping agent the hyphen forms adjectives, as in *face-saving action*, *newly-married couple* and *public-spirited council*. Of these examples, *face-saving* and *public-spirited* are always adjectives, so that the hyphen is still necessary if we write "His action was face-saving" or "The council was public-spirited". *Newly married*, however, need not be a compound adjective but simply a pair of independent words, so that if we write "They are newly married" there is no hyphen.

Similar examples are provided by the following pairs of sentences:

"She walked up the stairs to her office on the third floor."

"She walked up the stairs to her third-floor office."

"She is well dressed."

"She is a well-dressed woman."

"He gave an entertaining speech after dinner."

"He was an entertaining after-dinner speaker."

"His car was up to date but his ideas were out of date."

"He had an up-to-date car but out-of-date ideas."

"The circuit is rated at 250 volts."

"It is a 250-volt circuit."

"The journey is twenty miles."

"It is a twenty-mile journey."

In the last two examples you will notice the change from plural to singular when the quantitative words are compounded into adjectives. Similarly we should write of "a six-man committee", not "a six-men committee".

## WORDS WITH PREFIXES

A prefix is something placed *before* a word to modify the meaning. The following is a list of prefixes in common use:

| | |
|---|---|
| *pre-* (before) | *supra-* (above) |
| *ante-* (before) | *super-* (above) |
| *post-* (after) | *infra-* (below) |
| *anti-* (against) | *ex-* (former) |
| *pro-* (for) | *ex-* (out of) |
| *contra-* (against, opposite to) | *ultra-* (more than) |

Sometimes, but not always, the prefix is linked with the main word by a hyphen. There seems to be no law determining which words are to have the hyphen, but most probably all the words with prefixes originally had hyphens which have been discarded by general and tacit agreement in the course of time.

Thus, today we have *prehistoric* but *pre-Christian*, *postnatal* but *post-nuptial*, *antipathetic* but *anti-ethnic*.

*Infrared*, *ultraviolet* and most of the *contra-*, *supra-* and *super-* words are written without the hyphen, examples being *contradict*, *supranational*, *supernatural*. *Ex* may or may not be given the hyphen.

When a prefix is linked by a hyphen with a proper name, it is usual to start the prefix with a small letter even though the proper name starts with a capital. An example included in the foregoing lists is *pre-Christian*. A compound adjective which has become independent of the main word, however, is the geological name *Precambrian*, which logically should be *pre-Cambrian*.

Be careful how you use hyphened prefixes with double words. For example, think how absurd are written expressions like these:

"The ex-Home Secretary was at the reception."

"In spite of his anti-trade union attitude, he is a militant champion of the masses."

"Before becoming pro-Free Churches, the Bishop was a staunch High Anglican."

"Ex-Home-Secretary" would look peculiar, but why not use "former Home Secretary"? "Anti-trade-union" is all right, as it is a compound adjective preceding a noun. "Pro-Free-Churches" is not satisfactory, and here some reconstruction is necessary: "Before becoming a supporter of Free Churches, the Bishop was a staunch High Anglican."

## THE EFFECT OF OMITTING THE HYPHEN

The omission of the hyphen can produce absurd ambiguities like "small business heads", "obsolete food contamination regulations", "galloping inflation sufferers", "edible oil technologist" and "fine tooth comb". The logical way of writing these, as should be obvious after a little thought, is: "small-business heads", "obsolete food-contamination regulations", "galloping-inflation sufferers", "edible-oil technologist" and "fine-tooth comb". You should have a toothbrush, but a tooth-comb is unnecessary.

We have already seen some of the odd effects that can be produced by the omission of the hyphen, as in *writing desk* and *walking stick*.

What about the headline, "Man Eating Tiger in Zoo"? The omission of the hyphen between *man* and *eating* is a comical mistake, but it is by no means rare.

A vapour-lamp was advertised as "producing a germ destroying vapour". Literally interpreted, this meant that the lamp produced a germ which destroyed vapour. All that was needed to give the right sense was a hyphen in "germ destroying".

"French polisher" means a polisher of French nationality, but if the reference is to a man who does French polishing he should be described as a "French-polisher".

113

There is justification for the hyphen in words like **tinminer**. Similarly, the hyphen is necessary in the following words and all others like them, even if there is no following noun as in **man-eating tiger**:

| | | |
|---|---|---|
| *copper-mining* | *steel-production* | *tool-making* |
| *coal-mining* | *gas-manufacture* | *house-hunting* |
| *tea-planting* | *novel-writing* | *portrait-painting* |

It should be noted that words like **nickel plating** are *not* in this category, as **nickel** is an adjective and the **plating** is not done on the nickel but on the underlying metal. **Nickel-plating** would imply that the nickel itself was plated. **Tin plate** does not normally need a hyphen, but the accepted term is **tinplate**.

We may have an enumeration of hyphenated words, as in the sentence: "He is interested in gold-mining, silver-mining and copper-mining." If we wanted to write this as it would probably be said, we should be perfectly justified in writing: "He is interested in gold-, silver- and copper-mining."

While it is important to use it where it is justified, the hyphen should not be used unnecessarily. The use of too many hyphens is nearly as bad as the use of too few.

## OTHER MEANS OF ADJECTIVAL GROUPING

"Adjectival grouping" simply means the grouping of two or more words to form a compound adjective, as in "six-man committee" and "sabre-toothed tiger".

We have seen that the usual method of grouping is by means of the hyphen. There are, however, three other ways which must be mentioned.

If the group of words forming the adjective happens to be in quotation marks for one reason or another, hyphens are superfluous. Suitable examples are in the following sentences:

"The extraordinary meeting of the council resulted in the formation of a special 'coordination of committees' plan."

"For the purpose of attracting tourists it was decided to inaugurate a 'Welcome to Dulltown' campaign."

"The magnificent 'Daily Drummer' trophy was won by Mrs Queetch."

In the last example, "Daily Drummer" would probably have been printed in *italics*, as is the custom of most publishers, but in such cases there are no quotation marks. The use of italics, in fact, is the second method of grouping without the hyphen, and in writing or typing it is customary to underline any words which are to be set in italics.

Foreign phrases are usually printed in italics, and when they are used as adjectives it is not necessary to use the hyphen. We need not write *"bona-fide* claim" as the italics in *"bona fide* claim" provide sufficient grouping. Similarly, we should write *"à la carte* menu" and *"hors de combat* army".

There is a third system of grouping where omission of the hyphen is justified. "North Atlantic Treaty Organisation countries" does not have hyphens as the four words are a well-known group in themselves without any further aid, especially as each word is started with a capital letter. The capital initials, in fact, are frequently regarded as self-sufficient, and the organisation has developed into "NATO".

Note the absence of hyphens in these examples:

"A Foreign Office spokesman."

"The United States ambassador."

"A House of Lords debate."

"A Friends of the Earth representative."

## THE DASH

To many people, the dash (–) is the only punctuation mark known. They scatter dashes freely about their correspondence, to take the place of full stops, commas, colons and semicolons. If they do permit themselves a little relaxation from this dull practice it is probably only to use the double or treble exclamation mark.

The dash has three main functions – as a pause, as an indication of parenthesis, and as a link.

## THE DASH AS A PAUSE

When a dash is used to indicate a pause in a sentence, it is essential that after the pause the continuation is strongly linked with the part of the sentence preceding the dash. The reader or listener must *expect* something to follow the pause. In speech this expectation could be induced by the speaker's intonation, but in writing the best means of indication is the dash.

The following are typical examples of this function of the dash:

"It was not a lion – it was a tiger, furiously lashing its way through the undergrowth."

"That season Farmer Montgomery helped with my harvest – not before time, I thought."

The following is a *bad* example of this function of the dash:

"It will be for the Council to decide whether the property after improvement or conversion will have a useful life which will justify the spending of public money on it – the law requires that the expected life must be more than fifteen years."

It would have been better if a full stop had taken the place of the dash and a new sentence started with "The law . . ."

## THE DASH IN PARENTHESIS

The second function of the dash is parenthetical, and of course two dashes are required to give the parenthesis. (See page 74.) A pair of dashes may be equivalent to a pair of brackets or a pair of commas, but not always. Consider the following sentence:

"All night long they toiled – it was their third night without sleep – and by the morning they were completely exhausted."

Here, commas could not properly be used. Brackets could be used with the same effect as dashes:

"All night long they toiled (it was their third night without sleep) and by morning they were completely exhausted."

Often you find that a writer – even in print – will start a parenthesis with a dash and then forget to finish it. Such lapses can lead to this kind of writing:

"The Mayor's annual banquet – at which His Worship the Mayor, the Mayoress, the Sheriff, the Aldermen, the Councillors, and several visiting notabilities were present, was held today at the Town Hall."

Having chosen a dash to open his parenthesis the writer must use a dash to close it, and the right place for it in the above sentence is between *present* and *was*. If the writer had started with a bracket he would probably have noticed the need for a bracket at the other end.

Commas could have been used in this sentence instead of dashes or brackets, but the parenthesis is so long that the reader might have become confused. Refer also to the sections, "Commas in Enumeration", page 87, and "Parenthetical Use of Commas", page 89.

An interesting point arises when dashes or brackets are used with a legitimate comma. Consider the sentence:

"Harps are expensive, and harpists are scarce." The comma after *expensive* is justified.

Now, suppose that the writer wishes to interpolate in parenthesis some information about harps – for example, "a good harp costs well over a thousand pounds."

The most suitable place to put it is after *expensive*, so that the sentence takes either of the following forms:

"Harps are expensive – a good harp costs well over a thousand pounds –, and harpists are scarce."

"Harps are expensive (a good harp costs well over a thousand pounds), and harpists are scarce."

Now, although the comma after the second bracket looks all right, the comma after the second dash looks out of place. Actually, it is not out of place at all, and logically it should be there. However, parenthetical dashes are nowadays regarded as having the power of absorbing the second comma, or doing its job for it. In other words, the second dash fulfils the joint functions of a dash and a comma, so that the comma in such cases is not inserted.

## THE DASH AS A LINK

The third use of the dash is to indicate a connecting link. It may be between the general and the particular as on page 97 ("The Colon as a Link"), or before lists and summaries, or it may link a quotation with its source, for example:

" 'History is bunk.' – Henry Ford."

It can also be used to link breaks in speech:

"David, I've poured you a whisky and – oh, I forgot, you only drink orange juice, don't you?"

" 'Mr Johnson, I – ,' Smith broke off as Johnson's secretary entered the office."

The dash is used instead of a hyphen to link words where the first element is not a modifier of the second such as in, for example: "The Tyson–Bruno fight"; "The former Liberal–SDP alliance"; "The 1914–18 War"; "The Heathrow–Rome flight"; "The Chinese–Soviet border"; "The Jane Smith–Harold Jones wedding."

# BRACKETS

The use of brackets to indicate parenthesis has already been dealt with in Chapter 4 (under "Parenthesis") and in the foregoing section on dashes. There is therefore little further to say about brackets: their use is only parenthetical, they are always in pairs, and a bracket by itself has no reason for existence.

You should be careful when a closing bracket comes at the end of a sentence, a clause, or a phrase, in such a way that it is next to a full stop or a comma. Often, too often, you see mistakes in the order of punctuation, and the following examples are all wrong:

"The 5.30 will stop at Sheffield (Midland) and Leeds (City.)"

"The film is called 'To Shape Tomorrow.' (Subject: Plastics)."

"I thank you for your letter of the 15th and have pleasure in returning your plan (of which, incidentally, I have made a copy.)"

The comma seems to be less vulnerable than the full stop when used beside a closing bracket, but punctuation like this is sometimes seen:

"He showed me his bicycle (a very nice bicycle,) and let me have a ride."

The correct versions of the above four sentences are:

"The 5.30 will stop at Sheffield (Midland) and Leeds (City)."

"The film is called To Shape Tomorrow' (subject: Plastics)." An alternative is: "The film is called 'To Shape Tomorrow.' (Subject: Plastics.)"

"I thank you for your letter of the 15th and have pleasure in returning your plan (of which, incidentally, I have made a copy)."

"He showed me his bicycle (a very nice bicycle), and let me have a ride."

Strictly, the writer of the third example should not have used brackets, as the second part of his sentence is a relative clause rather than a parenthesis. The following would have been preferable:

"I thank you for your letter of the 15th, and have pleasure in returning your plan, of which, incidentally, I have made a copy."

SQUARE BRACKETS

While ordinary round brackets have their place in the course of a written sentence, and in fact are part of a written sentence, square brackets – [ ] – are generally used to enclose something that is put in, perhaps by way of explanation, but is not part of the sentence. (See also pages 74 and 116.)

"I live [*verb*] in a house."

The explanatory word ***verb*** is obviously not part of the sentence, and thus has to be distinguished somehow from the words of the sentence, "I live in a house."

If round brackets were used, it would mean that the word ***verb***, in parenthesis, was part of the sentence. To show its independence from the words of the sentence, therefore, it is enclosed in square brackets.

A common example of the use of square brackets is the interpolation of something into a quotation – the interpolation of a word or phrase which is not actually part of the quotation. The following example is from a book review:

"According to the author's preface, 'the book was planned to give the nation some idea of the conditions under which they [the pygmies] lived in the early nineteenth century.' If he has not succeeded, it is not his fault."

The words ***the pygmies*** are an explanatory note inserted by the reviewer. Round brackets would have made the words part of the quotation, but as they are not part of the quotation they are enclosed in square brackets.

You can do it another way – by breaking the quotation and using a pair of dashes:

"According to the author's preface, 'the book was planned to give the nation some idea of the conditions under which they' – the pygmies – 'lived in the early nineteenth century.' . . ."

## THE APOSTROPHE

The apostrophe is used to indicate possession (see page 19) and is also used to take the place, for the sake of abbreviation, of omitted letters. It is explained here when you should use apostrophe-*s* (*'s*) and *s*-apostrophe (*s'*).

## POSSESSION

Simple cases of possession include *Jim's dog, my uncle's book* and *St John's Church*. In each of these the possessor is singular, and the *s* follows the apostrophe. Where ownership is shared by two or more nouns the apostrophe comes after the *s*, as in *the girls' hats*, *the dogs' bones* and *the two nations' agreement*.

Most proper nouns ending in *s* take apostrophe-s, as in *Columbus's ship*, *Charles's reign*, *Frances's doll*, *Keats's poetry* and *Pythagoras's theorem*. Exceptions hallowed by tradition or euphony include *Achilles' heel*, *goodness' sake*, *Jesus' sake*, *Moses' law* and *Xerxes' fleet*. Another exception, in which the final sibilant acts as *s*, is *conscience' sake*. Classical poetry abounds in exceptions in this and other matters of grammar, but is usually exonerated by something called poetic licence.

Collective nouns are treated as singular, so that the apostrophe comes before the *s* in expressions like *the people's homes*, *the children's toys*, *the men's work* and *the mice's hole*.

Even some journalists are confused when writing about people's homes. You write *Mr Jones's house* or *Mrs Jones's house*, but if you want to refer to the joint ownership you treat the Jones household as plural and write *the Joneses' house*.

Commercial establishments should receive exactly the same treatment. If a firm is controlled by one man called Smith you can write that you do your shopping at *Smith's*. If there are two or more Smiths in a family business the correct form is *Smiths'*. If you do not know how many Smiths there are it is safe to stick to *Smith's*.

Of two newspaper reports one refers to "the Dean of St Paul's note" and the other to "the Serjeant-at-Arm's chair". Anything possessed by or attributed to the Dean of St Paul's should take the apostrophe-*s* in the normal way. The logical rendering of this phrase is "the Dean of St Paul's's note", but as this looks unwieldy it would be preferable to write "the note of the Dean of St Paul's".

The other phrase should be "the Serjeant-at-Arms's chair" or "the chair of the Serjeant-at-Arms".

On the subject of place-names where a possessive is involved, the best advice is to follow tradition or custom, wrong though it may be. For example, St Albans, St Andrews, St Annes, St Helens, St Ives, St Leonards and St Mawes, are not granted an apostrophe. St Michael's Mount, St John's Wood and Land's End are favoured, but Golders Green shuns the apostrophe.

The treatment of possessive pronouns has varied in the past, but today the accepted practice is to omit the apostrophe in *hers, ours, theirs* and *yours*. These possessive pronouns thus agree with *its*, which was never given an apostrophe.

## OMITTED LETTERS

Confusion between the possessive *its* and the abbreviation *it's* (*it is*) is one of the commonest mistakes in spelling. *It's* is one of the abbreviations, or contractions, in the same group as *can't, isn't, shouldn't, it'll, I'd, he's, we'll, they're*. *Won't* is a mysterious abbreviation of *will not*; it may be a corruption of "willn't", or it may owe its origin to the fact that it rhymes with *don't*. *Shan't*, meaning *shall not*, should have two apostrophes, and in many nineteenth-century books it is written *sha'n't*. George Bernard Shaw tried to assert his individuality by omitting the apostrophe from familiar contractions and wrote "didnt", "wont", "weve" and "shouldnt", but perversely he retained it in *I'm, I'll* and *he's*.

Then there are words like *'bus, 'phone, 'flu* (influenza), *'cello* (violoncello) and *'plane* (aeroplane or airplane). These started as definite abbreviations, but the apostrophe has subsequently been dropped as the abbreviated forms are accepted into the language as true words. *Bus, phone, flu, cello* and *plane* have now become as legitimate as *pram*.

# MARKS OF OMISSION

It is often necessary to copy an extract from something – from a report, an article, a book, a letter, or a speech. In the course of the extract you probably find that everything is not relevant to your present purpose, and that certain parts, having nothing to do with that purpose, can be omitted. What are you to do to avoid tedium for the reader?

The customary way of showing that something has been omitted from a quotation is by means of a row of three or four dots, not too closely spaced. If the end of a sentence falls immediately before the omission, the full stop should be shown in its proper place. If the omission starts in the middle of a sentence, a space must be left between the last word and the first dot. The following example shows both kinds of omission:

### Original version
"The Minister said that it had always been his aim to assist small shopkeepers. A large number of small purchases in a populous area could give a substantial turnover, but rural areas were less fortunate. Subsidies of the kind suggested by the Hon. Member would relieve hardship, but at the same time might tend to promote a certain lethargy. It was not his intention to set up a Royal Commission, but the Ministry would investigate any special claims of outstanding merit."

### Abbreviated version
"The Minister said that it had always been his aim to assist small shopkeepers. . . . Subsidies of the kind suggested . . . might tend to promote a certain lethargy. . . . the Ministry would investigate any special claims of outstanding merit."

Dots can also be used at the end of a quoted passage to show that the quotation is incomplete.

The use of dots is a device, too, of some novelists, to indicate perhaps a pause or an incomplete speech. Often, however, they are used for no particular reason, and can be misleading.

## CAPITAL LETTERS

Capital letters, being in a way a guide to the reader, can be included in a study of punctuation.

Far too many people use initial capital letters indiscriminately, not only in their personal correspondence but also in official, commercial and technical writing.

You should start a sentence with a capital letter, but you should not start one with a numeral. "£9 is barely sufficient to buy . . . ." should be written: "Nine pounds is barely sufficient . . . ."

Capitals should be used for the start of proper nouns – names of people and places. Personal titles should be graced with capitals, such as Her (or His) Majesty, Queen (or King) X, Lord Y, the Duke of Z, Mr, Mrs, Miss and Dr. The key words in titles of publications, stage productions and musical works should start with capitals, and so should the names of buildings, organisations, colleges and schools. These are the *basic* cases; there are innumerable optional cases in which words may start with capitals, but capitals must be used with care.

In the House of Commons the Member for Exton is invariably given a capital *M*, while his political Party sometimes gets a capital *P*. The newspaper and periodical Press is usually given the capital to distinguish it from the printing-press from which it sprang. The Navy has a capital *N*, while *naval* can have a small *n*. Besides Her Majesty's Army there can be unofficial armies of people or ants or frogs.

The cardinal points should not be given capitals unless used to specify a recognised geographical region:

"The road forked six miles west of the town, and when I reached the junction I turned north-west. After a while I left the road and followed a path which led eastwards over a hill, a hill which seemed to be one of the foothills of a great mountain range that traversed the island from north to south."

"A-town is six miles north of B-town", "Land's End is in the south-west of England", and "The mildest area in winter was eastern Scotland". Also correct, however, are: "New regions created by the Boundary Commission included West Sussex and East Yorkshire" and "The largest territory in southern Africa is the Republic of South Africa".

The four seasons – spring, summer, autumn, winter – do not normally require capitals.

Some people wonder, quite reasonably, if there is any rule about the writing of "French chalk" and "French polish", as the association of the terms with France is remote. There is no rule, and a small *f* is sometimes used, but it is conventional to use a capital *F* if only because the adjective ***French*** attracts it. As mentioned earlier the term "French polisher" is ambiguous. A person who engages in French polishing should be described with a hyphen, "French-polisher", to distinguish him from a Frenchman who polishes, "French polisher".

While you are advised to be sparing with capitals, do not adopt the practice which has developed in some "progressive" quarters of abolishing capitals altogether. It looks ridiculous and is to be condemned, not least because it is confusing to a child who is taught at school to use capitals.

## SMALL CAPITALS

If a word is printed completely in *ordinary* capitals the effect is one of CLUMSINESS, isn't it? You feel that the writer is shouting at you. Sometimes, however, it is necessary to print whole words or groups of words in capitals, and to get over the difficulty and yet give a quiet tone to the page the printer may use SMALL CAPITALS.

If you are sending anything to be printed, and want the compositor to use small capitals, you should rule a double line under the words affected.

It is usual, for instance, to use small capitals for BC and AD, which look much more tasteful in this form. It is worth remembering that the customary practice – though not the invariable practice – is to put "BC" after the date and "AD" before it, thus:

"Augustus Caesar (63 BC to AD 14) was the first Roman Emperor."

Academic qualifications such as BA or DD, and such designations as MP or PC (Privy Councillor), when written after someone's name, may also be set in small capitals.

## ITALICS

*Italics* are used in printing to emphasise something, to accentuate a word or group of words, to distinguish a word or group of words from the body of the text, and to show that a word or group of words is foreign. So much is generally known, and throughout this book there are dozens of examples of the use of italics.

If you want something to be printed in italics you underline it with a *single* line.

Most publishers use italics as an alternative to quotation marks for titles of books, periodicals, plays and films. In the case of a book or periodical, a reference to the title of anything contained *within* it should be in quotation marks, thus:

"In the author's new book of essays, *The Changing Seasons,* the one which impresses me most is the fragile little *belle-lettre* entitled 'In the Park.' "

"The article in yesterday's *Daily Trumpet,* 'Shall we have a new Party?', may lead to a barrage of questions when the House meets on Tuesday."

*Belle-lettre*, as a French word, is printed in italics. It is quite satisfactory to use italics for foreign words and phrases, but a whole sentence in a foreign language can be tedious to read if printed in italics and should preferably be printed in Roman type.

# 6

# COMMON MISTAKES

Many of these types of mistake have already been referred to, in earlier chapters, and page references are given.

## SUBJECT AND OBJECT

One of the most common mistakes is to confuse the subject and the object of a sentence. Should you want to refresh yourself, you will find references in Chapter 1 (page 27), Chapter 2 (page 48), Chapter 3 (pages 51 and 57) and Chapter 4 (pages 69 and 71).

To summarise, examples are given here of the confusion of subject and object with the necessary corrections:

| *Wrong* | *Right* |
|---|---|
| "He took Mother and I for a ride in the car." | "He took Mother and me for a ride in the car." |
| "The manager met my friend and I at the station." | "The manager met my friend and me at the station." |
| "Between you and I. . ." | "Between you and me . . ." |
| "Come and sit beside we girls." | "Come and sit beside us girls." |
| "Me and the wife went to the pictures." | "My wife and I went to the pictures." |
| "It's me." (This is now an accepted colloquialism.) | "It is I." |
| "Those are them." | "Those are they." |
| "Who shall I give it to?" | "Whom shall I give it to?" |
| "The person who I saw . . ." | "The person whom I saw . . ." |
| "Whom is the next speaker?" | "Who is the next speaker?" |

"The man who the policeman        "The man whom the
arrested . . ."                          policeman arrested . . ."

Finally, here is a gem from an estate agent's announcement:

". . . . presents his compliments to he (or she) seeking, south of
the Park, new, architect designed, freehold houses."

You will be aware that "he (or she)" should be "him (or her)". It should
also be pointed out that there should be a hyphen between "architect"
and "designed", for the two words form a compound adjective.

## "WHO" AND "WHOM"

*Who* is subjective, *whom* is objective.

"Who shall I give it to?" is wrong because the question is another form
of "I shall give it to whom?" or "To whom shall I give it?" The subject
is *I*, and a preposition – in this case *to* – is followed by the objective.

"Whom shall I take with me?" is right. "Who shall I take with
me?" is wrong. *I* am taking *someone* with me, so that *I* is the
subject, the *someone* is the object, and the someone in the question
is the unknown *whom*.

*Who*, as the subject, is correct in such questions as the following:

"Who goes home?"

"Who is coming with me?"

"Who did it?"

When *who* is used as a simple relative pronoun (see Chapter 3, page
57) it is immaterial whether its governing noun or pronoun is the
subject or the object, and both the following sentences are correct:

"The lady who dealt with your enquiry is away." ("The lady" is
the subject.)

"I saw the man who did it." ("The man" is the object.)

We could also say, correctly: "The lady who is loved by all is away."

Yet *who* would be changed to *whom* in the following kinds of
construction:

"The lady whom nothing could upset is away."

"The lady to whom you addressed your enquiry is away."

"The man whom the policeman arrested . . ." is right because it was the policeman who did the arresting. For **who** to be right, the man (subject) must himself have performed an action, or virtually performed it, as in "The man who was arrested . . ." Here, the man's action lay in being arrested.

The translators of the Psalms, though they sometimes erred in their English, made no mistake in the first verse of Psalm 27 (Prayer Book Version): "The Lord is my light, and my salvation; whom then shall I fear: the Lord is the strength of my life; of whom then shall I be afraid?"

## "WHOSE"

**Whose** can be used for something impersonal (see page 58), as in:

"At the outset of the meeting, whose agenda included a discussion on retirement pensions, the chairman gave a warning."

But the following is preferable:

"At the outset of the meeting, of which the agenda" – or "the agenda of which" – "included a discussion on retirement pensions . . . ."

The use of **whose** is better confined to persons, as in the following two examples:

"The man whose car was stolen reported the facts to the police."

"Mrs Elsie Jones, whose hundredth birthday fell yesterday, received presents from all her grandchildren and great-grandchildren."

## "EVERY" AND "EACH"

**Every, everyone** and **everything** have been dealt with fairly fully in Chapter 3 (page 64). The main thing to remember is that these are singular words, and it is a very common mistake to treat them as plurals.

Consider this example by a gossip-writer:

"I was most impressed by the reasonable prices and agreeable designs of everything on sale."

"Everything on sale" is singular, meaning *each* object, and each object had *its* own price and own design. The sentence should thus be:

"I was most impressed by the reasonable price and agreeable design of everything on sale."

"There are carpets in every room." This type of sentence is often heard. Each room *may* have more than one carpet, but the writer probably means that there is no room without a carpet. There are two correct ways of expressing the meaning:

"There is a carpet in every room."

"There are carpets in all the rooms."

*Each* is similarly maltreated, and the following are examples of common mistakes:

| *Wrong* | *Right* |
|---|---|
| "The hotel issues free guide books to each guest." | "The hotel issues a free guide-book to each guest." or "The hotel issues free guide-books to all guests." |
| "I foresee neat rows of tiny houses, with smooth lawns in each garden and prams at each front door." | "I foresee neat rows of tiny houses, with a smooth lawn in each garden and a pram at each front door." |

The following specimen is an extract from a bookseller's catalogue, following a list of novels by one author:

"Each are gripping examples of descriptive writing which many experienced writers in this genre might well envy."

The sentence should, of course, be like this:

"Each is a gripping example of descriptive writing . . ."

Incidentally, the writer of the catalogue goes on to say, still of the same novelist: "Putting such matters aside he is a remarkable stylist." You may know what is wrong with this sentence; if not, you will know later.

*Each* is singular, as explained, and is accompanied by the singular form of a verb. There is a pitfall, however, in this kind of sentence:

"Nigeria, Ghana, Sierra Leone and Gambia have each a part to play in the development of West Africa."

This is perfectly correct, but often you will find *has* instead of *have*. The plural verb *have* follows the enumeration of the different territories, but the singular *each* calls for *a part* (not *parts*). Alternatively, we could say:

"Nigeria, Ghana, Sierra Leone and Gambia all have parts to play in the development of West Africa."

## "BETWEEN EACH"

It is strange that one of the commonest mistakes is also one of the most obvious. Too often we read this kind of thing:

"Sow the plants in rows, with at least 60cm between each row."

"The buttonholes should next be cut, with 15cm between each."

"The Yorkshire Pennines are traversed by the Swale, the Ure and the Wharfe, between each of which is a range of hills forming a watershed."

It should be clear to anyone that the preposition *between* cannot exist with one singular word, and "between each" is nonsense. Correct versions of the foregoing sentences would be:

"Sow the plants in rows, with at least 60cm between adjacent rows", *or* ". . . with at least 60cm between each pair of rows", *or* "Sow the plants in rows, the rows being at least 60cm apart."

"The buttonholes should next be cut, 15cm apart."

"The Yorkshire Pennines are traversed by the Swale, the Ure and the Wharfe, each river being separated from the next by a range of hills forming a watershed."

The temptation is irresistible to conclude this section by quoting a lapse of William Combe from his rich long poem, which is almost an epic, *Dr Syntax's Tour in Search of the Picturesque* (1812):

"Whoe'er has passed an idle hour, In following Syntax through his Tour, Must have perceiv'd he did not balk His fancy, when he wish'd to talk: Nay, more – that he was often prone To make long speeches when alone: And while he quaff'd th' inspiring ale, Between each glass to tell a tale: . . . ."

If Combe had substituted **between** by **after**, logic would have been satisfied and the line would still have scanned.

## CONFUSION OF SINGULAR AND PLURAL

From consideration of **every** and **each** it is convenient to pass to the confusion of singular and plural within a sentence. Here are some examples of wrong and right:

| *Wrong* | *Right* |
|---|---|
| "You cross all the rivers by a bridge." | "You cross all the rivers by bridges." |
| "There is a crisis in the life of all men." | "There are crises in the lives of all men." |
| "Scotland was made poorer by the death of Bruce and Wallace." | "Scotland was made poorer by the deaths of Bruce and Wallace." |
| "When leaving fields, please see that the gate is fastened." | "When leaving fields, please see that the gates are fastened." |
| "The towers are 6m square at their base." | "The towers are 6m square at their bases." |

The conclusion is, then, that associated words in a sentence should usually agree *in number* – that is, singular with singular and plural with plural.

There are exceptions. Some words, for example, cannot be considered as plural, as the following sentences show:

"The dryness of the deserts is an adverse factor in their development" (not **drynesses**).

"The staff representation on the boards of the different companies is extremely active" (not *representations*).

"The atmosphere of West African countries is, in general, somewhat humid." (We should not use *atmospheres* here, although *atmosphere* has a plural in a quantitative scientific sense.)

An example of the plural use of *death* is given in the sentence: "Scotland was made poorer by the deaths of Bruce and Wallace." Here, the death of each man is considered as a separate event. But if we refer to death in a general sense it can be singular, as in: "Death overtakes all men." "Deaths overtake all men" would sound odd.

There are doubtful cases – for example, "The foliage at the bottom of the mountains is different from that at the top."

If the mountains are altogether, it may be presumed that they have a common bottom, in which case "the bottom of the mountains" is right. But if the mountains are separated, each with its own bottom, then we should say "the bottoms of the mountains".

## "EITHER" AND "NEITHER"

As explained in Chapter 3 (page 54) while *either* is generally correctly used *neither* is often abused.

Glaring examples of "neither are" appear in print frequently.

Here is an example:

"One can expect an immediate reaction from the Anti-Noise League, but neither the Clerk to the Magistrates nor the transport association's solicitor know of any regulations forbidding such cacophony."

As *Clerk* is singular, and *solicitor* is singular, *know* should be *knows*. *Know* would have been correct if both had been plural, as in: "Neither the Clerks nor the solicitors know."

If one had been singular and the other plural there would have been a difficulty. Should we say "Neither the Clerks nor the solicitor know" or ". . .knows"?

There is no solution, but you could reconstruct the passage thus: "The Clerks do not know and the solicitor does not know."

Here is a very confused passage from a leading article:

"Neither the British nor the American Governments, who supply the major part of the country's national income, nor the French Government, which also contributes to her exchequer, were aware of the discussions until Sept. 25."

As pointed out on page 55, "neither . . . nor" should not be used if there are more than two items. Yet here we have three items – the British, American and French Governments. That is one mistake. Another mistake is to say "neither . . . were."

A third mistake is to say "Neither the British nor the American Governments" (instead of "Government"). A fourth is to use *who* for the British and American Governments and *which* for the French Government; there should be consistency, especially when there is a reference to *her* exchequer.

The sentence is so hopelessly confused that it is beyond simple correction. It is a case that needs drastic rewriting, and, not forgetting to change "major part" for "most", you should do it thus:

"The British and the American Governments, who supply most of the country's national income, and the French Government, who also contributes to her exchequer, were not aware of the discussions until Sept. 25."

## THE USE OF ADJECTIVES AS ADVERBS

"Do it quick" is wrong. *Quick* is an adjective, and the verb *do* demands an adverb. The correct version is "Do it quickly". Similarly, "Drive slow" should be "Drive slowly".

While it is colloquial to say "Walk quicker" and "Drive slower", the correct forms are "Walk more quickly" and "Drive more slowly".

*Fast*, on the other hand, is both adjective and adverb. Another curious inconsistency concerns *wrong* and *right*. We say "He did his sums wrongly" but "He did his sums right". Yet if both terms are used together we say "Rightly or wrongly".

We speak of a tradition or a convention as "dying hard", meaning that the tradition or convention finds it hard to die. It would seem strange to say "die hardly", as *hardly* means *scarcely* or *nearly*.

*Well* is the adverb corresponding with the adjective *good*. Thus, we say "She is a good singer" or "She sings well". Some people, unfortunately, think it sounds polite to use *well* when they mean *good*, and frequently we hear: "It looks well on her, doesn't it?"

This construction is wrong. The word *well* is not associated with the verb *looks* but with the pronoun *it*, so that the adjective *good* should be used. The correct form of the sentence, in the sense meant by the polite speaker, is: "It looks good on her, doesn't it?" The same speaker would have no doubts at all about saying, correctly, "It looks splendid" or "It looks horrible" or "It looks old-fashioned".

Literally, "It looks well" means that *it* performs the *act of looking* well. *Well* is also an adjective meaning healthy, and although "He looks well" usually means that he looks healthy, it could also mean that he is a good performer in the act of looking.

## REDUNDANT CONDITIONALS

The redundant conditional is the name given in this book to the laboured form of construction described on page 42, Chapter 2. An example is the following:

"I should have thought that it would have been better the other way."

This is logically wrong as well as grammatically wrong. You cannot have two conditionals with one compound clause. There are two correct alternatives:

"I should have thought that it was better the other way."

"I think it would have been better the other way."

A somewhat similar form of redundancy is exhibited in the use of past participles, but that will come later.

## UNFORMED SENTENCES

Some examples of unformed "sentences" (though they are not sentences) appear under the heading "Sentences" in Chapter 4. Besides these examples, there are those groups of words that start with *which*, like these:

"The Government of Notaland, though lethargic in the implementation of its foreign policy, is at least stable. Which cannot be said for the Government of the neighbouring territory."

"My uncle gave me a five pound note and told me to go and enjoy myself. Which I proceeded to do with alacrity."

"Defending counsel described his client as industrious and honest, a man of integrity. Which, of course, he isn't."

There are two main errors of thought and grammar in passages like these. One error lies in the fact that in each case the "sentence" starting with *which* is not a sentence at all, but is a secondary clause dependent on the previous sentence. There should, therefore, be neither a full stop after the previous sentence nor a capital *W*.

The second error is in the assumption that the relative pronoun *which* can be used to relate a clause to something other than a noun or pronoun. This "something", in the first example, is the statement that the Government is stable. In the second example it is the uncle's command "to go and enjoy myself". In the third example the "something" is defending counsel's opinon of his client's virtues.

*Which*, as a relative pronoun, can only be used directly with a noun or a pronoun. The three examples above, then, cannot be corrected simply by the changing of each full stop to a comma and of each capital *W* to a small *w*. The passages must be reconstructed, and my suggestions would be the following:

"The Government of Notaland, though lethargic in the implementation of its foreign policy, is at least stable, and that is something that cannot be said for the Government of the neighbouring territory."

"My uncle gave me a five pound note and told me to go and enjoy myself. I proceeded to do so with alacrity."

"Defending counsel described his client as industrious and honest, a man of integrity. He is, in fact, nothing of the sort."

The examples given, of unformed sentences starting with **Which**, are similar to the example given on page 68: "To whom the book may be recommended".

There are other kinds of unformed sentences, and here are some curious examples from newspapers:

"The setting was an interview between Mr X, the MP who has recently been conducting a stormy correspondence in *The Times* about workmen on a building site spending too much time making tea." (How could Mr X have an interview between himself?)

"They prove that . . . one can do it beautifully. Or at any rate, with attractive accessories. Also practically."

## "INCLUDE" AND "INCLUDING"

Though it is debatable whether the verb "to include" was originally meant to embrace a whole or only a part, present usage generally carries the second implication.

"The CBI included many thousands of smaller firms which were not directly represented on its councils."

Obviously the thousands of smaller firms did not make up the whole of the CBI. There is nothing wrong, however, in giving the verb "to include" a much more comprehensive meaning, and we are equally justified in saying:

"The CBI included such industrial giants as The Rover Group, ICI, Courtaulds, as well as many thousands of smaller firms which were not directly represented on its councils."

It is possible to make a mistake with **include**, as in this short extract from a cookery guide:

"Some of the Chinese foods you can buy include: . . ."

*Some* and *include* are similar in implication, and the cookery writer should have written either of the following:

"Some of the Chinese foods you can buy are: . . ."

"The Chinese foods you can buy include: . . ."

The modern understanding that the verb "to include" embraces only a part, and not the whole, is obvious from the very common use of the present participle *including*.

"The members, including children, number over a thousand." Not all the members are children. Incidentally, it is important to note that the present participle *including* must be related to a noun or a pronoun, the related word in this case being the noun *members*.

## "CHART" AND "CHARTER"

A *chart* is a map or a plan. Thus, the verb "to chart" means to map, or to plot a survey. An uncharted reef is a reef not shown on a chart, or nautical map.

Yet here is an extract from a newspaper:

"A party of holidaymakers, rescued in motor launches when their boat struck an unchartered reef, were landed at Southampton."

The word should be *uncharted*. The verb "to charter" means to hire, and the noun "charter" is a Royal documentary instrument.

Some people, when they see *Magna Charta*, point out that it should be *Magna Carta*, the Great Charter. However, in Latin the two words are synonymous. *Magna Carta* happens to be the commoner form.

## "DUE TO"

"The scheme was not approved due to the absence of water in the vicinity."

"Due to the inclement weather, the annual outing has been postponed till next week."

*Both these are wrong.* Such sentences are quite common, making *due to* grammatically like *because of* and *owing to*, but strict grammarians say that *due* is always an adjective and that *due to* can only be used to link two nouns or noun phrases. Only "something" can be *due to* something else, and the following are quite right:

"His sleeplessness was due to late meals."

"General resentment, due mainly to the high-handed actions of the committee, was felt by all the members."

"Can the incidence of juvenile delinquency be due to the lack of parental interest?"

Consider the first two sentences again. Could the first be written thus? "Disapproval of the scheme was due to the absence of water."

This is correct structurally, but not quite correct logically. The listener or reader is first *being told* of something, namely, that the scheme was not approved, the reason for the disapproval following.

To say or write the sentence in the manner just given would imply that the listener already knows of the disapproval and is now being told the reason. If we wanted to use *due to* here, one way would be this:

"The scheme was not approved, the disapproval being due to the absence of water in the vicinity."

The other example could be rewritten thus:

"The annual outing has been postponed till next week, the postponement being due to the inclement weather."

If, however, we want to stick to the same kind of construction but avoid the misuse of *due to*, the following are the simplest ways:

"The scheme was not approved, because of the absence of water in the vicinity." (The comma is essential. If it is omitted the sentence can imply that the scheme *was* approved but for other reasons than the absence of water.)

"Because of the inclement weather, the annual outing has been postponed till next week."

Dr J. Bronowski, reviewing a book by Dr Fred Hoyle, rightly castigated the author for having written: "Stars can collapse catastrophically due to this cause."

*Owing to* can sometimes be used instead of *because of*, but can sometimes be clumsy if not used with care. *On account of* lends itself to Americanisms such as: "I went home from the office on account of I was feeling ill." It is acceptable in the following example:

"They wanted to live near the sea on account of the boy's health."

## "REASON"

From consideration of *due to* we pass conveniently to some observations on the associated constructions containing *reason*.

"The reason I am going home" is equivalent to "Why I am going home". It is just another way of saying it.

"The reason why I am going home", therefore, contains a redundancy, or duplication of meaning.

*Why* should not be used after the noun *reason* unless it is necessary as a convenient link for the sake of smoothness. "There is no reason I should go home" sounds awkward, and it is more usual to say "There is no reason why I should go home". The use of *why* could be avoided if the speaker said "There is no reason for my going home".

Another common error of duplication to avoid with the noun *reason* is its use in such constructions as "The reason is because . . ." and "The reason is due to . . ." The reason for something obviously cannot be because of or due to anything.

A mother may write to a schoolteacher: "The reason for my boy's absence was due to an attack of measles." This kind of mistake is not uncommon, and either of the following two correct forms could be used:

"The reason for my boy's absence was an attack of measles." "My boy's absence was due to an attack of measles."

The verb *to reason why* can be quite correct. The verb implies a particular reasoning, a reasoning of some problem, while *to reason* simply implies reasoning in general. *To reason why* implies that the object of the reasoning is to find out the cause of something, so that when Tennyson wrote "Theirs not to reason why" he was probably justified. (Tennyson, wrongly, wrote "their's", and many editors omit the apostrophe.)

## "CIRCUMSTANCES"

Circumstances are the events *around* something. Therefore to say "under the circumstances" is wrong. The correct use is "in the circumstances".

## OMISSION OF ARTICLES

In Chapter 1, page 22, the unpleasant custom of omitting the definite article *the* and the indefinite articles *a* and *an* is mentioned. Here is an example of this kind of writing:

"Best part for holiday this year is South Coast. If weather is good there are several resorts to give you variety of entertainment. At Seacliff try miniature village. At Sun-beach don't miss hanging gardens. Eastwater offers marble bathing pool. Westwater boasts biggest roller-coaster ride in Europe. Special attraction at Mudflat Kursaal this year is thriller *Hamlet* on ice with all-star skating cast. All these exciting places are honoured by Holiday Guide recommends."

This poor piece of writing badly needs its articles. You may notice two things, however. "Bathing-pool" needs a hyphen; otherwise it means a pool which is bathing. Then, to make the verb "recommend" into a noun is atrocious, for there happens to be a noun, "recommendation." You will hear, similarly, an invitation called an "invite," but these practices are indefensible.

## "THOSE KIND"

As noted in Chapter 3, you must never say "those kind" of anything. You can say "those kinds", "these kinds", "this kind" or "that kind". But to say "those kind" is to apply a plural adjective to a singular noun.

## THE MISUSE OF "AN"

The indefinite article *an* is used before a word starting with a *vowel sound* – not necessarily with a vowel.

*Unique*, for example, starts with a vowel but a vowel having the effect of a *y*. To say or write "an unique" is a mistake which is incomprehensible, for nobody would ever think of saying "an unicorn".

It is equally wrong and incomprehensible to say or write "an hotel", yet you come across this fault every day. It is right to say "an hour" and "an honour", when the *h* is silent, but please say "*a* hotel" and "*a* herbaceous plant".

## "AT ABOUT"

"I shall expect you about five o'clock."

"I shall expect you at about five o'clock."

Which of these is correct?

Strictly, *at* applies to a definite time; *about* applies to an approximate time. Therefore, *at about* is a confusion of two unlikes, and should be avoided. Logically-minded people say: "I shall expect you at or about five o'clock."

## VERBS WITH PREPOSITIONS

What is wrong with the verb "to face"? Why should "up to" be added?

"I could not face up to the problem."

Is this an improvement on "I could not face the problem"?

Additions to a language can only be justified if they are necessities or improvements, and "face up to" is in neither category.

"Stand for", instead of simply "stand", meaning "tolerate", is another expression in the same class as "face up to". The addition of the preposition "for" is quite needless.

"I'm not standing for it."

"Stand for", of course, has legitimate meanings, too, as in:

"He is standing for Parliament."

"BBC stands for British Broadcasting Corporation."

" 'I stand for righteousness and justice,' said the street-corner orator."

There are many similar compound verbs. Examples of such verbs are the following: "start up", "stop up", "speed up", "slow down", "heat up", "try out", "add up" and "seek out".

There is no defence of the use of the prepositions in these examples. On the other hand, "give up" and "cough up" are different from "give" and "cough". There is an Americanism – "visit with" for "visit", as in "We visited with some friends in New York". The habit of saying "consult with" (for "consult") has also spread, and there is "meet up with", instead of the simple "meet". None is attractive.

## "PERPENDICULAR" AND "VERTICAL"

*Perpendicular* is often misused for **vertical** (see page 300).

## "PARALLEL WITH"

Two lines can be *parallel with* one another (or each other), not *parallel to* one another. The preposition *to* signifies approach, and the moment the lines start approaching each other they cease to be parallel.

## "COMPARE"

There is some confusion about "compare with" and "compare to". To take a logical view *with* seems more suitable for comparison of likes, or subjects which are supposedly similar, and *to* for comparison of subjects in which the likeness is somewhat remote. The following are examples:

"Can Marlowe by compared *with* Shakespeare?"

"A bicycle cannot compare *with* a motorbike." (That is to say, a motorbike is much better.)

"The English master, praising Jim Brown's essays, jocularly compared the boy *to* Bacon."

"As the rabbit dodged into the bracken I compared the little animal *to* a cunning lion in the African jungle."

Sometimes you may be uncertain whether the compared subjects are like or unlike each other, and in such cases **with** is safer. **With** is invariably used in such constructions as: "For durability of footwear, nothing can compare **with** leather."

## "USED TO"

"He used to live in London" means "He formerly lived in London" or "He once lived in London".

That is understood. But neither the past tense nor the negative is generally understood, and we hear constructions like these:

"He didn't use to live in London."

"Did he use to live in London?"

"Used to" is itself a peculiar idiom, but there is no point in making its variations even more peculiar. The correct versions of the two examples are:

"He used not to live in London."

"Used he to live in London?"

Although many people find this formal and use **didn't use to** and **did he use to** in speech, these phrases look ugly in print.

## "PROMISE"

To **promise** means to engage oneself to perform a future act, to give a definite undertaking for the future. But in recent years the verb has acquired a further meaning and is now used, quite wrongly, to indicate that one is telling the truth at the moment. You may hear this kind of sentence:

"As I was coming home I saw a pink monkey, I promise you."

This use of **promise** is unjustified. To be correct the speaker could have said: "As I was coming home I saw a pink monkey, I swear."

## "OUGHT TO"

"He ought to, didn't he?" is something we often hear. The correct construction, of course, is "He ought to, oughtn't he?" or ". . .ought he not?"

## "LAY" AND "LIE"

For the use of *lay* and *lie* and their derivatives see Chapter 2, page 45 and the summary on page 296.

## "ATTAIN"

*To attain* means to reach, or to arrive, in the sense of reaching a height or arriving at a goal. Often it is used figuratively, as in "He attained the Presidency" or "He attained his dearest ambition".

Sometimes, however, *to* is added unnecessarily. "You can attain to something higher" is wrong. It is equivalent to saying "You can reach to something higher". Mountaineers do not try to attain to the summit; they try to attain the summit.

## "DIFFERENT FROM"

In spite of various feeble attempts at defence, "different to" is wrong simply because it is illogical. Nobody would dream of saying "similar from".

It is unfortunate that "different to" has penetrated such respectable quarters as Parliament, literature and the Press, for in matters of English many people accept the guidance of these mentors. They are even guilty of using an import from America, "different than", which is meaningless rather than illogical.

## "TRY AND"

Many people say "try and" when they mean "try to". Mistakes apart, however, there is a subtle difference between the two expressions.

Logically, if you try *and* do something you *try* first, making a general attempt in the right direction and finding out how to do it. Having found out the best way of doing it, you *do* it. Thus there are two actions involved, the trying and the doing, and in this sense "try and" can be quite right.

"Try to", on the other hand, implies the single combined action of trying and doing. Usually the correct expression is "try to", and when people say "try and" they seldom have the logical meaning in mind.

## "TIMES GREATER THAN"

"Production this year is six times greater than production last year."

What exactly does this mean?

If production is *once* greater, it is as much again, or twice as much as before. If it is *twice* greater, it is three times as much as before.

Therefore, if production (or anything else) is $x$ times greater, it is $(x + 1)$ times as great as before.

This is simple, isn't it? Nothing could be more logical. And yet, the person who wrote that sentence – "Production this year is six times greater than production last year" – actually meant that production is *six times as great.*

If the sentence is interpreted literally, it means that production this year is seven times production last year.

This is a very common type of mistake, especially in journalism, and you must be careful about it.

## "EXTENDED TOUR"

When a bus company advertises "Extended tours to the Highlands" it is writing nonsense.

"Extended" means "made longer" or "lengthened". Thus an *extended* tour is a tour which has been increased above its original length. In other words, the company originally meant it to last for a certain time but has now decided to extend or prolong it.

Nothing could be further, of course, from the company's mind, or minds. The intended meaning is that the tour to the Highlands (or the South-West, or the Lake District, or the Continent) is quite long as tours go, and the word that should be used is *extensive*.

## "BUT, HOWEVER"

Occasionally, one comes across this kind of construction:

"A blizzard had raged all morning, our limbs were numbed and our bodies exhausted. We expected to find a roaring fire of comfort in the cabin. But when we arrived, however, and opened the door, all we found was a cold heap of ashes in the hearth."

*But* and *however* are similar in effect, and should not be used together. The second sentence of this passage can be expressed in either of the following two ways:

"But when we arrived, and opened the door, all we found was a cold heap of ashes. . . ."

"When we arrived, however, and opened the door, all we found was a cold heap of ashes. . . ."

## "LOAN" AND "LEND"

*Loan* is a noun. *Lend* is a verb. It is a common mistake, however, to use *loan* as a verb, as in "I loaned him a fiver" instead of "I lent him a fiver". When something is *on loan* it is *lent*.

## "LEARN" FOR "TEACH"

The misuse of *learn* for *teach* is even found in the *Book of Common Prayer,* and is a warning that the text of the Prayer Book is not to be accepted in its entirety as good English, even as good mediaeval English.

In the Prayer Book, verse 4 of Psalm 25 is thus:

"Lead me forth in thy truth, and learn me: for thou art the God of my salvation; . . . ."

In the Bible, the fifth verse of Psalm 25 is thus:

"Lead me in thy truth, and teach me: for thou art the God of my salvation; . . . ."

(The first two verses of the Biblical version are condensed into the first verse of the Prayer Book version; hence the Bible's verse 5 is the Prayer Book's verse 4.)

## THE MISUSE OF "THAT"

Informally *that* is used as an emphatic adverb:

"I had no idea the house was that small."

"As a pianist he isn't really that good."

"If the weather is that bad you had better stay at home."

But in spite of common acceptance, this use of *that* is wrong and is to be avoided. The correct forms of the above sentences are:

"I had no idea that the house was as small as that." (The omission of "that" after "idea" is a permissible colloquialism.)

"As a pianist he isn't really as good as that."

"If the weather is as bad as that you had better stay at home."

*That* is often used instead of a simple *so:*

"I was that happy I could have cried."

"I went to the pictures three times that week, the film was that exciting."

"That happy" and "that exciting" should be "so happy" and "so exciting".

The common expressions "that much" and "that many" should be "as much as that" and "as many as that."

## "RIGHT HERE"

"Right here", "right there" and "right now" are Americanisms which can hardly be called mistakes. *Right* is used before adverbs and prepositions to emphasise them:

"She was wearing a skirt right down to her ankles."

"The house is right on the road and very noisy."

"If you wait for me right here, I'll be right back."

It is often preferable to substitute words like "completely", "directly", "exactly" or "immediately".

## "CHRISTMAS"

The only excuse for writing "Xmas" for "Christmas" is that *X* was the Greek symbol for Jesus Christ. Some people, aware of this, do it deliberately, but most writers of "Xmas" are merely lazy.

## "MOOT POINT"

Many people confuse the word **moot** with **mute** (silent), and wrongly talk about a "mute point" instead of a "moot point". See page 298.

## "ALL RIGHT"

*Already*, *almost*, *almighty* and *altogether* are right, but *alright* is wrong. There seems to be no fair reason for this, but if you want your written English to be correct, you must write "all right".

## "AVERSE FROM"

You cannot be *averse to*, or show an *aversion to*, anything. The suffix *to* signifies approach, when the opposite is intended. You can only be *averse from*, or show an *aversion from*, something.

## CONFUSED WORDS

Certain pairs of similar words are often confused and wrongly used, one word of a pair being used in place of the other. The following cases are the most common, and details will be found in Chapter 10, "Notes on Selected Words":

*adapt* and *adopt* (page 275)
*affect* and *effect* (page 276)

*balmy* and *barmy* (page 279)
*dependant* and *dependent* (page 285)
*deprecate* and *depreciate* (page 285)
*forebear* and *forbear* (page 291)
*forego* and *forgo* (page 292)
*licence* and *license* (page 297)
*loathe* and *loath* (page 297)
*prescribe* and *proscribe* (see page 302)

## REDUNDANT PAST PARTICIPLES

Redundant past participles are rather similar to redundant conditionals (page 42).

"He would have had to have waited" contains two past participles (*had* and *waited*) when only one is necessary. The meaning of this sentence should be expressed thus:

"He would have had to wait."

## UNATTACHED PARTICIPLES

Now we come to a class of error which is probably the most common of all.

Always remember this: a present participle must be logically attached to a noun or a pronoun.

Participles in general are dealt with in Chapter 2 (page 36). An example of an unattached present participle is given in Chapter 4 (page 68) in the sentence:

"Referring to your letter of the 16th November, the horse was sold last Monday."

If this is strictly interpreted, the present participle **referring** is attached to **the horse**. But the writer does not really mean that the horse was referring to the letter of the 16th November. He means that he himself is referring to the letter. There are several ways in which the sentence could be made sensible, and here is one:

"Referring to your letter of the 16th November, I have to state that the horse was sold last Monday."

"I have to state" is commercial English, but at least the sentence is now grammatical, with the participle **referring** attached to the pronoun **I**.

This silly kind of mistake is prevalent in commercial correspondence. Think, too, of the common misuse of **providing**, as in:

"Providing the goods are despatched by the end of December we shall pay in full by the end of January."

Literally, this means that **we** are doing the **providing**, and this, of course, is nonsense. The word here should be the past participle **provided**.

Here is a newspaper paragraph:

"Providing the weather is suitable, the Queen and the Duke of Edinburgh intend to take next month a week's cruise in the Mediterranean."

The Queen and the Duke have enough to think about without providing that the weather is suitable, and here, too, the word should be **provided**.

## "ASSUMING"

We are still in our study of unattached participles, and our next target is *assuming*. This kind of construction is common:

"Assuming it does not rain, the match will take place as arranged."

This means that the match will do the assuming, when actually the assuming is done by the organisers of the match. If the writer wants to use the word *assuming* he should write the sentence this way:

"Assuming it does not rain, the organisers will see that the match takes place as arranged."

It is preferable, however, to call in the aid of the past participle *assumed*, like this:

"It being assumed that it does not rain" – or "will not rain" – "the match will take place as arranged."

Here is another example:

"The stage is set for a dramatic dénouement of the crisis in the Middle East by the deadline of Monday next, assuming – which is far from certain – that the great gamble by the President of the United States comes off."

The present participle *assuming* is not attached to anything. And it is difficult to see what the relative pronoun *which* is related to. The writer should have expressed this passage something like this:

"The stage is set for a dramatic dénouement of the crisis in the Middle East by the deadline of Monday next, it being assumed that the great gamble by the President of the United States comes off. It is, however, far from certain if it will."

## "JUDGING"

Many professional journalists are fond of the present participle *judging* and often use it wrongly. Here is one example:

"Judging by accounts in the British Press, the opening night of *The Phantom of the Opera* in New York seems to have been successful."

This means that the opening night did the judging. The use of *judged* would have saved the situation.

Here is another passage where *judged* should have been used instead of *judging*:

"Judging by the department stores' sales, this looks like being France's most prosperous Christmas ever."

## MISCELLANEOUS EXAMPLES OF UNATTACHED PARTICIPLES

Prevalent errors are in the use of "broadly speaking", "strictly speaking", "generally speaking", and all the other kinds of speaking.

"Broadly speaking, the fortunes of the catering trade depend on the weather."

Can it be the fortunes of the catering trade which speak broadly? This sentence would have made sense if "speaking" had been omitted.

Then there is the other old friend which frequently appears in newspapers and on picture postcards: 'Beach at Seahampton, looking east."

The reader or viewer is meant to assume that *he* is looking east. But the literal meaning is that the beach itself is looking east – the direct opposite to the meaning intended.

The following is from a literary article by a *former editor:* "Looking back, then, two editors are outstanding . . . ."

The passage should be reconstructed: "If we look back," or "If one looks back, then, two editors are outstanding . . . ."

How do you like the following confused passage?

"Having made this quite clear it can be stated, for what it is worth, that since nationalization Bolivian tin has been sold at unit prices averaging a dollar and less and has cost from a dollar and a half to two dollars to produce, converting costs at the official exchange rate."

As it stands, the present participle **having** is attached to the pronoun **it**. Nobody knows what **it** is, but whatever it is it is not the thing that has made "this quite clear". It is hard to find anything at all to which **converting** might be attached.

Here is a grammatical reconstruction:

"This having been made quite clear, it can be stated, for what it is worth, that although, since nationalisation, Bolivian tin has cost one and a half to two dollars per unit to produce, it has been sold at prices (costs being converted at the official exchange rate) averaging a dollar and less."

This is a grammatical reconstruction, but it still is not very good prose. Several commas have been inserted to divide the long sentence into logical groups, but the effect is jerky. A much better way of writing the passage would be thus:

"The foregoing has been made quite clear. It may be of interest that although, since nationalisation, Bolivian tin has cost one and a half to two dollars to produce, its unit selling price at the official exchange rate has averaged a dollar or even less."

The present participles have now been cut out altogether. Incidentally, the *z* of "nationalisation" has been changed to *s* simply because it is preferred that way in this book. Some publishing houses favour *z* in such words.

For the following sentence some slight excuse may be found:

"Berlin, taking East and West together, was the undoubted theatrical capital of Germany again, and one of the leading theatre cities of the world."

It may be argued by the writer that he meant the ***taking*** to be interpreted as done by Berlin. It is doubtful, however, and this is preferred:

"East and West taken together, Berlin was the undoubted theatrical capital of Germany . . . ."

The following is an extract from a eulogy of a leader of a nationalised industry:

"When talking to X, the future of nationalisation seems a lot more important than the past."

Surely the future of nationalisation has not been talking to X! Yet that is just what it means. What the writer intended, of course, was this:

"When one talks to X, the future of nationalisation . . . ."

A university professor might be expected to be aware of the pitfalls in the use of participles, but here is an extract from a professor's foreword to a text-book on mining engineering:

"Having practised mining engineering for over thirty years and taught it for five, existing text-books had long seemed unsatisfactory."

If the professor wanted to use the participle he should have used it like this:

"Having practised mining engineering for over thirty years and taught it for five, I have long found existing text-books apparently unsatisfactory."

An excellent article in a scientific journal bore this title: "Exploration of the Earth's Upper Atmosphere Using High-Altitude Rockets".

Now, it was not the exploration which was using the rockets, but the experimenters. The title should have been: "Exploration of the Earth's Upper Atmosphere by the Use of High-Altitude Rockets".

## Unintentional Humour

Some examples of unattached participles are unintentionally funny. Some are tragically funny, as in this extract from the transactions of a historical society:

"In carrying out this dreadful punishment, the victim was fastened into a stool or chair at the end of a sort of see-saw, and was raised and lowered into a pool of water, in which she was completely submerged . . . ."

The poor victim was not carrying out this dreadful punishment, but that is the meaning of the sentence. One way of correcting the construction would be thus:

"In the carrying-out of this dreadful punishment, the victim was fastened into a stool or chair . . . ."

This is from a reader's letter to an editor, many years ago:

"Arising out of the Suez crisis, we are about to be made to realise what it means to be short of oil and petrol, the two fuels to which some of our brilliant politicians have confined road transport."

The letter means that *we* are arising out of the Suez crisis, like Venus arising out of the foam, and it is surprising that it was published as written. It should have been corrected, perhaps in this fashion:

"As a result of the Suez crisis, we are about to be made to realise . . . ."

A high-ranking officer in the police force wrote this in a communiqué:

"Failing to find the keys, forcible entry was effected." Did forcible entry fail to find the keys? Of course not. What the officer meant to say could have been written like this:

"Failing to find the keys, the intruders made a forcible entry", or like this clumsy alternative,

"Failure to find the keys resulted in the effecting of a forcible entry."

The following unfortunate example is from a book:

"Having eaten our dinner . . . and drunk our wines, the ladies have withdrawn and we have been left alone in the dining room."

Lest the reader may gather that the ladies were greedy, I now give the writer's intention:

"We have eaten our dinner and drunk our wines. The ladies have withdrawn and we have been left alone in the dining-room." (Notice the hyphen.)


## UNATTACHED PAST PARTICIPLES

Most examples of the misuse of participles are concerned with present participles. But even past participles can lead people astray, and two examples are given here. The first is from a magazine concerned with motoring:

"The picnic table is within easy reach when seated on camp stools."

Logically, this means that when the picnic-table is seated on camp-stools it is within easy reach. This kind of thing takes us into a world of nonsense, for the writer does not even say that he is referring to the picnickers. No doubt what he means is this:

"The picnic-table is within easy reach when the picnickers are seated on camp-stools."

But there is no need to go to this length, and the following would be quite adequate: "The picnic-table is within easy reach of the camp-stools."

The second example is from the catalogue of a building exhibition:

"Strong, clean and economically priced, we have strong conviction in recommending this product."

Let this be the last, before we go beyond amusement. A suitable reconstruction of this example would be:

"We have strong conviction in recommending this product, which is strong, clean and cheap."

## OTHER MISUSES OF THE PRESENT PARTICIPLE

There is one form of construction with the present participle which, frankly, presents a problem – the instructional or informative type of sentence which reads something like this:

"The machine is started by switching on the current and moving the control arm over to the extreme left."

This is not right as it stands, as the participles **switching** and **moving** are not disciplined by anything. The sentence would be quite correct, however, in this form:

"The operator starts the machine by switching on the current and moving the control arm over to the extreme left." Here, the participles are disciplined by the words **the operator**, which are, in fact, the subject of the sentence. In the example as given, it is difficult to analyse the sentence into subject, verb and object, and, in fact, if a sentence cannot be so analysed it is suspect.

If the example is an instruction to operators, it could just as well have been written, quite correctly, in the imperative mood:

"Start the machine by switching on the current and moving the control arm over to the extreme left."

Such sentences are not always instructions to operators, and the imperative mood cannot always be used. One solution is to treat such awkward participles as nouns, like this:

"The machine is started by the switching-on of the current and the moving of the control arm over to the extreme left."

This sentence, though correct, is clumsy. Some sentences, if treated in this way with present participles as nouns, are even worse. How, for instance, could the following be corrected?

1. "A new lawn may be made either by laying turves or by sowing seed."

2. "Cut as shown in the illustration, the centre cut being made by pressing the knife-blade down and pulling it out."

3. "There is an electronic wheel-balancing machine that enables the wheels to be balanced without removing them from the car."

4. "Any misadjustment may be gauged by grasping the centre ring firmly with both hands and pushing it down and pulling it up along the length of the shaft."

First, let us see the effect of treating the present participles as nouns.

1. "A new lawn may be made either by the laying of turves or by the sowing of seed."

2. "Cut as shown in the illustration, the centre cut being made by a pressing of the knife-blade down and a pulling of it out."

3. "There is an electronic wheel-balancing machine that enables the wheels to be balanced without the removing of them from the car."

4. "Any misadjustment may be gauged by a grasping of the centre ring firmly with both hands and a pushing of it down and a pulling of it up along the length of the shaft."

No. 1 now sounds satisfactory. Nos. 2, 3 and 4, however, are too cumbersome, and it would be better to rewrite the sentences. As No. 2 starts in the imperative mood ("Cut as shown") it might as well continue in this mood. Here are some suggestions:

2. "Cut as shown in the illustration, making the centre cut by pressing the knife-blade down and pulling it out."

3. "There is an electronic wheel-balancing machine that enables the wheels to be balanced without their removal from the car."

4. "Any misadjustment may be gauged if the centre ring is grasped firmly with both hands and pushed down and pulled up along the length of the shaft."

The present participle *being* is often maltreated, as in the following examples:

1. "The possibility of strong head winds being encountered is not precluded."
2. "The skid appears to have been precipitated by oil being sprayed on to a rear wheel by a defective oil breather pipe."
3. "Upon it being explained to him, he agreed with the proposal."

All these examples can be easily corrected by the treatment of present participles as nouns, in this way:

1. "The possibility of the encountering of strong head winds is not precluded."
2. "The skid appears to have been precipitated by the spraying of oil on to a rear wheel by a defective oil breather pipe."
3. "Upon its being explained to him, he agreed with the proposal."

Sometimes the correct manipulation of a present participle makes the sentence sound clumsy, as we have seen, and you might argue that ungrammatical sentences like those quoted are justified by common usage. Common usage, however, can occasionally be a good servant but is never a master. If common usage is to be our only guide in grammar we leave the way open to all kinds of slipshod writing and speech.

## UNRELATED WORDS

Lastly, we come to misconstructions of sentences by the use of unrelated words other than participles.

This is from an article on a celebrated man:

"Though shy of personal publicity, most people find him friendly and easy to get on with."

This means that most people are shy of personal publicity. The writer, on the other hand, really means that the celebrated man is shy. If the writer had read the passage carefully before sending it for publication he should have realised that readers would be hoodwinked by the false relation of "Though shy" with "most people". The sentence could have been corrected simply by the insertion of "he is" after "Though".

## "A VERBAL AGREEMENT"

People say this when they mean an oral agreement, that is, a spoken agreement. Everything involving words is verbal: if they are not written down they are oral. Thus a spoken agreement is an oral agreement.

## "PERSUADE" AND "CONVINCE"

"Convince" is often wrongly used for "persuade". You hear sentences such as "He convinced me to take a holiday", instead of "He persuaded me . . . ." I was persuaded to take the holiday, he was convinced that I should.

## "DISINTERESTED" AND "UNINTERESTED"

"Disinterested" means impartial, not uninterested. "Uninterested" means bored.

## "CENTRED"

As "centre" means the middle point of a circle or sphere you cannot centre *around* something, only *on* it. "His concentration was centred on the ball."

# 7

# ODDITIES OF THE LANGUAGE

In English there are numerous peculiar constructions and uses of words which cannot be classed as mistakes but which are interesting enough to deserve discussion. While many of these are acceptable in literate society, some are not recommended for regular use and may, in fact, be frowned upon.

## CLICHÉS

*Cliché* is the past participle of the French verb *clicher,* "to stereotype". Thus, in English, a cliché is a word, phrase, clause or sentence that has become figuratively stereotyped, or so overworked that it has ceased to be effective. Clichés are often used innocently by ingenuous people and are apt to provoke tolerant smiles or, at the worst, impolite sniggers.

The thing to remember about any cliché is that originally it was a clever, pungent, economical, euphonious or even witty expression. Whoever started it, other people copied it because they liked the sound of it or because of its handiness in saving thought and in expressing much in little.

Through constant use, however, clichés lose their originality and become hackneyed. They are to be avoided as far as possible although certain useful words like "incidentally" and phrases like "as a matter of fact", which are undeniable clichés, are so truly useful that they do not bring "the ghost of a smile" (this is a cliché) to the face of a listener or reader. Nobody, try as he may, can avoid clichés altogether.

Below is a list of clichés, some of them old, some not so old. If any of these expressions, or others like them, come into your mind while you are writing or speaking, you must be cautious. In writing you have time to hunt for ways of escape, but in speech you are liable to say the first thing you think of.

"I couldn't care less."

"Prior to" (before)

"Raining cats and dogs"

"A step in the right direction"

"The major part of" (most of)

"I read him like a book."

"Smoking like a house on fire"

"The letter of the law"

"By and large"

"Reading-matter"

"Exploring every avenue"

"Leave well alone"

"In his heart of hearts"

"It stands to reason."

"This hurts me more than it hurts you."

"Conspicuous by his absence"

"At this moment in time"

"In this day and age"

"Quite frankly . . . . to tell you the truth"

"This is a once only, unrepeatable bargain offer."

"We must give of our best."

"Each and every one of us."

"Finally, and in conclusion."

"This is a memorable occasion for the company."

You will be able to add many clichés to this list.

## COMMERCIAL ENGLISH

"Commercial English" bristles with clichés, and a business letter written in straightforward language is usually much appreciated.

These clichés are of a particular and strange kind of "business-speak". Why do people in business choose important-sounding phrases rather than simple precise words? A business letter in simple English shows that the writer has cleared his mind of, or has never acquired, those lifeless collections of words.

"Yours to hand", for instance – this is absurd. "The work is in hand" is only slightly better. Then there is our old friend *inst*. which is indefensible. There is no reason at all why dates should not be given as the 15th June or the 20th December. The expression "even date", for "today", is inexplicable, for it does not even have the virtue of saving space.

"I acknowledge receipt of your letter" is ungrammatical. You receive a letter, or you acknowledge a letter, but you cannot acknowledge receipt.

So many writers of business letters think it a sin to repeat anything that they are prone to writing about "the same", or even "same". This quaint practice is so unnecessary as to be comical.

"We regret" is often used where it would be more polite or more feeling to say "We are sorry", and it is used where more homely yet precise words would do.

"We regret that at this juncture we cannot see our way clear to accede to your request", sounds patronising compared with:

"We are sorry that we cannot, at present, do as you ask."

There may be a difference between "tell" and "inform", but in cases where there is no difference "tell" is preferable. "Forward" and "despatch" are used where "send" would be better. "Begin" or "start" is usually better than "commence".

As for the cliché "My grateful thanks", have you ever heard of thanks being ungrateful?

## "AS TO", "AS REGARDS", "WITH REGARD TO"

"So far as concerns this committee, greater understanding would result from an improvement with regard to communication."

Simplified this sentence becomes:

"Greater understanding for us would result from an improvement in communication."

"As to the children," we might read, "they are enjoying their holiday immensely."

The writer could have written simply:

"The children are enjoying their holiday immensely." Let us suppose, however, that he had a genuine reason; for example, he might have begun writing about the other members of the family and wanted to make a special point of adding something about the children.

Instead of "As to", then, he might have used "As for", "As regards", "With regard to", or, ungrammatically, "Regarding". "Regarding" is wrong because it is an unattached present participle; the children are not regarding themselves.

Anyway, the five expressions, similar in meaning, are clumsy. They are, however, shorter than the full and more explanatory construction:

"On the subject of the children, I can report that they are enjoying their holiday immensely."

Are the expressions acceptable? "Regarding" is not acceptable, as we have seen. "As regards" is the most awkward, for it is difficult to find any logical basis for it. "As to" and "As for" are better, and "With regard to" the most acceptable of all.

## "THE FORMER" AND "THE LATTER"

Too much use is made of "the former" and "the latter", in the mistaken belief that it is bad English to repeat a word. It *may* be bad English if the repetition can be avoided, but the use of "the former" and "the latter" is a poor way of avoiding it.

"The two greatest men in the history of Stonechester were Emmanuel Scamper and Benjamin Thwaites. Both were staunch councillors and noted philanthropists, but while the former was noted also for his horse-racing interests the latter's aversion from all kinds of gambling was particularly well known."

When the reader comes across "the former" and "the latter" he has to look back to see what is meant, and this is one factor against their use. In the above passage, for instance, the reader cannot be expected to grasp immediately that "the former" is Scamper and "the latter" Thwaites.

"The former" and "the latter" also tend to make a passage sound stilted. It sounds better written in this way:

"The two greatest men in the history of Stonechester were Emmanuel Scamper and Benjamin Thwaites. Both were staunch councillors and noted philanthropists, but while Scamper was noted also for his horse-racing interests Thwaites's aversion from all kinds of gambling was particularly well known."

"Aversion from", incidentally, is right. The common "aversion to" is wrong, "to" (as explained elsewhere) signifying approach.

Everybody uses "the former" and "the latter" sometimes, but their use should be minimised and confined as far as possible to complicated items consisting of groups of words. One important thing to remember is that "the former" and "the latter" can be used only for a *pair* of items, and the following examples are wrong:

"Problems which still have to be faced by our big cities include housing of increasing populations, provision of more schools, smooth and balanced organisation of public transport, and elimination of traffic congestion. Of these problems, the former is perhaps the most urgent."

"Speaking of Marlowe, Bacon and Shakespeare himself, I think there is no doubt that the latter was responsible for all the plays."

In the first example, the use of "the former" would be quite justified if there had been only two items, as each item consists of a group of words which could not be conveniently repeated. As there are more than two items, however, it is wrong to use "the former", and in such cases we should say "the first" and "the last" or "the first-named" and "the last-named".

In the second example "the last" or "the last-named" should have been used if this kind of construction had been wanted, but the sentence would be better in this form:

"Speaking of Marlowe, Bacon and Shakespeare, I think there is no doubt that Shakespeare himself was responsible for all the plays."

## ELLIPSIS IN COMPARISONS

Ellipsis (page 49) is simply a shortening by the omission of certain words which are understood, and "ellipsis in comparisons" means sentences like this:

"Temperatures today will be lower than yesterday." This is a shortened form of each of the following:

"Temperatures today will be lower than yesterday's."

"Temperatures today will be lower than they were yesterday."

"Temperatures today will be lower than those of yesterday."

The ellipsis is generally acceptable, but it is preferable to use the full form if it is not too unwieldy.

## SWITCHED ADJECTIVES

When we speak of a "generous gift" we do not mean that the gift is generous but that the giver is generous. The adjective *generous* has been switched from one thing to another and becomes a "switched adjective".

There is no harm in this practice as long as the reader or listener understands the intention of the writer or speaker. Other examples of switched adjectives are "glad tidings", "sad news" and even "happy Christmas".

## "LOST TO"

The phrase *lost to* is strangely used in two ways, as the following sentences show:

"When Jack retired from business after fifty years of hard work he felt that the commercial world was lost to him for ever."

"When Jack played in the bowls match this year he lost the championship to Bob."

In each case it is Jack who is the loser, but while in the first instance the thing lost (the commercial world) is lost to himself, in the second instance the thing lost (the championship) is lost to somebody else.

The general conclusion seems to be that if the thing lost is not gained by anyone else in particular it is *lost to* the loser. If the thing lost is gained by somebody it is *lost to* the gainer.

Here are some more examples:

"All that she had cherished was lost to her."

"Ruritania's once-prosperous trade in string bags had been lost to her go-ahead neighbour, Petularia."

"As he wandered through the streets of London, destitute, he bitterly resented the way his fortune had dwindled away and was now completely lost to him."

"As he wandered through the streets of London, destitute, he bitterly resented the way his legitimate fortune had been lost to his cunning and malevolent brother."

When the phrase *lose to* is used (instead of *lost to*) the thing lost can *only* be lost to the gainer:

"You must not lose your business to that terrible shop across the road."

## "AS FROM"

Two prepositions side by side are often frowned upon, but "as from" can be a useful and legitimate phrase.

"Order of 25th January. As from 1st January, salaries will be increased by 5 per cent."

"As from" here indicates precisely that the order takes effect from a date earlier than the date on which it is written, and there is no quarrel with anyone who uses it in this sense. But there seems no point in its use if, for example, the effective date is *after* the date of the order, in which case "as" should be omitted:

"Order of 25th January. From 1st February, salaries will be increased by 5 per cent."

If we come to another kind of writing, there is this:

"He heard a voice as from a great distance, and, waking from his dream, saw his father beside him."

There is nothing wrong with "as from" if it is regarded as an ellipsis. Thus in the first example it could be "as [if it is] from", and in the last example "as [if it came] from".

## LATIN ABBREVIATIONS

*Etc* (or *&c*) is an abbreviation of "etcetera", which is Latin for "and the rest". It should have no place in ordinary prose and its use should be confined to notes and jottings. If, after giving a list of items, a writer wants to imply the existence of more, he should use some such expression as "and so forth", "and so on", or "and others".

Other Latin abbreviations include *et al.* (*et alibi,* "and elsewhere", or *et alii,* "and others") and *et seq.* (*et sequens,* "and the following"). Note the original meaning of *alibi.*

## "AND/OR"

The term "and/or" has appeared for many years not only in official publications but also in more general writing. It may be convenient in certain limited circumstances, but it is not good English.

"*Instructions to Council.* The presentation of the Aldermen to His Grace will be made by the Lord Mayor and/or the Sheriff."

Now, in that official instruction, where brevity and clarity are both desirable "and/or" is justified. There is no justification, however, for "and/or" in the following:

"The features we look for in the ideal novel include accurate characterisation, an attractive literary style, the power of holding the reader's attention, a reasonable degree of probability and/or a good plot skilfully woven."

The writer means that if we cannot have a reasonable degree of probability we want a good plot skilfully woven, but preferably we should have both. He should say so, then. It will take longer, but the reader does not expect to find lack of meaning in his prose. One way of expressing the writer's intentions would be like this:

"The features we look for in the ideal novel include accurate characterisation, an attractive literary style and the power of holding the reader's attention. We also look for a reasonable degree of probability, with the addition or alternative of a good plot skilfully woven."

Here is another example:

"I should be obliged if you would kindly send me all your books, manuscripts and/or typescripts for examination."

This would be more pleasing thus:

"I should be obliged if you would kindly send me, for examination, all your books and scripts (whether manuscript or typescript)."

## "LITTLE" AND "A LITTLE"

There is a distinct difference between the following two sentences:

"He had little difficulty in finding the address."

"He had a little difficulty in finding the address."

The first means that he found the address easily. The second means that he did not find it easily. The little word *a* makes all the difference, but this is just one of the funny things about English.

## "TO BUILD"

The verb "to build" means "to erect". And yet we read about various things being built which are not built at all – things like tunnels, canals, and underground shelters, which are dug or (if we want a longer word) excavated.

If you are tempted to use the word ***build***, therefore, stop to ask yourself if you are doing right or wrong.

## POSSESSIVE PROBLEMS

Several place-names are prefixed by "Saint" or "St". Strictly, the name of the saint in each case where possession is implied should be given an apostrophe-*s*, as the place is supposed to be *his* place. There are other places, of course, where no possession is implied – St Asaph in Wales, for example – but these present no problem of apostrophe.

Unfortunately, the official names, no doubt as adopted by the town councils, do not always follow the rules of grammar, and the resulting inconsistency must be confusing to foreigners. It is especially unfortunate that St Andrew's, one of our oldest university towns, is officially St Andrews.

The following are the *official* names of some of the "St" places in English-speaking countries: St Abb's Head, St Albans, St Andrews, St Anne's, St Bees, St Bride's Bay, St Catherines (Ontario), St Catherine's Point, St Davids, St Fillans, St George's Channel, St Helens, St Ives, St John's (Newfoundland), St Leonards, St Mary's (Scilly Isles), St Neots.

## PROBLEMS OF PLURALS

We may be confronted with alternatives of the following kinds:

"The United States are important allies."

"The United States is an important ally."

"The Straits of Gibraltar were crowded with vessels."

"The Straits of Gibraltar was crowded with vessels."

"Ten thousand tons of ore were produced in the month."

"Ten thousand tons of ore was produced in the month."

It is commonly accepted practice to treat the United States as singular, so that the first example should be:

"The United States is an important ally."

The Straits of Gibraltar, on the other hand, are treated as plural, so that here we should say:

"The Straits of Gibraltar were crowded with vessels."

Quantities expressed in tons, and in all other units, are treated as singular, the point being that it is the substance which is grammatically significant, not the number of units. Thus, in "tons of ore", the governing word is "ore", not "tons", so that the sentence should be:

"Ten thousand tons of ore was produced in the month." If, however, both the units and the substance are plural, it is natural to say (for example), "Six pounds of peas are wanted", or "Twelve acres of daffodils were destroyed by frost."

Plural problems of a different kind arise with collective nouns like *company*, *committee*, *board*, *society* and so forth. Do we say "The committee is agreed" or "The committee are agreed"?

There is no rule about this, and procedure largely depends on the sense. If the sense implies – as it usually does – that the company, committee, board or society *as a whole* is involved, the singular form of the verb should be used, as in the following two examples:

"The Board in its annual report has shown a profit for the year, in spite of serious strikes and increased costs."

"The Company has decided in the interests of safety to install special protective devices in the factory."

But if the sense implies that the *individual members* of the organisation are involved, the plural of the verb should be used, as in the following two examples:

"After prolonged deliberations the Committee were unanimously agreed that the scheme should be adopted."

"Following recent criticism an extraordinary meeting of the Society was held on the 31st August. At first there was considerable evidence that the Society were divided among themselves. After some discussion, however, and the reading of supporting letters from representative bodies of kindred societies, it was decided that there was no substance in the unfavourable allegations. The meeting closed with the Society convinced of their unity."

## "MESSRS"

"Messrs" is the abbreviation of the French "Messieurs", or "Gentlemen". As such, it is a plural, so that Messrs J. & A. Smith means the combination of Mr J. Smith and Mr A. Smith.

But once Messrs J. & A. Smith form themselves into a limited company, perhaps under the name of J. & A. Smith Ltd, they become a *single legal person*. It is therefore incorrect to address the firm as Messrs J. & A. Smith Ltd.

The rule is simple. "Messrs" should not be used in addressing a limited company. For a company which is not limited it should only be used if the title of the company includes a surname or surnames. Thus, you would be correct in writing "Messrs J. & A. Smith" or "Messrs Robinson & Co.", but you would be wrong in writing "Messrs The Apex Jamjar Co." or "Messrs Happifoot Shoes". Letters addressed to the last two firms would be inscribed "The Apex Jamjar Co." and "Happifoot Shoes".

## "SCOTCH", "SCOTTISH", "SCOTS"

Do not imagine that "Scotch" is a vulgarism, or, in the facetious words of some Englishmen, "only the name of a drink". Reputable Scotch writers up to the nineteenth century, notably Burns and Scott, were not afraid of the adjective "Scotch", although natives of Scotland could be called Scotsmen.

"Scottish" may be the older form and seems to be generally favoured by many English people, perhaps to distinguish it from the verb "to scotch" and perhaps from a mistaken fancy that "Scotch" sounds inelegant.

Attempts have been made to effect a compromise by the use of "Scots" as an adjective. These attempts certainly have historical and literary validity, but one objection to "Scots" is the possibility of awkwardness if, for instance, it should be mistaken for the possessive "Scot's" (singular) or the possessive "Scots'" (plural). Thus, the title of the excellent *Scots Magazine* never was meant to imply that the magazine belonged to or was published for Scots (Scotsmen and Scotswomen) but that it was the Scottish or Scotch magazine.

## SCOTTISH USAGE

Some Scots use certain words and phrases in ways which sound peculiar to many English people unfamiliar with Scotch usage.

### "PRESENTLY"

There is a distinct difference in meaning between the Englishman's *presently* and the Scotsman's. In England it means "soon, in a little while". In Scotland it means "at present, now, at this very moment". Thus to people of either nation, unused to their neighbours' habits, it can lead to misunderstanding.

When a Scotsman, in a business letter, writes, "We are dealing with the matter presently", he means that his firm are dealing with the matter at the moment, but the English recipients of the letter would conclude that the matter was to be dealt with in a short while.

Yet, strangely, the legal language of both countries still gives *presently* its Scottish meaning, and you can find it used in this way in numerous legal documents.

## "MISTRESS"

The title "Mrs" is an abbreviation of "Mistress", but only among some old-fashioned Scots will you hear the abbreviation pronounced as "Mistress". The usual pronunciation of "Mrs" is the only way of distinguishing the meaning of the word as a title from its other meanings.

## "WHAT LIKE"

Englishmen will say "What is the park like?" Some Scotsmen will say "What like is the park?"

There is nothing wrong with this syntax. Indeed, where there is some distance between the Englishman's "What is" and "like", the Scottish practice has much to commend it. Thus, "What like are the gardens at the other end of the park?" is much neater than "What are the gardens at the other end of the park like?"

## "PURPOSE"

"I purpose to apply for permission next week" used to be both English and Scotch usage, but now the use of **purpose** for **propose** is found mainly in Scotland.

## "RETIRAL"

In England a man speaks of his "retirement", but in Scotland he speaks of his "retiral".

## "SHOCK"

While, medically, **shock** in England means something definite, in Scotland it has an additional meaning, the meaning of **stroke**. Thus, "He died of a stroke" in England would be "He died of shock" among some Scots.

## "OUTWITH"

**Outwith** is sometimes used by Scotsmen for **outside**, as in the sentence, "The subject is outwith the committee's terms of reference".

## ELLIPSIS

Most Scottish linguistic curiosities are technically sound, but this does not apply to the habit of unjustified ellipsis (omission of certain words). Some Scots may say "Have you plenty money?" when they mean "Have you plenty of money?" They may say "He wants in" instead of "He wants to come in", or "He wants out" instead of "He wants to go out".

A fairly common example of such ellipsis is, "She said to tell you to come home", instead of "She said I was to tell you to come home".

## GREAT BRITAIN

It is annoying to hear people refer to "England" when they mean Great Britain or the United Kingdom. The media is not immune from the vice, and we even read of "the island of England".

Use "England" and "English" when you mean "England" and "English". Use "Wales" and "Welsh" when you mean precisely these things. Use "Scotland" and "Scottish" (or "Scotch" or "Scots") when these are the words you really mean.

## INTRUDERS

Additions to or modifications of a language can be necessary, logical, mellifluous or all three. Such innovations are healthy and welcome, but there are others which, being unnecessary, illogical or discordant, are certainly unwelcome. Examples spring to the mind.

The word **like**, which has several legitimate uses, is now often misused by being commonly substituted for **as**, as in "Like I said", "It should offend him like it offends me". Some misusages are so grotesque that only complete reconstruction would rectify the offending passages. Thus, a woman publisher, interviewed about her interests, is reported to have said: "I've several, like I go to the theatre a lot."

Here are other examples of strange construction which may make you wince:

"At this point in time" for "now" or "at present".

"Overly" instead of a simple "over", as in "over-anxious".

"For real" and "for free" instead of "real" and "free".

"From whence" instead of "whence" (literally "where from?").

"But" for emphasis, as in: "It was disastrous, *but* disastrous."

# PART 2

# SPELLING
# AND VOCABULARY

# INTRODUCTION

It is, of course, the spelling of *English* (or *orthography*) with which we are concerned in this section, but English-writers should know that users of other languages have their difficulties, too, so that writers of English unsure of their spelling need not think themselves unique. As it is only in writing that incorrect spelling shows itself, the most fluent speaker may be quite inadequate when he puts pen to paper or fingers to keyboard.

With the gradual spread of literacy and the invention of printing came the development of written English, with its confusing and inconsistent spellings becoming more and more apparent.

The first potential reformer was Sir Thomas Smith, who in 1568 published a book (in Latin!) on English spelling. He was followed by several other scholars in the sixteenth and seventeenth centuries.

Even as late as the eighteenth century many people did not seem to concern themselves greatly with rules or accepted practices, the general feeling perhaps being that, as long as a writer's meaning was understood, spelling did not matter. Ephraim Chambers in his *Cyclopaedia* (1743) wrote:

> "In the English, the orthography is more vague and unascertained, than in any other language we know of. Every author, and almost every printer, has his particular system. Nay, it is scarce so well with us as that: we not only differ from one another; but there is scarce any that consists with himself. The same word shall frequently appear with two or three different faces in the same page, not to say line."

English spelling remains inconsistent in part and can be puzzling. Why, for example, should *English* itself sound as if it began with an *I*? The word *England* is derived from *Englaland,* the land of the Angles or Engles, not the Ingles. Numerous other examples of inconsistency in pronunciation and spelling could be cited, but examples which spring readily to mind are the following: *clerk*, *jerk*; *full*, *dull*; *work*, *fork*; *worm*, *form*; *put*, *but*; *gone*, *done*, *bone*; *four*, *dour*; *said*, *laid*, *plaid*; *cow*, *low*; *treat*, *threat*; the two meanings of *tear*; the two tenses of *read*; *names*, *Thames*; *love*, *strove*; and all the different sounds made by *-ough*.

Inconsistencies such as these, however, contribute to the fascination of the language.

Interest in spelling reform was revived in the 1840s, largely through the work of Sir Isaac Pitman. His scheme for reform was rivalled by others but none found acceptance, perhaps because there were too many. There were attempts at reform in the twentieth century, not only by the Simplified Spelling Society but also by Robert Bridges (Poet Laureate from 1912 to 1930) and George Bernard Shaw. In 1961 Sir James Pitman (Isaac's grandson) introduced his Initial Teaching Alphabet, which, however, is not a reformed spelling system but a teaching method.

Several dictionaries appeared before the publication of Dr Samuel Johnson's in 1755, and although this great work contained many inconsistencies it established the basis of our spelling of today, which we accept with all its imperfections.

Observance of consistency led to the limited formulation of rules. Most of the rules developed from within, out of tradition, convention, general understanding and common practice. The rules were not imposed from without, and it is noteworthy that there is no organisation in Great Britain similar to the two language academies of Italy (founded in 1582) and France (founded in 1635). There are various bodies which concern themselves with language, such as the British Academy, the Philological Society and the English Association, but, admirable though these institutions are, they do not give *authoritative* linguistic advice in the manner of the two Continental Academies. The members of the French Academy, for example, meet periodically to *decide* – amongst many other matters concerned with the French language – how words, especially new words, are to be spelt.

Agreement to stick to rules developed in the nineteenth century, when more people discovered the joys of reading and writing. Hand-in-hand with the Industrial Revolution came a surge in the publication of books, newspapers, periodicals and the transactions of learned societies. The necessity of discipline in spelling was accompanied by an appreciation of discipline in grammar, but grammar is different from spelling as much of it depends on logical thought, and most of the great writers of the past, however loose their spelling (and unlike many of today's ephemeral writers) were good grammarians.

In spite of the evolution of rules in spelling there are anomalies which cannot be satisfactorily explained, such as alternative spellings for some words and a deliberate legality in the breaking of some rules. Some irregularities are legacies of the past, perhaps results of writers' or printers' carelessness which, unnoticed at the time, have been assimilated into the written language.

American spelling of today, on the whole, is the result of years of deliberation, of trial and error, of advance and retreat, the result of labour initiated by the great lexicographer Noah Webster (1758–1843). Webster made several attempts at standardisation, would discard, revive and discard again until he, and his successors, reached forms of spelling that were to be adopted as standard American, forms which in many cases are more logical than our own.

This section on spelling and vocabulary offers more than mere lists of words which can be found in dictionaries. It is meant to help the reader to enjoy the fascination of words *as words*, to induce an interest in their history, to appreciate how they are formed, to listen to their sounds, and to be aware of strange inconsistencies.

While keeping the needs of the doubtful speller in the forefront, considerable attention has been given to the formation of words. A general list of words at the end of the section – words which can raise doubts in spellings, words which can be misspelt, and words which are interesting – is preceded by notes on selected words which deserve discursive comment.

Spelling is based on the alphabet, and in a delightful little book, *Origins of the Alphabet* Joseph Naveh writes:

> "But bad as English spelling may be, it still retains most of the principles of alphabetic writing. It takes only a year or two of study to learn to spell English. The Chinese, on the other hand, have to devote many years to learning characters if they are to have a complete command of their literature."

You may be relieved, then, to be studying English rather than Chinese.

# 8

# WORD FORMATION

Anybody really interested in spelling will naturally want to know how words are formed and how, despite numerous inconsistencies, the mode of formation can influence the spelling. Some people have an innate instinct for words, but others not so blessed can develop a retentive visual memory and keep it in sound working condition by intelligent reading. A "good speller" need not be well versed in etymology, but the detection of irregularities and similarities, and awareness of their existence, add to the fun of language-study. Notes on the formation of words, therefore, will be necessary as a foundation, and remarks on the "rules" will be given where appropriate.

## WORD-CONVERSIONS

Basic words are generally changed into related words by the addition of prefixes or suffixes, more often by suffixes. In the case of verbs, for example, *talk* (present tense) becomes *talked* (past tense and past participle) and *talking* (present participle). We say "generally" because "rules" of grammar and of spelling are often disturbed by exceptions. *Eat*, for instance, gives *ate*, not "eated", *sit* gives *sat*, *hold* gives *held*, and *sleep* gives *slept*.

In this section the expression "basic verb" is used rather than "indicative" and terms like "infinitive" and "present tense, first person". Technical terms will be avoided as far as possible, but it is essential to use "past tense", "past participle" and "present participle". The meaning of past tense, generally understood, is obvious, but of "participle" less so.

It will be evident from the examples in Chapter 2 and later in this section that past participles can take many forms, but for a great many verbs the past participle is the same as the past tense.

Despite the vagaries of the past participle, the present participle is constant, always ending in *ing* and presenting no spelling puzzles.

## BASIC VERBS ENDING IN CONSONANTS

Sometimes the rules for converting the present tense of verbs into past tense, past participle and present participle can appear so involved that it is easier to remember the "look" of the words themselves than to try to remember the rules. As we noted in Chapter 2 the addition of *ed* or *ing* to the present tense sometimes needs a connecting link, and the nature of the link (according to the rules) depends on the structure of the basic word and the placing of the stressed syllable.

Verbs of one short (unsustained) syllable ending in a consonant are usually converted by doubling the last letter before the *ed* or *ing*. Thus we get: *hug*, *hugged*, *hugging*; *pet*, *petted*, *petting*; *trap*, *trapped*, *trapping*. One exception is *tread*, which gives *trod* (past tense), *trodden* (past participle) and *treading* (present participle). Other strange exceptions are *cut* and *put*, where the past tense and past participle are still *cut* and *put* but the present participles *cutting* and *putting*. *Jut*, on the other hand (just to be awkward), gives *jutted* and *jutting*. Yet another inconsistent *u* verb is *run*, with its past tense *ran*, its past participle *run*, and its present participle *running*.

Where the monosyllable is sustained (or long) the final consonant remains single, but there are inconsistencies. *Lead* and *read* might be expected to behave similarly, yet the past tenses and past participles are *led* and *read*. *Feed* and *need* make *fed* and *needed*. *Bear* and *near* (in the sense of "nearing one's goal") should follow parallel paths, but *bear* makes *bore* (past tense), *borne* (past participle) and *bearing* (present participle), while *near* follows the regular pattern of *neared* (past tense and past participle) and *nearing* (present participle). (The spelling of the past participle, *borne*, distinguishes it from *born* in the sense of birth.)

Still on the subject of exceptions, remember the correct usage of the verb *lend*, of which the related noun is *loan* (see page 147).

The past tense and past participle of *bend* are both *bent*, but occasionally you may hear the archaic (old-fashioned) form *bended*, as in "on my bended knees".

Verbs of two syllables (occasionally three) ending in a hard consonant take the final double consonant if the stress is on the second (or last) syllable, as in: *abut*, *abutted*, *abutting*; *overlap*, *overlapped*, *overlapping*; *prod*, *prodded*, *prodding*; *regret*, *regretted*, *regretting*. If the stress is on the first syllable of a basic two-syllable verb the final consonant usually stays single, as in: *gallop*, *galloped*, *galloping*; *limit*, *limited*, *limiting.* The rule breaks down in the case of (for example) *ballot*, where, although the stress is on the first syllable, the related words *ballotted* and *ballotting* have a double *t*. Likewise there are *combat*, *combatted* and *combatting*, and *rivet*, *rivetted* and *rivetting*.

In the three-syllable verbs *elicit* and *solicit*, where the stress is on the middle syllable, the *t* stays single to give *elicited*, *eliciting*, *solicited* and *soliciting*. Shorter -*it* verbs are inconsistent. Although *sit* makes *sat* and *sitting*, the past tense and past participle of *quit* are both *quitted*, and the present participle *quitting* agrees with *sitting*. ("I have quit" is said colloquially.) As for *hit*, "hitted" would sound strange, and the past tense and past participle are both *hit*, with *hitting* as the present participle. The verbs *emit*, *fit*, *grit* and *knit* all follow the -*itted* and -*itting* pattern.

There are several nouns and adjectives ending in *ight* but few verbs. Examples of verbs which spring to mind are: *alight* (in the sense of getting off a vehicle); *delight*; *light*; *right* (righting a wrong); and *sight*. All follow the *-ighted* and *-ighting* pattern, but in the case of the verb *light* the past tense and past participle can be *lighted* or *lit*.

## BASIC VERBS ENDING IN Y

With most basic verbs ending in *y* after a consonant or after *h* (not that there are many) the past tense and past participle are obtained by substituting the *y* by *ied*, but in the present participle the *y* is retained and *ing* is added. Examples are: *chivvy*, *chivvied*, *chivvying*; *cry*, *cried*, *crying*; *lobby*, *lobbied*, *lobbying*; *ply*, *plied*, *plying*; *shy*, *shied*, *shying*.

If the *y* follows a vowel it is not normally dropped, and we have: *betray*, *betrayed*, *betraying*; *cloy*, *cloyed*, *cloying*; *play*, *played*, *playing*; *toy*, *toyed*, *toying*. There are exceptions; for example, *buy* gives *bought* and *buying*, and *-ay* exceptions are *say* (*said*), *pay* (*paid*) and *lay* (*laid*).

## OTHER EXAMPLES OF DOUBLING

A few examples of the doubling of the final consonants *d*, *g*, *p* and *t* are given. Other consonants which are usually (but not always) doubled after appearing as single last letters are *b*, *l*, *m*, *n*, *r* and *s*, but there is option in two *s* cases as the following examples will show:

| Case | Basic verb | Past tense & past participle | Present participle |
|------|-----------|------------------------------|--------------------|
| b | ebb | ebbed | ebbing |
| b | rob | robbed | robbing |
| b | stab | stabbed | stabbing |
| m | dim | dimmed | dimming |
| m | gum | gummed | gumming |
| m | ram | rammed | ramming |

| | | | |
|---|---|---|---|
| n | ban | banned | banning |
| n | shun | shunned | shunning |
| n | sin | sinned | sinning |
| r | abhor | abhorred | abhorring |
| r | demur | demurred | demurring |
| r | occur | occurred | occurring |
| s | gas | gassed | gassing |
| s | bias | biased *or* biassed | biasing *or* biassing |
| s | focus | focused *or* focussed | focusing *or* focussing |

Exceptions include verbs ending in *en* (such as *open*, *opened* and *opening*, and *sharpen*, *sharpened* and *sharpening*), and verbs ending in *er* (such as *offer*, *offered* and *offering*, and *temper*, *tempered* and *tempering*). The irregular verb *run* (*ran*, *running*) was mentioned earlier, and another irregular verb is *win* (*won*, *winning*).

Inadequate spellers often find difficulty in deciding whether to put one *r* or two in *occurred*, *occurring*, *recurred* and *recurring*. There is never any doubt about the spelling of *gassed* and *gassing*, but *biased*, *biasing*, *focused* and *focusing* are more commonly spelt with one *s*.

## BASIC VERBS ENDING IN L

The following are examples of British practice (not necessarily American):

| *Basic verb* | *Past tense and past participle* | *Present participle* | *Related noun (if any)* |
|---|---|---|---|
| | | | |
| *l* preceded by one vowel: | | | |
| cancel | cancelled | cancelling | cancellation |
| gel | gelled | gelling | |
| travel | travelled | travelling | travel |

*l* preceded by two vowels:

| | | | |
|---|---|---|---|
| feel | felt | feeling | feeling |
| heal | healed | healing | |
| kneel | knelt | kneeling | |
| maul | mauled | mauling | |
| sail | sailed | sailing | |
| steal | stole (*past participle* stolen) | stealing | |

*l* preceded by a vowel and a consonant:

| | | | |
|---|---|---|---|
| crawl | crawled | crawling | crawl |
| curl | curled | curling | curl |
| hurl | hurled | hurling | |
| trawl | trawled | trawling | trawl |

*l* doubled already:

| | | | |
|---|---|---|---|
| cull | culled | culling | cull |
| pall | palled | palling | |
| sell | sold | selling | sale |
| spell | spelled (*past participle* spelt) | spelling | |
| tell | told | telling | |

Some verbs can be spelt with one *l* or two, but the past tense and the participles have the double *l*, examples being **enthral(l)** and **marshal(l)**. Further examples of the construction of words based on verbs ending in *l* or *ll* are given on page 254.

A favourite example of irregularity with verbs ending in *l* is **parallel**, of which the past tense has a single *l* to give **paralleled**. (Although **parallel** is usually an adjective, it is also used as a verb.) This irregularity conforms with standard American practice, which allows the final *l* in all such verbs to remain single. It is curious, in passing, to note that the epithet **unparalleled** is used far more often than **paralleled**, as in "unparalleled magnificence".

## BASIC VERBS ENDING IN E

Basic verbs ending in *e* usually take *d* for the past tense, as in **elope(*d*)**, **love(*d*)**, **moralise(*d*)**, **rule(*d*)**. For the present participle the *e* is dropped and replaced by ***ing*** (**eloping**, **loving**, **moralising**, **ruling**), but special cases are dealt with below.

Exceptions include **take**, of which the past tense is **took** but the past participle **taken** and the present participle **taking**. By this system, **make** should be converted to "mook" and "maken", but by one of our pleasant little quirks the past tense and past participle are **made**, in spite of consistency in **making**. Another exception is **hide**, of which the past tense is **hid**, the past participle **hidden**, and the present participle **hiding**. **Chide** should behave similarly but has alternatives, its past tense being **chided** or **chid**, its past participle **chided** or **chidden**, and its present participle **chiding**.

Another exception is **bite**, of which the past tense is **bit** (not "bited"), the past participle **bitten**, and the present participle **biting**. For **prove** the past tense is always **proved**, but there is another past participle, **proven**, which has a limited use in technical and legal language.

From **strike** are derived **struck** (past tense and usual past participle) and **striking** (present participle). An archaic form of past participle, **stricken**, is sometimes found in such sentences as "I am stricken in years" and such hackneyed expressions as "poverty-stricken" and "panic-stricken". These applications exemplify the common use of old-fashioned words by people who do not think about them. Another good example is provided by the obsolescent **bereft** (from **bereave**), as in "I was bereft of my senses". Even the commonest verbs can display irregularities. Thus, the past tense of **come** is **came** but the past participle is still **come**. The past tense and past participle of **lose** are both **lost**.

## VERBS ENDING IN EAVE

The derivation of *bereft* from *bereave*, which means "to deprive, rob, spoil, or render desolate", has been referred to. In its association with the death of near relatives the past participle has gradually been replaced in popular usage by *bereaved*, which means the same. In *The Tempest* Ariel speaks to the King of Naples about Ferdinand: "Thee of thy son, Alonso,/They have bereft;. . ."

Disagreement among the *-eave* words is shown in the following list, and in some cases an alternative form of the past tense or past participle is permissible. The present participle follows the regular *-ing* construction with the *e* dropped. *Cleave*, incidentally, has two meanings which in a sense are opposites: (1) to split asunder; (2) to adhere.

| Basic verb | Past tense | Past participle | Present participle |
|---|---|---|---|
| bereave | bereaved | bereaved or bereft | bereaving |
| cleave (1) | cleaved, clove or cleft | cloven or cleft | cleaving |
| cleave (2) | cleaved or clave | cleaved | cleaving |
| heaved | heaved or hove | heaved or hove | heaving |
| leave | left | left | leaving |
| reave | reaved or reft | reaved or reft | reaving |
| weave | wove | woven | weaving |

Common expressions using the archaic forms of the *cleave* (1) words are "cloven hoof" and "in a cleft stick", where the past participle serves as an adjective. *Heave* has a nautical sense in

"Heave to" and "The boat hove in sight". Although the past participle of *weave* is *woven* commerce talks about "wove paper"; "finely-wove fabric" and many other woven materials.

## SPECIAL CASES OF -ING

The doubtful speller often finds difficulty in deciding whether or not to retain the final *e* in converting the present tense of a verb to the present participle. For example, in that sentence, why is "decideing" not written when *decide* ends in *e*?

Some words are easy, and nobody gives a thought to common words like *dying* and *tying* from *die* and *tie*. *Dyeing* and *singeing*, likewise, should present no problems; if the *e* were omitted the results would be *dying* and *singing*, which are words already. Another irregularity is seen in the verb *hie* ("Hie you thither"), of which the past tense is certainly *hied*. *Hying* is given as the present participle in some dictionaries, but the usual spelling is *hieing*.

The *e* is retained in some cases, as in *swingeing* ("swingeing increases in inflation") and *shoeing*. Curiously, *ageing* is right but so are *foraging*, *managing* and *raging*.

*Centre*, when used as a verb, gives *centred* as past tense and past participle, but some people are puzzled about the present participle. Should it be *centreing* or (as the Americans have it) *centering*? The accepted spelling in British English is *centring*, with the *e* dropped. Verbs of similar construction include *accoutre* (*accoutring*), *manoeuvre* (*manoeuvring*) and *mitre* (*mitring*).

Verbs ending in *c* are given a gratuitous *k*, as in *bivouac*(*king*), *panic*(*king*), *picnic*(*king*) and *mimic*(*king*).

The needs of modern English have given rise to certain verbs from nouns which were originally considered only as nouns. *Service*, for instance, led to the *servicing* of cars and many other things, and the invention of the *torpedo* made *torpedoing* necessary. These spellings have developed from common custom, the accepted past tense and past participle being *serviced* and *torpedoed*. To put something through a *process* is now a verb *to process*, with *processed* as past tense and past participle and *processing* as present participle.

In most cases there is nothing reprehensible in the adoption of nouns as verbs with the same spelling, for the practice can be convenient and save circumlocution. If on the other hand the use of a noun as a verb grates on the ear it should be avoided. "I am taking a bus home" is more pleasant than "I am bussing home", but "bussing" seems to be used in the United States. Already referred to is the malpractice of using *loan* as a verb instead of *lend*.

## VERBS ENDING IN VOWEL SOUNDS

Reference to the noun and verb *torpedo* naturally leads to the consideration of other verbs ending in the vowel sound *o*. Apart from *torpedo*, only three need to be considered, of which two are from nouns, *radio* and *veto*. *Radio* is given an *e* in *radioed* but not in the present participle *radioing*. *Veto* is similar, giving *vetoed* and *vetoing*.

The third is one of the most frequently used verbs in the language, *go*. Dealing with *come*, it was remarked that even the commonest verbs can show irregularities, and *go* is as irregular as *come*. Its past tense is *went* (not a bit like *go*), its past participle *gone*, and its present participle *going*.

Some other verbs are less common. *Shanghai* (to get a man drunk and put him aboard a ship needing a crew), for instance, nowadays has little need of application. If its past tense and participles must be used, the forms are *shanghaied* and *shanghaieing*. Some people prefer the apostrophe to *e*, as in *shanghai'd* and *shanghai'ing*. Even less commonly heard or read is the past participle (used as an adjective) *moustachioed* or *moustachio'd*.

## BASIC VERBS ENDING IN IVE

Basic verbs ending in *ive* are regular or irregular. By "regular" is meant verbs of which the past tense and past participle are made by adding *d* to the basic verb and the present participle by dropping the *e* and adding *ing*. Examples of regular -*ive* verbs are: *connive*, *connived*, *conniving*; *dive*, *dived*, *diving*; *live*, *lived*, *living*. Examples of irregular -*ive* verbs are given in the following list:

| Basic verb | Past tense | Past participle | Present participle |
|---|---|---|---|
| drive | drove | driven | driving |
| give | gave | given | giving |
| rive | rived | riven | riving |
| shrive | shrove | shriven | shriving |
| strive | strove | striven | striving |
| thrive | thrived *or* throve | thrived *or* thriven | thriving |

There are, of course, many other English verbs ending in *ive*, and the above are given only as examples of regularity and irregularity. The unique pronunciation of *give* and *live* (different from that of other -*ive* verbs) is one of the charming oddities of the language. The Scots have a special verb, *to gift*, meaning to give or bequeath a handsome contribution to a worthy cause.

## BASIC VERBS ENDING IN W

Basic verbs ending in *w*, too, are regular or irregular in pattern. By "regular" in this case is meant the pattern in which the past tense and past participle are made by adding *ed* to the basic verb and the present participle by adding *ing*. Examples of regular -*w* verbs are: *brew*, *brewed*, *brewing*; *endow*, *endowed*, *endowing*; *row*, *rowed*, *rowing*; *view*, *viewed*, *viewing*. Examples of irregular *-w* verbs are listed below:

| Basic verb | Past tense | Past participle | Present participle |
|---|---|---|---|
| draw | drew | drawn | drawing |
| grow | grew | grown | growing |
| hew | hewed | hewn | hewing |
| sew | sewed | sewn | sewing |
| show | showed | shown | showing |
| strew | strewed | strewn | strewing |
| throw | threw | thrown | throwing |

It should be pointed out that, although *crow* now follows the regular pattern of *crowed* and *crowing*, the archaic past tense *crew* is not to be ignored. ("And immediately the cock crew." Matthew, xxvi. 74, *A. V.*)

*Shew* as an alternative to *show* is obsolete, even if still seen occasionally.

## BASIC VERBS CONTAINING I WITH N

Some people are confused when they have to use the past tense or past participle of certain verbs containing the vowel *i* followed by *n*. They struggle mentally as they wonder if they should write or say "I sank it" or "I sunk it", when they know that "I wrang my washing" sounds all wrong. Their confusion is excusable, for such verbs are infuriatingly inconsistent.

The only *-in* verb which follows a normal pattern is *sin*, from which even the similar *win* differs. *Wring*, with past tense *wrung*, is different even from *ring*, with past tense *rang*.

Apart from *-in* verbs there is *swim*, which is included in the list below as it is similar in behaviour to some of the *-in* verbs.

| Basic verb | Past tense | Past participle | Present participle |
| --- | --- | --- | --- |
| begin | began | begun | beginning |
| bring | brought | brought | bringing |
| cling | clung | clung | clinging |
| drink | drank | drunk | drinking |
| fling | flung | flung | flinging |
| ring | rang | rung | ringing |
| shrink | shrank | shrunk | shrinking |
| sin | sinned | sinned | sinning |
| sing | sang | sung | singing |
| sink | sank | sunk | sinking |
| spin | spun | spun | spinning |
| spring | sprang | sprung | springing |
| swim | swam | swum | swimming |
| swing | swung | swung | swinging |
| think | thought | thought | thinking |
| win | won | won | winning |
| wring | wrung | wrung | wringing |

The past participles **drunk**, **shrunk** and **sunk** have alternative forms used as adjectives: **drunken** ("drunken man"), **shrunken** ("shrunken head") and **sunken** ("sunken garden").

You must not be misled by Byron, who wrote:

"The isles of Greece, the isles of Greece!
Where burning Sappho loved and sung,
Where grew the arts of war and peace,
Where Delos rose, and Phoebus sprung!"

The past tense of **spin** has an archaic form, **span**, as in John Ball's rhetoric of 1381, "When Adam delved and Eve span..."

# CONVERSION OF VERBS TO NOUNS

Some verbs can be changed into nouns simply by a change of spelling. From the verb *pursue*, for example, the noun is *pursuit*, and *sue* leads to *suit*. The noun from the verb *breathe* is *breath*, and the noun from *die* is *death*. *Inquire* (or *enquire*) leads to *inquiry* (or *enquiry*).

Many other verbs can be converted to nouns only by the addition of suffixes, in some cases with slight modifications. While to some extent one carries out a conversion unconsciously it is interesting and entertaining to review the various suffixes which have appeared in our language: *-ment, -ion, -tion; -ant, -ent; -ance, -ence; -ism, -ysis, -asm; -al; -age; -ry, -ery; -ure; -acy; -er, -ster; -ar; -ing; -ee, -and*.

## -MENT, -ION, -TION

Some verbs can take either of the two suffixes *-ment* and *-ion*, but the meanings of the two resulting formations are usually different. For example, *commitment* and *commission*, both from *commit*, have different meanings; *excitement* and *excitation*, both from *excite*, are different; and *complement* and *completion*, both from *complete*, are different.

The *-ment* ending is usually straightforward, being simply attached to the basic verb. With verbs ending in consonants, for example, there are: *amend(ment)*; *detach(ment)*; *embellish(ment)*; *harass(ment)*; *resent(ment)*. With verbs ending in *e* there are: *abate(ment)*; *defile(ment)*; *encase(ment)*; *incite(ment)*. An exception is *argue*, the final *e* of which is dropped to give *argument*.

There is no need for *bewilder(ment)* if you come across *retiral*, which is the Scottish equivalent of *retirement*.

The *-ment* suffix cannot be discussed without a reference to those verbs ending in *dge*, such as *abridge*, *acknowledge*, *judge* and *lodge*. Although the conversions of all these are often spelt with the *e* included (*abridgement*, *acknowledgement*, *judgement*, *lodgement*), a common practice is to omit it from the first three (*abridgment*, *acknowledgment*, *judgment*) and include it only in *lodgement*. The Americans nearly always omit the *e*.

Normally, the *-ion* suffix is simply added to the basic verb, as in *collect(ion)*, *obstruct(ion)*, *repress(ion)*. Where the basic verb ends in *e*, the *e* is dropped, as in: *accumulate*, *accumulation*; *devote*, *devotion*; *pollute*, *pollution*; *secrete*, *secretion*.

There are numerous special cases. The noun from the verb *destroy* is *destruction*, and many thriller-writers have licensed themselves to use an unpleasant back-formation verb "destruct". ("Read the message quickly, for it will self-destruct in one minute".) *Recognise* should make "recognision", but the noun is *recognition*. *Reconcile* makes the long noun *reconciliation*, and *resolve* makes *resolution*.

While on the subject of the *-ion* suffix for conversion of verbs to nouns, verbs ending in *-tend*: *contend*, *distend*, *extend*, *intend*, *portend* and *pretend* must be dealt with. Uncertain spellers (understandably) often find difficulty with these, as the derived nouns follow no consistent pattern. There may be a problem in choosing between *s* and *t*, and the following list shows the correct conversions:

| Basic verb | Derived noun |
| --- | --- |
| contend | contention |
| distend | distension |
| extend | extension |
| intend | intention |
| portend | portent |
| pretend | pretension |

*Extend* is also related to the noun *extent*, which has a different meaning from *extension*. *Pretend* is related to *pretence*, which is not quite the same as *pretension* and not the same as the continuing state of *pretentiousness* (a noun derived from the adjective *pretentious*).

As adjectives have entered our discussion it is appropriate to point out that the adjective from *contend* is *contentious*, and this leads to another noun *contentiousness*. Although the verb *portend* gives the noun *portent* the adjective is *portentous* (often mispronounced "portentious"), and this gives another noun *portentousness*.

We have seen that the noun *destruction* comes from the verb *destroy*. *Construction*, however, is from *construct*, and *instruction* from *instruct*.

The noun *declension*, strangely, is derived not from an imaginary "declend" but from *decline* a word which has several different meanings as a verb and is also used as a noun. *Prevention* is derived from *prevent*; there is no problem about this, but the preferred adjective is *preventive,* not, as many seem to think, the longer "preventative".

It is a mystery to many that while the noun from *adopt* is *adoption* the noun from *adapt* is *adaptation*, although the incorrect "adaption" is sometimes seen and heard. The verb *absorb* is unique in the replacement of its *b* by *p* to form *absorption*.

A note on the conflict between *-ection* and *-exion* will be found on page 257.

Numerous verbs in English end in *ate*, and for conversion to nouns the *e* is dropped and replaced by *ion*. A few examples are given here for the sake of illustration (from *illustrate*): *demonstrate*, *demonstration*; *enumerate*, *enumeration*; *meditate*, *meditation*; *pollinate*, *pollination*; *stagnate*, *stagnation*.

The suffix *-ation* is applied to some verbs ending in *ise*; for example: *authorise*, *authorisation*; *civilise*, *civilisation*;

*improvise*, *improvisation*; *polarise*, *polarisation*. Conversion to the noun in each case requires the dropping of the final *e*. (The question of *-ise* and *-ize* is discussed on page 253.)

The suffix *-ation* can be a suffix in its own right even when the verb does *not* end in *ate*, examples (apart from *adaptation* mentioned above) being: *afforest*, *afforestation*; *crown*, *coronation*; *deprive*, *deprivation*; *derive*, *derivation*; *divine*, *divination*; *fix*, *fixation*; *inhale*, *inhalation*. It is obvious that where the verb ends in *e* the *e* is dropped in the conversion.

(It is curious, incidentally, that, although *derive* makes *derivation*, *contrive* makes *contrivance* and *survive* makes *survival* – three different suffixes used with similar verbs.)

Still on the subject of the suffix *-ation*, it is interesting to observe that in the case of verbs ending in *ke* the *ke* is replaced by *c* before the suffix in the conversion to give the following nouns: *convoke*, *convocation*; *evoke*, *evocation*; *invoke*, *invocation*; *provoke*, *provocation*; *revoke*, *revocation*. *Revoke* also makes the nouns *revocability* and *irrevocability*.

Where some basic verbs end in *ain* or *aim* the *i* is dropped to give, for example: *declaim*, *declamation*; *exclaim*, *exclamation*; *explain*, *explanation*; *proclaim*, *proclamation*. Other verbs in this group behave differently, such as: *abstain*, *abstention*; *entertain*, *entertainment*; *maintain*, *maintenance*; *sustain*, *sustenance*.

It might have been thought that the verb *remonstrate* would have led without question to the noun "remonstration", just as, *demonstrate* gives *demonstration*. So it does, but this word is hardly ever used. The common noun is *remonstrance*, a word with a history which is given on page 304.

There is a wide range of *-ation* nouns derived from verbs, but here four in particular are dealt with – those from the verbs *announce*, *denounce*, *enounce* and *pronounce*. *Announce* makes two nouns, *announcement* and *annunciation*, but the second is used almost solely in reference to the announcement of the Incarnation made by the Archangel Gabriel to the Virgin Mary. It will be noticed that in the conversion to this noun the *o* has been dropped before the *u*, and the same practice is followed in conversion to the nouns *denunciation, enunciation* and *pronunciation.* The last is a fairly common word, yet (and in spite of its meaning) some people persist in mispronouncing it "pronounciation". There is also a noun *pronouncement*, usually taken to mean an important announcement, a proclamation.

In the case of some nouns ending in *ation* there is another possible ending, *ative*, which does not give the same meaning as the *ation* ending. Examples are: *accuse, accusation, accusative; affirm, affirmation, affirmative; derive, derivation, derivative; indicate, indication, indicative; preserve, preservation, preservative. Direct* gives not "directation" but *direction* and *directive*.

There is another series of *-ation* nouns, admittedly rather long nouns because of their construction, which are derived from verbs ending in *ify* which in turn are derived from other, shorter, nouns. In each case the *y* is dropped and replaced by *ication*. A few examples among many such constructions are: *beatify, beatification; gasify, gasification; glory, glorification; sanctify, sanctification; solidify, solidification.*

Not surprisingly, there are exceptions. The noun *liquid* leads to the verb *liquefy*, not "liquify", and the verb leads in turn to *liquefaction*, not "liquidification". (For further notes on derivatives from *liquid*, the reader is referred to page 244.) The verb *putrefy* (not "putrify") leads to the noun *putrefaction*. The verb *crucify* leads to neither "crucification" nor "crucifaction" but to *crucifixion*. Although *perform* gives *performance, deform* gives *deformation*. Although *condole* gives *condolence, console* gives *consolation*.

Besides *-ation* nouns there are nouns in which the *tion* is preceded by other vowels, and already dealt with is the dropping of the final *e* from basic verbs in their conversion to such nouns. The following notes are an extension of the discussion, with, when appropriate, remarks on special cases.

The verb *complete* forms, besides *completion*, two other nouns with different meanings – *completeness* and *complement*. *Complement* is often confused with *compliment*, and more is said about it later (page 283).

The suffix *-ition* is attached to several verbs ending in *ish*, where *sh* is dropped and replaced by *ition*. Thus, *abolish* is converted to *abolition*, *admonish* to *admonition*, and *demolish* to *demolition*. The suffix is not limited to *-ish* verbs, however; it can be attached to some verbs ending in *-it*, such as *exhibit(ion)*, *fruit(ion)*, *inhibit(ion)* and *prohibit(ion)*. Other verbs ending in *it* take *ssion*, as we shall soon see.

There are several verbs ending in *ish* which do *not* take the suffix *–ition*; for example, *banish*, and *embellish* both take *ment* to form the nouns. *Furnish* forms *furniture* and *furnishing*, a present participle used as a noun.

The noun *condition*, by a back-formation, has given rise to a verb which is the same word.

Already given are examples of *-otion* nouns formed from *-ote* verbs (such as *devotion* from *devote*), but a notable exception is *denote*, which gives not "denotion" but *denotation*.

Also given are examples of *-ution* nouns formed from *-ute* verbs (such *as pollution* from *pollute*). *Diminution*, however, is not from a non-existent word "diminute" but from *diminish*. This verb should have led to "diminition" but some long-forgotten printer may have been nodding and unwittingly inaugurated a new spelling.

*Dissolve* gives two nouns – *dissolution* (of Parliament, for example) and *solution* (in chemistry). Other verbs ending in *olve*, with the *ve* replaced by *ution*, are: *absolve, absolution; devolve, devolution; evolve, evolution; resolve, resolution; revolve, revolution.* The usual noun from *involve* is *involvement*, but there is an archaic noun *involution*.

Despite the fact that most *-ute* verbs form *-ution* nouns (such as *comminution* from *comminute*), it is as well to remember in this computer age that the noun from the verb *compute* is not "compution" but *computation.* Similar constructions are: *depute, deputation; impute, imputation; refute, refutation.*

Already dealt with is the suffix *-sion* in *pretension* from *pretend* and similar constructions, but the suffix is applied also to some verbs ending in *ise*, with the *e* dropped, as in: *excise, excision; revise, revision; supervise, supervision. Televise* is not the verb from which *television* is derived, but is a back-formation – that is, the noun appeared before the verb.

There is an interesting group of verbs ending in *de* (preceded by a vowel) in which this ending is dropped and replaced by *sion* to form nouns. This is a large group, but the following are selected examples: *collide, collision; conclude, conclusion; decide, decision; divide, division; evade, evasion; extrude, extrusion; invade, invasion; persuade, persuasion; provide, provision.*

The suffix *-sion* is also applied to some verbs ending in *rt*, when the *t* is dropped and replaced by *sion*. The following are examples: *avert, aversion; convert, conversion; divert, diversion; invert, inversion; revert, reversion.*

As well as *-sion* there is the double-*s* suffix *-ssion*, often occurring with verbs ending in *eed* or *ede*. There are, for example: *accede, accession; concede, concession; intercede, intercession; proceed, procession; secede, secession.* Yet *precede* gives not "precession" but *precedence.*

Now here is a warning. Many people fall down with *supersede*, understandably giving it a *c* instead of an *s*. The noun, too, is spelt with an *s*: *supersession.*

The suffix *-ssion* is also attracted by some verbs ending in *it*, such as: *emit*, *emission*; *omit*, *omission*; *transmit*, *transmission*. *Remit* gives *remission*, but it also gives *remittance*, and the suffix *-ance* will be considered later.

To conclude our survey of the *-ion* suffix we shall deal with the series of nouns in which the suffix is preceded by a vowel and *ct* (*-action*, *-ection*, *-iction*, *-oction*, *-uction*). In some cases the vowel and *ct* form part of the basic verb itself, as in *protract(ion)* and *retract(ion)*. In other cases the vowel and *ct* do not form part of the basic verb, which then suffers some amendment. Already referred to are *liquefy* (*liquefaction*) and *putrefy* (*putrefaction*). *Rarefy* gives both *rarefaction* and *rarefication*, but *satisfy* gives only *satisfaction*.

Following are examples of verbs ending in *ect*, *ict* and *oct* with corresponding nouns:

*ect*: *bisect(ion)*; *direct(ion)*; *protect(ion)*.

*ict*: *constrict(ion)*; *contradict(ion)*; *derelict(ion)*; *predict(ion)*; *restrict(ion)*.

*oct*: *concoct(ion)*; *decoct(ion)*.

Most of the verbs producing nouns ending in *uction* end in *e*, which is dropped to give, for example, the following: *deduce*, *deduction*; *induce*, *induction*; *produce*, *production*; *seduce*, *seduction*. (*Induce* produces another electrical noun, *inductance*.) *Conduct*, which does not end in *e*, leads to *conduction*, but there is also *conductivity*. *Abduct* (no final *e*) gives *abduction*. The peculiarity of *destroy* and *destruction* was considered earlier.

We have seen what happens to *adopt* and *adapt* when they are converted to nouns (page 198). Other verbs ending in *pt* behave like *adopt* in taking the suffix *-ion* without any amendments, as in *corrupt(ion)*, *intercept(ion)* and *interrupt(ion)*. *Concept* is a noun, not a verb, and the noun *conception* is from the verb *conceive*. There is no verb "percept", and *perception* is from the verb *perceive*. Similarly, *reception* is from *receive* and *deception* from *deceive*.

## -ANT, -ENT

Compared with the suffixes *-ment* and *-ion* for converting verbs to nouns, consideration of which has taken much space, other suffixes for the same purpose are few in number. Among them are *-ant* and *-ent*, which justify only a brief mention.

The suffix *-ant* forms (for example) the following: *celebrate*, *celebrant*; *coagulate*, *coagulant*; *confide*, *confidant* (not to be confused with the adjective *confident*); *depend*, *dependant* (not to be confused with the adjective *dependent*); *lubricate*, *lubricant*; *migrate*, *migrant*; *mutate*, *mutant*; *occupy*, *occupant*; *serve*, *servant*.

The suffix *-ent* forms (for example) the following: *adhere*, *adherent* (a different noun from *adhesion*); *antecede*, *antecedent*; *correspond*, *correspondent*; *deter*, *deterrent* (*r* doubled); *precede*, *precedent*; *preside*, *president*. Indirect *-ent* formations include *agent* (from *act*), *recipient* (from *receive*), and *student* (from *study*).

Both *-ant* and *-ent* suffixes can also be attached to verbs to form adjectives, and we shall consider this function later.

## -ANCE, -ENCE

Nouns are formed from some verbs with the suffixes *-ance* and *-ence*, and spellers sometimes find difficulty in remembering which to use of the two. There is no absolute rule about this, and the existence of a final *e* has no bearing on the decision, as is obvious from the lists below. It will be appreciated that these words are merely examples and that there are, in fact, very many others ending in *-ance* or *-ence*.

*-ance* nouns:
verbs with final *e*

| | |
|---|---|
| dominate | dominance |
| grieve | grievance |
| ignore | ignorance |
| reassure | reassurance |
| remonstrate | remonstrance |
| tolerate | tolerance |

*-ance* nouns:
verbs without final *e*

| | |
|---|---|
| attend | attendance |
| clear | clearance |
| convey | conveyance |
| forbear | forbearance |
| inherit | inheritance |
| maintain | maintenance |
| perform | performance |
| remit | remittance |

*-ence* nouns:
verbs with final *e*

| | |
|---|---|
| adhere | adherence |
| coincide | coincidence |
| condole | condolence |
| confide | confidence |
| precede | precedence |
| subserve | subservience |
| subside | subsidence |

*-ence* nouns:
verbs without final *e*

| | |
|---|---|
| abhor | abhorrence |
| defer | deference |
| excel | excellence |
| infer | inference |
| obey | obedience |
| refer | reference |
| subsist | subsistence |

It is odd that the verb *obey* gives not "obeyence" or "obeyance" as a noun but *obedience*. If spelling were logical it should at least correspond with *convey(ance)*. Another anomaly in the lists is the formation of *maintenance* (not "maintainance") from *maintain*. In *subservience* an unnecessary *i* has been inserted. In *abhorrence* the *r* is doubled, but in *deference*, *inference* and *reference* it remains single.

The suffixes *-ance* and *-ence* are also applied in the conversion of some adjectives to nouns.

## -ISM, -YSIS, -ASM

In this heading *-ism* and *-ysis* are written for the sake of clarity. Strictly, the effective suffixes are *-m* and *-is*, but the word-endings to be considered are as above.

Although the ending *ism* is usually applied to adjectives and nouns it is also applied to some verbs in their conversion to nouns. For example, the verb *criticise* leads to the noun *criticism*, *dogmatise* to *dogmatism*, and *plagiarise* to *plagiarism*. In each case the final *e* is dropped and replaced simply by *m*.

The ending *ysis* is found mostly in the vocabulary of scientists. It is applied to verbs ending in *yse*, in which the *e* is dropped and replaced by *is*. For instance, the verb *analyse* leads to *analysis*, and *electrolyse* leads to *electrolysis*. In *synthesise*, when the *e* is dropped, there is no need for any replacement to give the noun *synthesis*.

Mention of *-asm* is given only as an incidental opportunity to point out that *enthusiasm* is not derived from a verb "enthuse". This verb, used colloquially, is a back-formation from the noun.

## -AL

It has already been remarked that *retirement* in England means the same as *retiral* in Scotland. It might be conjectured from this that other *-ment* words in England can alternatively take *-al* in Scotland, but *retire* is probably alone in this treatment.

Other examples of *-al* nouns from verbs include: *acquit*, *acquittal*; *arouse*, *arousal*; *avow*, *avowal*; *betray*, *betrayal*; *carouse*, *carousal*; *rebut*, *rebuttal*; *rehearse*, *rehearsal*; *withdraw*, *withdrawal*. It will be seen that where the basic verb ends in *e* the *e* is dropped, and where it ends in *t* the *t* is doubled. *Rebut* can also form *rebutment*.

Most verbs ending in *ate* are converted to nouns by the use of such suffixes as *-ment* and *-ion*. An example of the rare use of *-al* with a verb ending in *ate* is *reciprocal* (as a noun) from *reciprocate*.

It may seem confusing that verbs similar to those mentioned, when converted to nouns, take not *-al* but some other suffix. For example, although *withdraw* takes *-al* to form *withdrawal*, *draw* takes *-ing* to form *drawing*. In spite of *arousal* and *carousal* there are *sousing* and *delousing*. In spite of *betrayal* there are *playing* and *payment*.

The suffix *-al* can also form adjectives.

## -AGE

The suffix *-age* is generally attached to nouns, but in a few cases it is attached to verbs. The geological term *cleavage*, for example, comes from the basic verb *cleave* (with the final *e* dropped). *Usage* (a noun often employed by writers on language) may be from the verb or noun *use*, again with the *e* dropped. *Waste* and *post*, too, can be regarded either as verbs or nouns in their conversion to *wastage* and *postage*.

There are modernisms, manufactured from verbs for the sake of convenience, such as *coverage* and *reportage*. When the introduction of such words into the language arises out of necessity their use cannot be condemned, for nearly all words have appeared from necessity at some time or other. Legitimate reasons for condemnation include confusion of structure (for example, mixture of roots) and lack of euphony.

Some users of the suffix *-age* show remarkable ingenuity, as, for example, on an invoice I saw on which the various additions to the basic amount – sales tax, allowance for inflation and other charges – were entered as "total plussage".

The suffix *-age* is found more frequently in French than in English, perhaps because in its pronunciation it comes easily to the tongue.

## -RY, -ERY

A few verbs are converted to nouns by the suffix *-ry* to result, for example, in *bake(ry)*, *husband(ry)*, *mimic(ry)*, *outlaw(ry)* and *revel(ry)*. (Here, *husband* is the verb "to manage or cultivate", and *outlaw* is in its verbal sense.) In some cases *e* precedes the *ry* to give words like *brew*(*ery*), *hatch*(*ery*) and *wash*(*ery*). In the case of *launder* the *e* is dropped to give *laundry*. These two suffixes are usually attached to nouns, however, as shall be shown later.

## -URE

The suffix *-ure* is used for converting a few verbs to nouns. If the basic verb ends in a consonant the suffix is a simple addition, as in *fail*(*ure*). Similarly, *forfeit*, which is both noun and verb, gives *forfeit*(*ure*). In *proceed* there is slight modification to form *procedure*. There is also modification in the conversion of *invest* to *investiture*, where *it* has been inserted, unnecessarily. (The word does not mean the same as *investment*.)

If the verb ends in *e* this is dropped, as in: *erase*, *erasure*; *legislate*, *legislature*; *pose*, *posture* (with *t* inserted); *seize*, *seizure*. In the case of *ligature* there is a verb *ligate*, which, however, is probably a back-formation. Another back-formation is a verb *sculpt* from the noun *sculpture*. The formation of *furniture* from *furnish* was mentioned earlier.

The suffix *-ure* is applied to a few adjectives but usually to nouns, and it shall be considered again later.

## -ACY

Some verbs can be converted into nouns by the use of *-acy*, with slight attention to the ending of the original. Thus, from the verb *conspire* the noun is *conspiracy*, and from *advocate* the noun is *advocacy*. The suffix is also attached to nouns and adjectives, and these uses will receive our attention at the appropriate times.

## -ER, -STER

*Laughter*, a noun in a class by itself, is more likely to come from the verb *laugh* than from the noun, but whatever the origin the result is the same. The suffix *-er*, however, is used in an "action" or "occupation" sense as explained in the next section.

The suffix *-ster* is usually attached to adjectives or nouns, but an example of its use with a verb is ***spinster***. Incidentally, why was it once apparently assumed that only unmarried ladies did the spinning?

## "ACTION" SUFFIXES

Several suffixes are used to describe the actions or occupations of people or the uses of things. Most of them are added to nouns, but some are added to verbs, sometimes with slight alterations to the verb-endings. The suffixes generally in use are *-er*, *-or*, *-ant* and *-ist* (or *-yst*), and there is the rarer *-ar*. Where the *-ist* suffix is used with a verb ending in *ise* the real suffix is *-t*, the final *e* being dropped. There are several inconsistencies in the application of these suffixes, and the commonest cause of doubt is the choice between *er* and *or*.

Such suffixes have here been called "action" suffixes for the sake of convenience, and examples of their applications are given in the lists below. The verbs selected, of course, are only a few out of hundreds.

| *Verb* *-er* | *Related noun* | *Verb* *-or* | *Related noun* |
|---|---|---|---|
| betray | betrayer | act | actor |
| buy | buyer | convey | conveyor |
| carry | carrier | decorate | decorator |
| cool | cooler | distribute | distributor |
| defend | defender | lease | lessor |
| haul | haulier | mediate | mediator |
| inform | informer | pave | pavior (paviour) |
| magnify | magnifier | purvey | purveyor |

| | | | |
|---|---|---|---|
| plaster | plasterer | sail | sailor |
| send | sender | survey | surveyor |
| spell | speller | vend | vendor |
| upholster | upholsterer | | |
| write | writer | | |

| Verb | Related noun | Verb | Related noun |
|---|---|---|---|
| *-ant* | | *-ist*, *-yst* | |
| aspire | aspirant | anaesthetize | anaesthetist |
| celebrate | celebrant | analyse | analyst |
| coagulate | coagulant | apologise | apologist |
| cool | coolant | catalyse | catalyst |
| defend | defendant | dogmatise | dogmatist |
| defoliate | defoliant | dramatise | dramatist |
| depend | dependant | pacify | pacifist |
| enter | entrant | plagiarise | plagiarist |
| inform | informant | | |
| inhabit | inhabitant | *-ar* | |
| pollute | pollutant | beg | beggar |
| | | lie | liar |

Some examples from these lists demand attention. It is curious, for instance, that, although **send** leads to **sender**, **vend** leads to **vendor**. There is no logical reason why **haulier** and **pavior** (or **paviour**) should have an *i* inserted, and there is no apparent justification for **lessor** instead of "leasor". A near parallel to **pavior** (or **paviour**) is **saviour** from the verb **save**; in American English the noun is **savior**, but **Saviour** is retained in the Christian sense.

The verb **inform** is deliberately given two places in the lists, because an **informer**, with its forensic connotation, is not the same as **informant**. The verb **cool** also is given two places; a **cooler** is usually understood as a place into which something is put to be cooled, and a **coolant** is a medium (a liquid, for instance) which circulates around something (such as machinery) to keep it cool. The duplication of **defend** is justified because a **defender** supports the interests of a **defendant**.

Excluded from the **-ant** list are the verb **confide** and the noun **confidant**. A **confidant** (contrary to the opinion of some misusers of the word) is not the person who confides but the person who receives the confidential information.

A **dependant** (noun) is a person who **depends** (verb) on someone else and is therefore **dependent** (adjective) on him.

To include **burglar** and **pedlar** in the short **-ar** list would not be strictly legitimate, as these nouns appeared before the verbs **burgle** and **peddle** which are thus back-formations.

Verbs ending in **y** are not consistent in their behaviour. Thus, although **magnify** leads to **magnifier**, **pacify** leads to **pacifist**. A minor irregularity is observed in the treatment of the verb **enter**, which perhaps should give the noun "enterant", but tradition has reduced the word to **entrant**.

The connection of action suffixes with nouns will be considered later.

## -ING

Very often the present participle of a verb is used as a noun ending in the suffix **-ing**. For example, the following are legitimate: "The **giving** of donations is welcome" (as an alternative to **gift**); "From the **rising** of the sun . . ."; "His **comings** and **goings** are difficult to trace"; "As a leader he has a tremendous **following**".

## -EE, -AND

The suffix **-ee** is a relic of the French suffix **é** (masculine) or **ée** (feminine). Originally it was adopted in English in the same form, but gradually the acute accent was dropped and *ee* retained to cover both sexes. The following are examples of its use: ***address*, *addressee*; *employ*, *employee*; *lease*** (as verb), ***lessee*** (the other party being the ***lessor***); ***pay*, *payee*; *vend*, *vendee*** (the party at the selling end being the ***vendor***). Occasionally you find the meanings reversed, particularly with the two nouns derived from the verb ***mortgage***. The party who lends money on the security of an estate is the ***mortgagee***; the borrowing party is the ***mortgagor*** (or, less commonly, ***mortgager***).

A beneficiary under a will is a ***legatee***, and although this is derived from a verb ***legate*** the verb has largely fallen into disuse in favour of ***bequeath***.

The suffix *-and* is of limited application. An undergraduate about to receive his degree, and thus become a graduate, is a ***graduand***. An aspiring clerk in holy orders offering himself for ordination is an ***ordinand***.

## CONVERSION OF VERBS TO ADJECTIVES

Verbs are converted to adjectives by the addition of suffixes which may or may not require some alteration to the ending of the basic verb. These suffixes include the following: *-able*, *-ible*; *-ous*; *-ory*; *-ive*; *-al*; *-ant*, *-ent*; *-some*; *-ful*.

### -ABLE, -IBLE

These two suffixes, applied to some verbs and some nouns to make adjectives, give rise to confusion even in newspapers. The following are *general* rules.

Some verbs ending in consonants take ***able*** without any alteration, as in: ***accept*(*able*)**, ***book*(*able*)**. ("All seats are bookable"), ***comfort*(*able*)**, ***favour*(*able*)** and ***honour*(*able*)**. ***Explain*** should lead to "explainable", but there is no such word. The derived adjective is ***explicable***, from a basic verb ***explicate*** which means the same as ***explain*** but is never used.

If the basic verb ends in *ate* this ending is dropped and replaced by *able*. Common results of this treatment include: *abominate*, *abominable*; *appreciate*, *appreciable*; *calculate*, *calculable*; *demonstrate*, *demonstrable*; *educate*, *educable*; *irritate*, *irritable*.

If the basic verb ends in *e* after a consonant (or after *s*) the *e* is usually dropped, to give, for example: *admire*, *admirable*; *debate*, *debatable*; *prove*, *provable*; *use*, *usable*. Although *movable* is standard, *moveable* is sometimes accepted. *Despise* should make "despisable", but the adjective is *despicable*.

If the basic verb ends in *ce* the *e* is retained, as in *enforce(able)*, *pronounce(able)* and *trace(able)*.

Words ending in *age* are usually nouns, some of which attract the suffix *-able* to form adjectives, which will be dealt with later. There are also a few verbs ending in *age* which take *-able*, and in these the final *e* is usually retained, as in *assuage(able)*, *damage(able)* and *manage(able)*. *Damage*, of course, is also a noun.

If the basic verb ends in *y* after a consonant, the *y* is replaced by *i*, as in: *descry*, *descriable*; *pity*, *pitiable*; *rely*, *reliable*. This rule, as usual, can break down. *Apply*, for example, should make "appliable", which is sometimes seen, but the adjective, used every day, is *applicable*. *Friable*, incidentally, has no connection with the verb *fry*; it is a scientific term meaning "easily crumbled". *Viable* ("practicable" in its commonest modern sense) has nothing to do with *vie* ("to rival, compete with").

If the basic verb ends in *y* after a vowel, the *y* is retained. There are few words of this kind, examples being *assay(able)*, *convey(able)*, *pay(able)* and *play(able)*.

There is an opportunity here to talk about the vexed adjective *inflammable*, which is derived from the basic verb *inflame* (with the *e* dropped and the *m* doubled). Unfortunately, the prefix *-in* can easily be regarded as *not*, to result in a complete misinterpretation of the word as "not liable to burst into flame" and therefore "safe". Confusion is now sometimes avoided by using the word *flammable* to convey the correct meaning.

The suffix *-ible* seems to be more attracted to nouns than to verbs, and the number of verbs taking this suffix is limited. Some of them end in *e*, in which case the *e* is dropped to give, for example: *collapse*, *collapsible*; *force*, *forcible*; *reverse*, *reversible*.

In some cases, if the basic verb ends in *t* or *d*, the last letter is dropped and replaced by *sible* or *ssible*. For example, *comprehend* makes *comprehensible*, *defend* makes *defensible*, and *reprehend* makes *reprehensible*. Use of the double *s* is exemplified by *admissible* (from *admit*), *omissible* (from *omit*) and *permissible* (from *permit*). Exceptions from this practice include *controvert(ible)* and *resist(ible)*, where the suffix is simply added to the basic verb without any alteration.

In cases where the basic verb ends in a consonant other than *t* or *d*, the suffix is again simply added to the base, as in *discern(ible)* and *gull(ible)*.

The adjectives *contemptible* and *contemptuous* are dealt with under noun-adjective conversions rather than verb-adjective conversions, as these adjectives are derived from the noun *contempt* and not directly from the verb *contemn*.

Irregularities are not hard to find. Thus, *neglect* makes not "neglectible" but *negligible*, and it may not be generally known, as a similarity, that *eligible* comes from the verb *elect*.

The verb *eat* makes use of both suffixes to give *eatable* and *edible*.

Although the verb *reduce* ends in *ce* it takes not *able* but *ible*, with the final *e* dropped, to give *reducible*.

The adjective *practicable*, though related to the noun *practice* and the verb *practise*, is not directly derived from either, and cannot readily be accommodated in any of the word-groups we have been considering. It should be remembered that it does not mean quite the same as *practical*, which, however, is sometimes used when *practicable* would be more suitable. (See Chapter 10, "Notes on Selected Words".)

It may seem anomalous that although *resolve* makes *resolvable* the similar verb *dissolve* makes not "dissolvable" but *dissoluble*. This means virtually the same as *soluble*, which is used in chemistry. (It is of incidental interest that *resolvable* has an archaic form, now never used, *resoluble*.) We shall be examining negative forms of words later, but it is appropriate here to point out that both *dissoluble* and *soluble* take the negative prefix *in-* to make *indissoluble* and *insoluble*.

Legitimate attempts have been made to differentiate between the use of *-able* and *-ible* on etymological grounds, but the attempts have partly broken down in the face of established tradition. Tradition may have been influenced by carelessness, but sometimes consistency may have been sacrificed to the more pleasant sound or attractive appearance of a word. The conclusion seems to be that the "correct" choice between *-able* and *-ible* depends less on rules than on a good visual memory, and for the benefit of the reader a list is included later in this section giving some fairly common *-able* and *-ible* adjectives made from verbs and nouns.

### -OUS

A few verbs (not many) can be converted to adjectives by the suffix *-ous*. We have already seen (page 197) how the verb *pretend* can form three nouns, one of which, *pretentiousness*, is an extension of the derived adjective *pretentious* (that is, derived from *pretence*). Most *-ous* adjectives, in fact, are made from nouns, as discussed on page 228.

One of the verbs taking *-ous* is *ponder*, which, originally meaning "to weigh carefully in the mind", has gradually come to be applied to deep thought generally and so given rise to the adjective *ponderous*. An irregularity is immediately evident, however, when it is realised that *wonder* (as a verb), though similar to *ponder*, does not make "wonderous" but *wondrous* (without an *e*).

A similar construction is seen in *cumbrous*, from *cumber* (an early form of *encumber*), for which another adjective is *cumbersome*. The noun *disaster* follows the same pattern, leading to *disastrous* (not "disasterous", a spelling of which even some journalists are guilty). The adjective *piteous* is derived from *pity*, which can be a noun or a verb, the *y* having been replaced by *e*. (A note on the misused *pity* adjectives will be found on page 301.)

The verb *tremble* should perhaps form an easy adjective "tremblous", but its adjective is *tremulous*, which sounds more pleasant. A similar treatment is given to the verb *bib* (to tipple, as in "wine-bibber"), of which the adjective is *bibulous*.

## -ORY

The suffix *-ory* can be applied to some verbs and some nouns. Applied to verbs, it is usually, but not always, part of *-atory*, as in: *declaim*, *declamatory*; *exclaim*, *exclamatory*; *explain*, *explanatory*; *retaliate*, *retaliatory*. It is seen from these words that where there is *ai* the *i* is dropped, and where the verb ends in *e* this is dropped.

A verb needing no alteration before the suffix is *inhibit*, which makes *inhibitory*. *Compel* needs modification to make *compulsory*. It might be thought that *repel*, a similar verb to *compel*, should make "repulsory", but the adjective is *repellent*, which is also a noun. (The suffixes *-ant* and *-ent* are discussed later.) In *promise* the *e* is dropped to form *promissory*.

There is a strange inconsistency with verbs ending in *ide*. Consider three rather similar verbs: *decide*, *divide* and *deride*. *Decide* makes the adjective *decisive*, *divide* makes *divisive*, and only *deride* nicely fits into this section with its adjective *derisory*.

## -IVE

There are many verbs which can be converted to adjectives by the suffix *-ive*. Where the basic verb ends in *e* the *e* is dropped to give, for example, the following: *cumulate* (an archaic form of *accumulate*), *cumulative*; *cure*, *curative*; *decorate*, *decorative*; *indicate*, *indicative*; *restore*, *restorative*; *speculate*, *speculative*. Irregularities, where *d* is replaced by *s*, include: *conclude*, *conclusive*; *decide*, *decisive*; *divide*, *divisive*; *exclude*, *exclusive*; *include*, *inclusive*.

Two of the verbs ending in *ke* (mentioned on page 199 in connection with the conversion of verbs to nouns), *evoke* and *provoke*, can also be converted to adjectives with the aid of the suffix *-ive*. The *e* is dropped, but in addition the *k*, strangely, is replaced by the hard *c* to give *evocative* and *provocative*. Although the verbs *invoke* and *revoke* are similar to the two just cited, they do not make *-ive* adjectives but *invocable* and *revocable*.

Where the basic verb ends in a consonant the suffix is simply added, in such cases, for example, as *construct(ive)*, *express(ive)*, *instruct(ive)*, *possess(ive)* and *prevent(ive)*. "Preventative", referred to elsewhere in this book, is to be discouraged as the repetition of the *t* makes the word less euphonious than *preventive*, and yet *represent(ative)* has only one form. The suffix is legitimately extended to *-ative* in *affirm(ative)* and *confirm(ative)*, but no repetition of *t* is involved.

The *-ative* adjectives listed in the first paragraph of this section are derived from verbs which themselves end in *ate*. *Conserve* and *preserve*, however, which do not end in *ate*, also form *-ative* adjectives (and nouns) – *conservative* and *preservative*. Two other *-erve* verbs take different suffixes to make adjectives, the adjective from *deserve* being the present participle *deserving* and the adjective from *reserve* the past participle *reserved*.

Other cases concern verbs ending in *end,* in which the *d* is replaced by *sive* to give the following: *apprehend*, *apprehensive*;

*comprehend*, *comprehensive*; *defend*, *defensive*; *offend*, *offensive*. (*Defensive* and *offensive* are also nouns.) The suffix *-ive* is also taken by some verbs ending in *it*, the *t* being replaced by *ss* to form: *admit*, *admissive*; *permit*, *permissive*; *submit*, *submissive*. The first two examples do not mean the same as the other related adjectives *admissible* and *permissible*.

## -AL

We have already examined the conversion of verbs to nouns by the suffix *-al*, and the suffix can also be used to convert verbs to adjectives. It has been pointed out that *practical* (as well as *practicable*) is associated with, but not directly derived from, the noun *practice* and the verb *practise*. Other adjectives formed with *-al*, which *are* directly derived from verbs, include the following: *criticise*, *critical*; *equivocate*, *equivocal*; *pontificate*, *pontifical*. The suffix is more commonly used in the conversion of nouns to adjectives, however, and this use will be considered later.

## -ANT, -ENT

We have seen how the suffixes *-ant* and *-ent* can be used to convert some verbs into related nouns, and the same suffixes can be used in the formation of some adjectives. Some adjectives are formed from nouns ending in *-ance* and *-ence*, but it cannot be concluded that all the derived nouns listed on page 205 can automatically be changed into adjectives by the replacement of *-ance* or *-ence* by *-ant* or *-ent*. Of the derived nouns listed, only the following (in alphabetical order) make *-ant* or *-ent* adjectives:

| Noun | Adjective | Noun | Adjective |
|------|-----------|------|-----------|
| abhorrence | abhorrent | ignorance | ignorant |
| adherence | adherent | obedience | obedient |
| attendance | attendant | precedence | precedent |

| coincidence | coincident | subservience | subservient |
| confidence | confident | subsistence | subsistent |
| dominance | dominant | tolerance | tolerant |
| excellence | excellent | | |

Other *-ant* adjectives (besides those mentioned above) are: *defy*, *defiant*; *please*, *pleasant*; *repent*, *repentant*; *vibrate*, *vibrant*. Some are independent of verbs, such as *adamant*, *brilliant* and *constant*. (*Adamant* was originally a noun meaning *diamond*.)

Adjectives ending in *-ent* made from verbs are commoner. Besides those already mentioned there are: *decay*, *decadent*; *deliquesce*, *deliquescent*; *effervesce*, *effervescent*; and others. The adjective *confident* (having confidence in something or someone) is different from the adjective *confidential* (secret, not to be disclosed). *Coincidental* is merely a longer form of *coincident*.

Included in the list on page 205 are the three similar verbs *defer*, *infer* and *refer*, which form the nouns *deference*, *inference* and *reference*. These nouns, however, do not lead to *-ent* adjectives but to *deferential*, *inferential* and *referential*.

## -SOME, -FUL

There are several adjectives ending in *-some*, but not all are derived from verbs. One is *cumbersome*, noted earlier as an alternative to *cumbrous*, which is derived from the verb *cumber* (or *encumber*). Others derived from verbs are *fear(some)*, *grue(some)*, *quarrel(some)*, *tire(some)* and *win(some)*. There are *-some* adjectives derived from nouns and others derived from other adjectives. Some of these, which have been with us for centuries, have the respectability of age; others of more modern origin sound artificial.

The following is a list of *-some* adjectives which are not derived from verbs but are included here for want of a suitable place elsewhere: *awesome*, *fulsome*, *gladsome*, *handsome*, *lightsome*, *lonesome*, *wholesome*. As a matter of interest, *gruesome* is from a verb *grue* which means "to shudder, to feel horror or dread".

Although the suffix *-ful* is attached to many nouns to form adjectives and other nouns, it is attracted by few verbs. One is *mourn*, which makes *mournful*. *Vengeful* is related to *revenge* (verb and noun) and to *vengeance* (noun).

## CONVERSION OF ADJECTIVES TO NOUNS

Adjectives are converted to nouns by use of the following suffixes: *-ness*; *-ity*; *-ion*; *-acy*; *-ery*, *-ry*; *-ment*; *-ism*; *-ance*, *-ancy*; *-ence*, *-ency*; *-escence* (an expansion of *-ence*); *-iety*.

These will be considered in turn.

### -NESS

*Most* adjectives can be converted into nouns by the straight-forward addition of the suffix *-ness*. To give examples would be unnecessary were it not for the opportunity to make several observations and point out exceptions.

Adjectives ending in *y* have the *y* replaced by *i* to give, for example, *beastliness*, *happiness*, *saintliness* and *sprightliness*. The adjective *busy* follows the same rule; its derived noun, *business*, is now hardly ever, if at all, connected with the adjective, being used as an isolated noun in itself.

It is possible to form two separate nouns from the same base. For example, there are *persuasiveness* and *persuasion*, but they have different meanings, the first being from the adjective *persuasive* and the second from the verb *persuade*. The verb *consider* gives *consideration*, while the adjective *considerate* gives *considerateness*. *Faithful* gives *faithfulness*, but it also gives *fidelity* which means the same.

-ITY

*Fidelity*, from the Latin form of the adjective *faithful*, brings us to the suffix *-ity*. Where the adjective does not end in *e*, the *ity* is normally a straightforward appendage, as in *fluid*(*ity*), *humid*(*ity*), *infirm*(*ity*), *morbid*(*ity*) and *senior*(*ity*). In the treatment of most nouns ending in *i* the *i* remains single, as in *jovial*(*ity*), *normal*(*ity*) and *plural*(*ity*). An exception is *tranquil*, where the *l* is doubled to give *tranquillity*.

*Irregular*, of course, leads to *irregularity*, and we find an irregularity in the conversion of the adjective *profound* to the noun *profundity*, where the *o* is lost. *Odd* forms *oddness* and *oddity*, the first being a general state of being odd and the second a particular peculiarity. It is strange that while the noun *longevity* is in fairly common use, the adjective from which it is derived, *longeval*, meaning long-lived, is hardly ever heard.

Where the basic adjective ends in *e* the *e* is dropped, as in the following examples: *agile*, *agility*; *diverse*, *diversity*; *ductile*, *ductility*; *infinite*, *infinity*; *profane*, *profanity*; *pure*, *purity*; *senile*, *senility*; *suave*, *suavity*. *Crude* and *nude*, by the same rule, make *crudity* and *nudity*, but tantalisingly *rude* makes not "rudity" but *rudeness*.

There is the rather long process by which the original basic verb is converted to an *-able* or *-ible* adjective which in turn is converted to a noun ending in the suffix *-ity*. In such cases the final *le* is dropped before replacement by the suffix. Examples are innumerable (this word would give *innumerability*), and rather than have examples here the reader is referred to the list of *-able* and *-ible* adjectives, made from verbs and nouns, on pages 267–268.

## INTERPOLATION: ADJECTIVES ENDING IN OUS

Where an adjective ends in *ous* it *may* be derived from the noun but not necessarily. I am sure that the adjective *monstrous* (with *u*) appeared before the noun *monstrosity* (without *u*), *curious* before *curiosity*, *ferocious* before *ferocity*, and *porous* before *porosity*, and that in the formation of the nouns the *u* was dropped for convenience. On the other hand there are instances where the noun probably appeared before the *-ous* adjective; for example, *fury* probably came before *furious* and *parsimony* before *parsimonious*.

The following *-ous* adjectives are given the benefit of any doubt and it is assumed that they appeared before their corresponding nouns: *ambiguous*, *ambiguity*; *ambitious*, *ambition*, *ambitiousness* (not quite the same as *ambition*); *devious*, *deviousness* (not the same as *deviation*); *fortuitous*, *fortuity*; *hilarious*, *hilarity*; *ingenious*, *ingenuity*; *ingenuous*, *ingenuousness*. (It is fortuitous that the similar adjectives *ingenious* and *ingenuous* make different noun-forms, as otherwise they would be even less understood than they are.) Another adjective which makes two different nouns is *precocious*, which leads to *precociousness* and *precocity*.

## -ION

Although, as we have seen, there are many verbs which can be converted to nouns by the suffix *-ion*, the direct process is applied to only a few adjectives. For example, *abject* gives *abjection* and *contrite* gives *contrition*. The noun *discretion* is from the adjective *discreet*, but there is also an adjective *discrete*, which means "distinct, discontinuous, detached, separate", the noun from which is *discreteness*.

The *-ion* suffix is also part of the involved process seen in the formation of words like *resolution*. This began as a verb, *resolve*, which led to an adjective, *resolute*, which in turn led to the noun *resolution*. The adjective and noun derived from *dissolve* (mentioned on page 201), however, – *dissolute* and *dissolution* – have connections far removed from the scientific sense of *dissolve*.

The verbs *devolve*, *evolve* and *revolve* miss the intermediate adjectival stage to result in the nouns *devolution*, *evolution* and *revolution*, but these can be carried a step further and form the adjectives *devolutionary*, *evolutionary* and *revolutionary*.

## -ACY

The suffix *-acy* can be applied to adjectives and verbs to form nouns and to nouns to form other nouns. For the present, however, we are concerned with the conversion of adjectives. We may be on delicate ground here, for in some instances it is questionable which came first, the adjective or the noun.

*Diplomacy* perhaps preceded *diplomatic*, and *fallacy* could have been on the scene before *fallacious*. In other cases, however, there is no doubt that the adjective came first, examples of these being: *accurate*, *accuracy*; *delicate*, *delicacy*; *obstinate*, *obstinacy*; *profligate*, *profligacy*; *supreme*, *supremacy*.

## -ERY, -RY

The suffixes *-ery* and *-ry*, which we have already seen in their association with verbs, can also be used occasionally in the conversion of adjectives to nouns. Examples are *bravery* from *brave* and *greenery* from *green*. The suffix *-ry* can also be used to convert nouns to other nouns, as we shall see later.

## -MENT

The suffix *-ment* readily attaches itself to verbs to form nouns but is not greatly attracted to adjectives. The adjective *merry* forms the noun *merriment*, but some dictionaries allow *merriness* to exist.

Another example of the use of *-ment* in the conversion of adjectives to nouns is in *betterment*, but a note of caution is necessary. *Better* is an adjective of comparison ("good, better, best"), and hence conversion to the noun *betterment* seems legitimate. The word is almost invariably applied to property, however, in the sense of "improvement", and **betterment** could be derived not from the adjective but from a back-formation verb **to better**.

-ISM

Apart from its use in converting nouns to other nouns (considered later) and verbs to nouns (page 206), the suffix **-ism** is used in several cases for converting adjectives to nouns. Some of the **-ism** nouns thus formed are names of practices, theories, cults and attitudes, but others are more ordinary nouns. In many cases the suffix is a simple appendage to the basic adjective, but in others modification is required. The following examples include both kinds: **altruistic**, **altruism**; **American(ism)**; **archaic**, **archaism**; **colloquial(ism)**; **didactic(ism)**; **monetary**, **monetarism**; **mystic(ism)**; **spiritual(ism)**; **true**, **truism**; **witty**, **witticism**.

There are inconsistencies. If **didactic** and **mystic** make **didacticism** and **mysticism** why do not **altruistic** and **archaic** make "altruisticism" and "archaicism"? In the formation of **witticism** the adjective **witty** has been treated as if it were "wittic".

-ANCE, -ANCY, -ENCE, -ENCY

In the conversion of some adjectives to nouns these four suffixes are common, **-ance** and **-ancy** replacing **-ant** and **-ence** and **-ency** replacing **-ent**. Spellers often find difficulty in deciding whether to use **a** or **e**, but, as in many other spelling problems, a good visual memory helps. The following are short lists of typical conversions.

| Adjective | Noun | Adjective | Noun |
|---|---|---|---|
| *-ant* | to *-ance* | *-ant* | to *-ancy* |
| abundant | abundance | constant | constancy |
| attendant | attendance | expectant | expectancy |
| clairvoyant | clairvoyance | hesitant | hesitancy |

| Adjective | Noun | Adjective | Noun |
|-----------|------|-----------|------|
| *-ant* | to *-ance* | *-ant* | to *-ancy* |
| dominant | dominance | infant | infancy |
| elegant | elegance | vacant | vacancy |
| fragrant | fragrance | | |
| relevant | relevance | | |

| Adjective | Noun | Adjective | Noun |
|-----------|------|-----------|------|
| *-ent* | to *-ence* | *-ent* | to *-ency* |
| corpulent | corpulence | absorbent | absorbency |
| prominent | prominence | clement | clemency |
| reticent | reticence | consistent | consistency |
| subsistent | subsistence | fervent | fervency |
| | | fluent | fluency |
| | | strident | stridency |

A few observations are necessary, for there is a certain laxity about some words of this kind. For example, ***attendant***, ***clairvoyant*** and ***infant*** can be nouns as well as adjectives. There is a noun ***ascendant*** used, for example, in astronomy, but there are two adjectives, ***ascendant*** and ***ascendent***, which are interchangeable and form both ***ascendancy*** and ***ascendency***. ***Brilliant*** forms both ***brilliance*** and ***brilliancy,*** ***eminent*** both ***eminence*** and ***eminency***, and ***repellent*** both ***repellence*** and ***repellency***. (For a note on ***dependent*** and ***dependant,*** see page 285.)

## -ESCENCE
A group of attractive words which could be placed in the "*-ent* to *-ence*" series is that in which adjectives ending in ***escent*** form nouns ending in ***escence***, the adjectives themselves being in most cases derived from verbs. A list of examples follows.

| Verb | Adjective | Noun |
|---|---|---|
| acquiesce | acquiescent | acquiescence |
| coalesce | coalescent | coalescence |
| convalesce | convalescent | convalescence |
| deliquesce | deliquescent | deliquescence |
| effervesce | effervescent | effervescence |
| evanesce | evanescent | evanescence |
| fluoresce | fluorescent | fluorescence |
| | iridescent | iridescence |
| | obsolescent | obsolescence |
| opalesce | opalescent | opalescence |
| phosphoresce | phosphorescent | phosphorescence |
| recrudesce | recrudescent | recrudescence |
| | senescent | senescence |

Where no verb is shown, a verb does not exist.

## -IETY

A little-used suffix for converting adjectives to nouns is *-iety*, which gives, for example, the following: *anxious*, *anxiety*; *dubious*, *dubiety*; *pious*, *piety*; *proper*, *propriety*; *sober*, *sobriety*; *various*, *variety*.

## OTHER ADJECTIVE-NOUN SUFFIXES

There are several other suffixes by which adjectives can be converted to nouns, some by means of simple appendage and others by modification of the basic word. Thus, *false* makes three nouns by the use of different suffixes, all with different meanings. The suffixes *-hood* and *-ness* are added to *false* to give *falsehood* and *falseness*, but in the case of *falsity* the *e* is dropped. The suffix *-hood* is usually applied to nouns, and examples will be given later.

Also applied to nouns is the suffix *-dom*, but it, too, can be applied to adjectives, as in the product *wisdom* from *wise*, the *e* being dropped. The suffix *-ship* is usually applied to nouns, but one adjective, *hard*, gives *hardship.* The addition of *-ster* to form nouns like *youngster* has little to recommend it except in certain cases, and the practice sounds somewhat contrived. I shall say no more about it here, as most of the *-ster* words are formed from nouns.

The suffix *-ure*, used mainly for converting verbs to nouns and nouns to other nouns, is used also for converting a few adjectives to nouns. One example is *rapture*, a noun formed from the adjective *rapt*. There is an obvious connection between the noun *literature* and the adjective *literate*, but evidence of actual conversion is lacking.

## CONVERSION OF NOUNS TO ADJECTIVES

There are many ways of carrying out the reverse of the last process – instead of converting adjectives to nouns, converting nouns to adjectives. We have examined the delicate question of deciding which came first, and the following notes try to concentrate on examples in which the noun preceded the adjective so that the adjective was genuinely formed from the noun.

The suffixes to be considered are: *-y, -ly; -ish; -ous; -ic, -ics, -ical; -ary; -ar; -ful; -less; -al, -ial, -eal; -ate; -ine; -ian, -ean, -ese; -en; -esque; -able, -ible; -ose; -iac.*

### -Y, -LY

The simplest method of conversion in the numerous cases where the noun does not end in *e* is that of adding *y* to the noun to give, for example, *greed(y)*, *meat(y)*, *rubber(y)* and *weight(y)* – the list is almost endless.

If the basic noun ends in *e* the *e* is dropped before the *y*, to give, for example, the following: *haze, hazy; lace, lacy; sauce, saucy; shale, shaly; treacle, treacly.* The word *clay* is awkward as it ends in *y*, but the accepted geological adjective is *clayey* with an *e* inserted. *Day* could hardly give "dayey", however, and so its adjective (as described below) is *daily*.

A variation of the *-y* suffix in the formation of adjectives is *-ly*, which is attracted to some nouns in the sense of "having the quality of". Examples are *beast(ly)*, *curmudgeon(ly)*, *friend(ly)*, *king(ly)*, *mother(ly)* and *rascal(ly)*. Still as an adjectival suffix it is applied to nouns to give a sense of "at regular intervals", such as *hourly*, *daily* and *weekly*.

The adjectival use of *-ly* is not to be confused with its adverbial use, which is referred to later.

## -ISH

Another suffix for noun-adjective conversion is *-ish*, which in most cases is simply added to the basic noun, as in *book(ish)*, *boy(ish)*, *fever(ish)* and *fiend(ish)*. In the case of nouns ending in *e* practice varies; for example, both *rogueish* and *roguish* are acceptable. The suffix is also attached to adjectives to form other adjectives in the sense of "not quite", as in *reddish*, *smallish* and *youngish*. There are also adjectives derived from no particular nouns, such as *outlandish*. Most commonly, of course, the suffix is applied to nationality, as in *British*, *Polish* and *Spanish*, and to language.

## -OUS

The suffix *-ous*, already noted as an agent for converting verbs to adjectives and adjectives to nouns, can also be used for converting nouns to adjectives. Here again, in the simplest cases, the suffix is added to the basic noun to give, for example, *bulb(ous)*, *cretin(ous)*, *peril(ous)*, *poison(ous)* and *portent(ous)*.

If the basic noun ends in *y* the *y* is dropped and replaced by *ous*, *ious* or *eous*, as in the following: *anomaly*, *anomalous*; *calamity*, *calamitous*; *glory*, *glorious*; *parsimony*, *parsimonious*; *pity*, *piteous*. *Pity*, it is important to remember, gives three different adjectives, the other two being *pitiful* and *pitiable*, and for further discussion the reader is referred to page 301. *Beauty*, which ends in *y*, gives *beauteous* as an adjective as well as *beautiful*. *Atrocity* should form "atrocitous", but the adjective is *atrocious*. *Efficacy* should form "efficacous", but for smoothness an *i* has been inserted to make *efficacious*.

In the case of nouns ending in *our* the *u* is dropped before the *r* to give, for example, the following: *clamour*, *clamorous*; *dolour*, *dolorous*; *glamour*, *glamorous*; *humour*, *humorous*; *odour*, *odorous*; *tumour*, *tumorous*; *vapour*, *vaporous*. It was remarked elsewhere that, in relation to the noun *amour*, there are two adjectives, *amorous* and *amatory*.

Two other nouns which need amendment before the suffix *-ous* are *number* and *mischief*. In *number* the *b* is dropped and *ous* added to give *numerous*. With *mischief*, the *f* is replaced by *v* to result in *mischievous*. Unfortunately in some parts of the British Isles the mispronunciation "mischievious" is heard.

In nouns ending in *er* the *e* is dropped in some cases and retained in others. With the *e* dropped we find the following: *disaster*, *disastrous*; *idolater*, *idolatrous*; *leper*, *leprous*; *monster*, *monstrous*; *wonder*, *wondrous*. With the *e* retained before the *r* we follow the practice already mentioned for the simplest cases and directly add the suffix to the basic noun, thereby reaching such words as *cancer(ous)*, *danger(ous)*, *murder(ous)*, *slander(ous)* and *thunder(ous)*. *Boisterous* and *obstreporous* are not related to any nouns. There is a reference to *ponderous* on page 215.

Where the noun ends in *ge* the *e* is retained and the suffix is a simple appendage, so that we find *courage(ous)* and *advantage(ous)*.

Nouns ending in *ce* take various suffixes to form adjectives, but, as far as *-ous* is concerned, the usual treatment is to replace the *e* by *ious* to give, for example: *avarice*, *avaricious*; *caprice*, *capricious*;

*malice*, *malicious*; *space*, *spacious*; *vice*, *vicious*. The adjective from the noun *licence* is not "licencious" but *licentious*.

In nouns ending in *re* the *e* is dropped to give, for example: *adventure*, *adventurous*; *fibre*, *fibrous*; *lustre*, *lustrous*; *pore*, *porous*. An exception is *ochre*, the adjective from which is *ochreous*.

Nouns ending in vowels seldom take *-ous* to form adjectives, but when they do the construction is not simple. *Vertigo*, for example, could lead to a direct adjective "vertigous", but the adjective is the long *vertiginous*.

From the noun *tumult* the adjective should be "tumultous" but an extra *u* has been inserted to make it *tumultuous*. An extra *u* has similarly been inserted into *contemptuous* from the noun *contempt*. This adjective, incidentally, is different from *contemptible*, which applies to the person who, or the behaviour which, deserves the contemptuous person's contempt. Then there is the splendid adjective *tempestuous* from *tempest*.

The adjective from the noun *science* is *scientific*. Yet if we add *con* at the beginning, to make *conscience*, the adjective is not "conscientific" (which sounds horrible) but *conscientious*. *Contagion* (meaning contact) leads to *contagious*.

There are many *-ous* adjectives which are not related to nouns, or are related to nouns only by tenuous association or etymological connection. Such adjectives include *conspicuous*, *deciduous*, *horrendous*, *illustrious*, *scabrous*, *stupendous* and *tremendous*. Not included in this list are two interesting adjectives *dextrous* and *vicarious*, on which there are special notes on pages 287 and 310.

A few lines above, the adjective *tenuous* is used. The associated noun is *tenuity*, but it is difficult to decide which appeared first. In the case of *pusillanimity* this could be the basic noun which gave rise to the adjective *pusillanimous*.

There are two extended *-ous* suffixes, *-iferous* and *-aceous*, the use of which is practically limited to science and technology.

Adjectives incorporating these are either derived directly from nouns or have strong etymological connections. They include *arenaceous* (sandy), *carbonaceous* (carbon-bearing), *Carboniferous*, *Cretaceous*, *farinaceous* (floury) and *metalliferous* (associated with metals). The third and fourth words in this list are given capital initial letters as they are the names of geological periods.

There are also *-ous* adjectives derived from nouns which themselves are derived from verbs. For example, the verb *contend* leads to the noun *contention* which in turn leads to the adjective *contentious*. Similarly we find *presume*, *presumption* and *presumptuous* (*not* "presumptious").

From these many examples it is clear that "rules" for conversion of nouns into *-ous* adjectives apply only in *some* cases, so that in effect there are not any rules. There will be further necessary discussion of the suffix after the next section.

## -IC, -ICS, -ICAL

The suffix *-ic* for conversion of nouns to adjectives is found in many words. Where the basic noun ends in *e* the *e* is usually dropped, so that we find: *aesthete*, *aesthetic*; *athlete*, *athletic*; *metre*, *metric*; *oolite*, *oolitic*; *tone*, *tonic*. Science, *pedagogue* and *romance* happen to end in *e*, but the adjectives are *scientific*, *pedagogic* and *romantic*.

Where the basic noun ends in a consonant the suffix may be simply added, to give, for example, *alcohol(ic)*, *choler(ic)*, *lithograph(ic)*, *magnet(ic)* and *monotheist(ic)*. Exceptions include *horrific* from *horror*, *terrific* from *terror*, and *chaotic* from *chaos*.

Nouns ending in vowels other than *e* usually take the straightforward suffix to form adjectives without any modification, as in *algebra(ic)*, *delta(ic)* and *hero(ic)*. *Aroma* should give "aromaic", but the adjective is *aromatic*, just as the adjective from *dogma* is *dogmatic* and the adjective from *drama*, *dramatic*. The adjective from *giant* should be "giantic", but an unnecessary *g* has been inserted to make *gigantic*. (The adjective *pragmatic* is derived from a Latin word, and there is no English noun "pragma".)

With nouns ending in *y* the *y* is dropped and replaced by *ic* to give (for example) the following: *economy*, *economic*; *geography*, *geographic*; *geometry*, *geometric*; *harmony*, *harmonic*; *history*, *historic*; *melody*, *melodic*; *strategy*, *strategic*. Exceptions with nouns ending in *y* include: *fantasy*, *fantastic*; *poetry*, *poetic*; *tragedy*, *tragic*. *Biology* and *geology* attract the extended forms *biological* and *geological*.

Some *-ic* adjectives are derived from proper nouns, or names, and should not really be counted as legitimate words until they have become firmly established. By this is meant that *Byronic* and *Miltonic* (with capital initials) do not have the same status as *plutonic* (small *p*), a geological adjective applied to certain igneous rocks. *Hebrew* is an established proper noun giving the adjective *Hebraic*. *Mosaic*, applied to the Law of Moses, is not to be confused with the design of small stones called mosaic.

The suffix *-ic* is part of some adjectives that are not directly derived from nouns, such as *automatic*, *bucolic*, *comic*, *domestic*, *exotic* and *linguistic*. *Electric* is derived from the Greek work for amber, *elektron*, the ancient Greeks having discovered that if amber is rubbed it produces static electricity.

Applied to some special studies the suffix *-ic* is pluralised, as in the nouns *acoustics*, *economics*, *ethics*, *logistics*, *mathematics*, *physics* and *politics*. Adjectives formed from some of these pluralised nouns drop the *s* and extend the *-ic* suffix to *-ical*, giving, for example: *acoustical*, *ethical*, *mathematical*, *physical* and *political*. *Economical* has a sense of its own (thrifty) not necessarily directly connected with the study of economics. There is no accepted adjective "logistical", the usual word being *logistic*.

The suffix *-ical* can also be applied to some adjectives already attracting *-ic*, as in **comic(al)**, **historic(al)** and **geographic(al)**. **Liturgy** does not make an adjective "liturgic" but **liturgical**. **Theatre** makes **theatrical**. The noun **pharmacy** obviously caused difficulty in the formation of a connected adjective, and eventually the peculiar **pharmaceutical** appeared.

Although a grammatical rather than a spelling matter, a subject for interesting debate is the treatment of those nouns ending in the plural form *ics*. Should we say "Mathematics *are* his strong point" or "Mathematics *is* . . ."? Should we say "Politics *was* the main topic of his conversation" or "Politics *were* . . ."? There is no fixed rule. Logically, *a* subject or *an* academic sphere of learning is regarded as singular, and takes the singular verb form. Our Canadian and American friends wonder why we abbreviate "mathematics" to the plural "maths" when they call the subject "math". The wonderment is mutual.

## INTERPOLATION: -OUS AND -IC

Although laymen may be hazy about the suffixes *-ous* and *-ic*, in chemistry scientists have been very cunning in seizing both to indicate definite differences in certain matters. For instance, most people know about **sulphuric** acid, and some may have heard about **sulphurous** acid and thought it was the same thing. There is a distinct chemical difference, however, just as there are differences between **ferric** and **ferrous** iron compounds, **cupric** and **cuprous** copper compounds, **nitric** and **nitrous** nitrogen compounds, and **phosphoric** and **phosphorous** phosphorus compounds. For the benefit of those readers who may follow newspapers in the matter of spelling, I emphasise that the element is **phosphorus,** not **phosphorous.**

Besides the adjective **metalliferous** mentioned earlier, there is another adjective, **metallic**, and in both the *i* is doubled. In some applications there is little or no difference; thus, a metalliferous mineral is the same as a metallic mineral, but if the noun "substance" is used rather than "mineral" the adjective is normally *metallic*. A mine producing ores is a metalliferous mine, not a metallic mine. It is customary to speak of a metallic sound, a metallic taste, or a metallic thread, when the other adjective would be unsuitable.

## -ARY

It has been pointed out (page 223) how from the nouns *devolution*, *evolution* and *revolution* we can obtain the adjectives *devolutionary*, *evolutionary* and *revolutionary*. In these examples the suffix *-ary* is directly attached to the noun to form the adjective, and, indeed, this is the usual practice, other examples being *budget(ary)*, *diet(ary)*, *element(ary)*, *inflation(ary)* and *unit(ary)*. In *exemplary* there is a slight modification of the noun *example*, and in *voluntary* there is modification of *volunteer*.

Some other *-ary* adjectives are not *directly* formed from nouns – for example, *contrary*, *culinary*, *literary*, *military*, *necessary*, *pulmonary* and *sumptuary*. The suffix also finds its way into nouns, by association or along etymological routes, examples being *antiquary*, *apothecary* and *luminary*.

## -AR

The suffix *-ar* is part of some nouns but is also attached to a number of nouns to make adjectives. Some conversions are regular, the suffix being simply added to the noun, as in *column(ar)* and *line(ar)*, without any amendment. Other nouns ending in *e*, however, unlike *line*, lose the *e* to give, for example: *molecule*, *molecular*, *nodule*, *nodular*, *vehicle*, *vehicular*. Some nouns ending in *e* not only lose it but adopt a *u*, making *angular* from *angle* and *titular* from *title*. In the case of some nouns ending in *us* these two letters are replaced by *ar*, as in: *annulus*, *annular*, *nucleus*, *nuclear*.

*Peninsula* makes *peninsular*, an adjective which unfortunately many people, and some newspapers, use as the noun. The noun *spatula* makes *spatular*, but another version of the adjective with the same meaning is *spatulate*. The adjective *regular* is not formed from a noun and a suffix but is derived from a Latin root meaning "rule". *Lunar* is derived etymologically from *moon*, and an adjective not found in older dictionaries is *sonar*, which is derived etymologically from *sound*.

## -FUL

There are many adjectives ending in *-ful* derived from nouns, the straightforward practice being to add the suffix to the basic word. There was a time when the suffix was given a double *l* as in the word *full* itself, but convenience – perhaps printers' convenience – led to its elimination. Examples are not hard to find. Here is a short list: *art(ful)*; *boast(ful)*; *care(ful)*; *doubt(ful)*; *event(ful)*; *fear(ful)*; *joy(ful)*; *master(ful)*; *sin(ful)*; *taste(ful)*; *wonder(ful)*.

*Awful* originally meant "inspiring awe" (with the *e* dropped), but because of its modern colloquial sense the word is now sometimes spelt "aweful" when the original meaning is required. *Dreadful* originally meant "inspiring dread" rather than, as now, "disagreeable" or "horrid".

In the case of some nouns ending in *y* the *y* is replaced by *i* before the suffix, to give: *beauty*, *beautiful*; *bounty*, *bountiful*; *fancy*, *fanciful*. In each of these, of course, the adjective means "full of . . .". Where the noun refers to a container, to form another noun, however, the *y* is retained, as in *lorryful*.

*Wilful* is the accepted form of "will(ful)" with an *l* eliminated. *Hateful* should mean "full of hate", but its application has been transferred to the thing hated. *Grateful*, from the noun *gratitude*, is simpler than "gratitudeful". It, too, is sometimes transferred; a person refers to his "grateful thanks" when it is *he* who is grateful. The misapplication of *pitiful is* discussed on page 301.

*Meaningful* should be as respectable as *meaningless*, but the word has got into the wrong hands and is used indiscriminately by people who indulge in meaningless verbiage.

The suffix *-ful* can be applied also to nouns to make other nouns, as we shall see later.

## -LESS

The common suffix *-less*, attached to nouns to make adjectives, gives the opposite meaning to the suffix *-ful*. Not that every *-ful* adjective can readily take *-less*. Consider the first list in the previous section.

*Artless*, *careless*, *doubtless*, *fearless*, *sinless* and *tasteless* are all acceptable. But there are no commonly recognisable words "boastless", "masterless" and "wonderless". Nor can we recognise the existence of "awless", "dreadless", "beautiless", "bountiless", "willess" and "hateless". The opposite of *grateful* is not "grateless" but *ungrateful*. *Meaningless*, as explained, is itself full of meaning.

## -AL, -IAL, -EAL

The suffix *-al* is not only an extension of *-ic* to form *-ical* in the manner explained on page 233, to give words such as *comical* and *historical*. It can also be independent of *-ic* and be a suffix in itself.

Unless the basic noun ends in *e* the suffix is usually a simple addition, as in *autumn(al)*, *exception(al)*, *function(al)*, *hexagon(al)*, *incident(al)*, *sensation(al)* and *verb(al)*. Interesting exceptions include: *abdomen*, *abdominal*; *benefit*, *beneficial*; *contract*, *contractual*; *crux*, *crucial*; *foetus*, *foetal*; *glottis*, *glottal*. In *glottis* there is a double *t* already, and although the verbs *acquit* and *rebut* (page 206) end in a single *t*, this is doubled to form the nouns *acquittal* and *rebuttal*. The noun *digit* also ends in a single *t*, but in the conversion to the adjective *digital* the *t* remains single.

Where the basic noun ends in *e* the *e* is usually dropped to give, for example, the following: *adjective*, *adjectival*; *agriculture*, *agricultural*; *anticline*, *anticlinical*; *centre*, *central*; *doctrine*, *doctrinal*; *spectre*, *spectral*. *Line* is an exception; besides making an adjective *linear* (already discussed) it makes another, *lineal*, which pertains to a line of family descent.

Some nouns ending in *ce* behave as in the following examples, with the *e* dropped: *face*, *facial*; *finance*, *financial*; *province*, *provincial*; *race*, *racial*; *sacrifice*, *sacrificial*; *truce*, *trucial*.

Yet other nouns ending in *ce* are given adjectival endings in *tial*, as in the following examples (again with the *e* dropped): *consequence*, *consequential*; *deference*, *deferential*; *essence*, *essential*; *influence*, *influential*; *palace*, *palatial*; *providence*, *providential*; *space*, *spatial*; *substance*, *substantial*.

As a direct suffix, *-ial* is found in *tangent(ial)* and *torrent(ial)*; yet the similar *monument* forms *monumental*. The direct *-eal* suffix is found in *ether(eal)*.

The construction of *spatial* from *space* is curious when the adjectives from *face* and *race* are *facial* and *racial*. As noted earlier, another adjective from *space* is *spacious*. *Spatial* pertains to the subject of space in general; *spacious* implies that there is plenty of room.

In the case of some nouns ending in *y* the *y* is dropped and replaced by *ial*, as in: *actuary*, *actuarial*; *artery*, *arterial*; *industry*, *industrial*; *remedy*, *remedial*. (*Industry* forms another adjective *industrious*, which is different from *industrial*.) *Periphery* is an exception, making not "peripherial" but *peripheral*.

There are several adjectives ending in *-al*, *-ial* or *-eal* which are not directly formed from nouns but have strong etymological connections, examples being *arboreal*, *diurnal*, *dual*, *fiscal*, *floral*, *funereal*, *legal*, *maternal*, *prandial*, *radial*, *sidereal* and *terrestrial*.

## -ATE

*Spatulate*, mentioned earlier as an alternative to *spatular*, is one of the few adjectives ending in the suffix *-ate* which are directly derived from nouns. Another is *roseate* (coloured rose-pink) as in "The roseate hues of early dawn" (C.F. Alexander). There are, however, several *-ate* adjectives which are not directly connected with nouns, such as *cognate*, *desolate*, *duplicate* and *oblate*. *Pulmonate*, meaning "equipped with lungs", is different from *pulmonary*, which means "pertaining to the lungs".

## -INE

A delta is one kind of river-mouth, an estuary is another. Yet the adjective from *delta* (page 231) is *deltaic*, and the adjective from *estuary* is *estuarine*. The suffix *-ine* is perhaps the most attractive of all, and gives rise to some lovely words; for example: *adamant*, *adamantine*; *alkali*, *alkaline*; *alp*, *alpine*; *coral*, *coralline*; *crystal*, *crystalline*; *Florence*, *Florentine*; *lake*, *lacustrine*. Admittedly *asinine* from *ass* is not very attractive. *Sanguine* is now only remotely connected with blood, its usual modern meaning being "hopeful, optimistic", this state of mind having originally been attributed to the state of one's blood. *Sanguinary* ("bloody, bloodthirsty") is a different word altogether.

## -IAN, -EAN, -ESE

Reference has been made to the suffix *-ish* in its application to nationality and language. The suffix *-ian*, also, can be attached to proper nouns – names of people or places – to form adjectives of nationality, of geography, of language, of kind, or of some connection. Such adjectives include: of people: *Christ(ian)*, *Churchill(ian)*, *Georg(ian)* (*e* dropped); and of places: *Boston(ian)*, *Eton(ian)*, *Paris(ian)*, *Mar(t)(ian)* (*s* of *Mars* replaced by *t*).

Where the *a* or *ia* is already part of the proper noun, *n* only is added, as in *Africa(n)*, *Australia(n)*, *Russia(n)*. This is especially the case with the English names of languages, such as *Persia(n)* and

*Yugoslavia(n)*. In the development of English special treatment has been given to the English spelling of such adjectives as *Norwegian* (from *Norway*) *and Flemish* (from *Flanders*). Where the English equivalent of a name ends in *y* the adjective is formed by replacing the *y* by *ian*, as in *Italian* and *Hungarian*.

Inhabitants of some British cities have given themselves names which have no *direct* spelling connection with the city-names but which are usually understood, examples being *Dundonian* (Dundee), *Glaswegian* (Glasgow), *Liverpudlian* (Liverpool), *Mancunian* (Manchester), and *Novocastrian* (Newcastle).

*Greek*, applied to nationality and language, is not the same as *Grecian*, which means "pertaining to Greece" or "having the characteristics of a Greek". For example, we speak of "a Grecian vase" and "a Grecian nose". The people of Etruria, incidentally, were not "Etrurians" but *Etruscans*.

The suffix *-eau* does similar work to *-ian*, but is largely restricted to adjectives connected with places and people. Where the basic proper noun ends in *es* this ending is replaced by *ean*, as in: *Antipodes*, *Antipodean*; *Archimedes*, *Archimedean*; *Hebrides*, *Hebridean*. Where the basic noun ends in *e, an* is added, as in *Europe(an)*. Where the basic noun ends in a consonant the suffix is a simple addendum, as in *Tyrol(ean)*. *Jacobean* is a derivative of *Jacobus*, *or James*.

The existence of two similar suffixes can be confusing, especially as some of the adjectives formed can be spelt either way. *Shakespeare*, for instance can form *Shakespearian* or *Shakesperean*. The master himself sometimes used the spelling "Shakespere".

Another suffix used in adjectives of nationality and language is *-ese*, as in *Chinese, Japanese, Portuguese*. It is also used in adjectives pertaining to styles of writing or of diction, as in *journalese*.

Apart from its use as a suffix in the formation of geographical and linguistic adjectives, *-ian* is used in the formation of many other words which can be either nouns or adjectives, such as *vegetarian* and *octogenarian*, but more often in the formation of nouns.

It is sometimes thought that because of its meaning, and the spelling, *riparian* is derived in a corrupt way from the noun *river*. It is true that the adjective means "associated with rivers", but the word is derived from a Latin root meaning the *bank* of the river, not the river itself; hence we have "riparian rights".

## -EN

The suffix *-en* attached to a few nouns conveys a meaning of "made of", "consisting of" or "of the nature of". Usually it is a simple addendum, as in *earth(en)*, *flax(en)*, *gold(en)*, *hemp(en)*, *wheat(en)* and *wood(en)*. In the case of *wool* the *l* is doubled to give *woollen*, and *brass* gives the irregular *brazen*. Archaic examples of the use of the suffix are *lead(en)*, *leather(n)* (no *e*), *oak(en)*, *oat(en)*, *silk(en)* and *wax(en)*, words which are so pleasant that it seems a pity that they are not seen more often.

## -ESQUE

There are a few adjectives converted from nouns by the unusual suffix *-esque*, which means "in the manner of" or "reminiscent of". The following examples are commonly seen or heard: *arab*, *arabesque*; *picture*, *picturesque*; *statue*, *statuesque*. *Arabesque*, when used as a noun, can refer to a fanciful type of decoration, to an elaborate musical composition, or to a ballet position. *Grotesque* was originally a *noun* applied to an extravagantly ornamental or distorted design, and its use as an adjective came later.

## -ABLE, -IBLE

These two suffixes, as we have seen, attach themselves to numerous verbs to form adjectives. They are attracted also to a great number of nouns, as in the following examples: *-able*: *action(able)*, *fashion(able)*, *honour(able)*, *marriage(able)*; *-ible*: *access(ible)*, *contempt(ible)*, *forc(ible)*.

It should be noted that the *e* of *marriage* is retained but the *e* of *force* dropped. The adjective *contemptible* (as explained earlier) does not mean the same as *contemptuous*.

Some *-able* and *-ible* adjectives are connected only etymologically, not directly, with verbs and nouns, but in view of the number of adjectives with these endings a list is given later in the book.

### -OSE

The suffix *-ose* (denoting fullness, abundance, or possession of a quality) forms adjectives from bases which can be nouns (occasionally), other adjectives, or related Latin root-words. For example, *bellicose* (warlike) is from *bellum* (war); *comatose* is from the noun *coma*; *grandiose* is from the adjective *grand*; *jocose* is from *jocus* (joke); *morose* is from *morosus* (sullen, peevishly self-willed); *verbose* is from *verbum* (word). Except for *comatose*, these adjectives can form nouns: *bellicosity*, *grandiosity*, *jocosity*, *moroseness*, *verbosity*.

The other application of *-ose* is in chemical words such as *cellulose*, *dextrose* and *glucose*.

### -IAC

The suffix *-iac* is found in adjectives derived from nouns and in nouns derived from other nouns. Adjectives from nouns include *demoniac* from *demon*, *elegiac* from *elegy*, and *iliac* (iliac artery) from *ilium*. Nouns formed from other nouns include *insomniac* from *insomnia*, *kleptomaniac* from *kleptomania*, and *maniac* from *mania*. *Cardiac*, which can be adjective or noun, has only an etymological connection with *heart*, and *maniac* leads to the adjective *maniacal*. In chemistry, *sal ammoniac* is a compound related to *ammonia*.

## PARTICIPLES AS ADJECTIVES

The present participle of a verb is often used as an adjective. Usually it ends in *ing*, as in *charming* (lady, for instance), *doting* (parents), *frightening* (incident), *moving* (experience), *spelling* (problem), *travelling* (salesman). Almost any present participle can be used as an adjective in some connection.

Past participles also can lend themselves to adjectival use, but less commonly than present participles. Past participles ending in *ed*, for example, give *cancelled* (appointment), *enthralled* (audience), *lapsed* (subscription), *rejected* (suitor), *unparalleled* (magnificence). Past participles ending in *en* give such expressions as *bitten* (apple), *cloven* (hoof), *stricken* (deer), *stolen* (purse).

The use of participles as adjectives, briefly outlined here for the sake of completeness, is generally understood, and no more need be said.

## CONVERSION OF NOUNS TO VERBS

We have seen how verbs can be converted to nouns by the addition of suffixes. Conversely, some nouns can be converted to related verbs by the addition of other suffixes, such as *-en* (or *-n*), *-ify* (or *-fy*), *-ise* (or *-ize*), and *-ate*. Not to be forgotten, however, are the prefixes, *en-*, *em-* and *dis-*.

### -EN (OR -N)

The suffix *-en* is more usually attached to adjectives than to nouns. It is true that the noun *length* produces *lengthen,* and *strength* produces *strengthen*, but it can be argued that the basic words are the adjectives *long* and *strong*. The verb *heighten* is legitimately regarded as being derived from the noun *height* rather than the adjective *high*. The constant use of this suffix does not warrant any more discussion, but the obvious rule may be mentioned that, if the basic noun ends in *e*, *n* only is added as in *haste(n)*.

## -IFY (OR -FY)

In the use of *-ify* modification of the basic noun is sometimes necessary, as in: *beauty*, *beautify*; *example*, *exemplify*; *fruit*, *fructify*; *glory*, *glorify*; *stupor*, *stupefy*. No modification is needed in cases like *person*(*ify*) and *solid*(*ify*). Notes on the verbs derived from *liquid* will be found opposite.

Some *-ify* verbs, though not directly derived from English nouns, have strong etymological connections, such as *deify*, *magnify*, *petrify* and *sanctify*.

The noun *modification* is derived from the verb *modify* ("to alter, but only moderately"), and this in turn is derived from the noun *mode* ("manner, way of doing"), the final *e* being dropped.

## -ISE (OR -IZE)

Examples of the use of the suffix as a direct appendage are: *carbon*(*ise*), *idol*(*ise*), *liquid*(*ise*). In *glamour* and *vapour* the *u* is dropped to give *glamorise* and *vaporise*.

The question of choice between *-ise* and *-ize* does not exist in *all* cases, and is discussed at greater length on page 253.

*Synthesis*, *synthesise*, and *analysis*, *analyse* would be reluctantly included as examples as it is probable that the verbs appeared before the nouns.

## -ATE

Most verbs ending in *ate* are not *directly* derived from nouns, but there are a few which are. Such direct conversions, in which the suffix is added to the basic noun, include: *carbon*(*ate*), *hyphen*(*ate*), *liquid*(*ate*). (*Carbon* forms two verbs, *carbonate* and *carbonise*, but *carbonate* is usually a noun.)

Conversions involving slight modification of the basic noun include: *action*, *activate*; *motion*, *motivate*; *vaccine*, *vaccinate*. *Acid* forms *acidulate*. An interesting example of unexpected construction is *filtrate*, which is *not* a verb. The verb is *filter*, and the filtrate is the liquid which passes through the filtering medium.

It is curious that although the verb *consolidate* is understood to mean "make solid" (*solid* being a noun or an adjective), there is neither a noun "consolid" nor a verb "solidate". The verb *decorate* is not derived from, but is etymologically related to, the French noun *décor*, the adoption of which in English is of fairly recent origin. Many *-ate* verbs, in fact, have only etymological connections with their basic nouns, such as *adumbrate*, *exculpate*, *legislate* and *terminate*. *Fenestrate* ("make a window") is derived from the French noun *fenêtre*.

A great many verbs ending in *ate* are not derived from nouns at all, and therefore have no place in our present discussion.

## INTERPOLATION: LIQUID

From the noun *liquid* are derived three different verbs with different meanings, each of which forms a secondary noun: *liquefy, liquefaction; liquidise, liquidisation; liquidate, liquidation*. Brief (not necessarily complete) definitions of the three verbs are as follows:

*liquefy*: convert solid to liquid, melt;

*liquidise*: convert solid to liquid by physical means, as in a mixer or pulveriser;

*liquidate*: bring to an end, pay off, wind up.

*Liquid* is also used as an adjective, and, in a linguistic sense, is found in such expressions as "liquid *l*". (See carillon, page 282.)

## PREFIXES EN-, EM-

Many nouns can be converted to verbs by the prefix *en-*, which is always a simple addition. Examples, not hard to find, are *en(case)*, *en(courage)*, *en(danger)*, *en(joy)*, *en(snare)* and *en(trust)*.

Allied to *en-* is the prefix *em-*, which, attracted to appropriate nouns, forms (for example) the verbs *em(balm)*, *em(bank)*, *em(body)*, *em(brace)* and *em(power)*.

PREFIX DIS-

*Dis-*, an exceedingly versatile prefix, can be attached to nouns to form verbs, to verbs to form other verbs, and to adjectives to form other adjectives. Essentially it is a negative-forming prefix, usually conveying a meaning of "opposite" or "away from", and as examples of its attachment to nouns to form verbs the following should suffice for illustration: *dis*(*band*), *dis*(*bar*), *dis*(*courage*) (opposite of *encourage*), *dis*(*cover*), *dis*(*grace*), *dis*(*honour*) and *dis*(*illusion*). Other examples are given on page 264.

CASES WHERE THE NOUN AND THE VERB ARE THE SAME WORD

There are numerous cases where a noun can be used as a verb, examples being *attack*, *cook*, *honour*, *manufacture*, *noise* ("noise it abroad"), *paper* ("paper the room"), *polish*, *service* and *sound*. *Summons* is a singular noun with a legal connotation giving a similar verb meaning "to issue a summons". The verb *summon* has a different meaning.

# CONVERSION OF NOUNS TO OTHER NOUNS

Several suffixes are used to convert nouns to other words which are still nouns but mean something different. The following will be considered: *-age*, *-ful*, *-ry* and *-y*, *-cy*, *-hood*, *-ship*, *-ate*, *-ure*, *-ic*, *-ster*, *-dom*, *-ism*, *-ee* and *-eer*.

-AGE

Sometimes the suffix is a direct addition, as in *acre*(*age*), *broker*(*age*) and *front*(*age*). In *usage* the *e* of the basic noun *use* has been dropped. (*Use* can also be a verb.) *Assembly* can be converted to *assemblage*, which admittedly means much the same.

-FUL

A *full spoon* (adjective and noun) contains a *spoonful* (noun). There are many such words, all ending in one *l*. If there is a problem, it lies in deciding on the plural form. Is it *spoonsful* or *spoonfuls*? As the derived noun is a measure of quantity it should be *spoonfuls*, just as we speak of pints, tons and miles, or, to fall in with metric custom, of litres, tonnes and kilometres. Other *-ful* nouns derived from other nouns include *cupful*, *handful*, *houseful* and *mouthful*. The construction of *-ful* adjectives from verbs and nouns has been considered (pages 220 and 235).

-RY, -Y

Examples of the use of either of these similar suffixes spring readily to the mind. Usually the suffix is a simple addition to the basic noun, even when this ends in *e*, as *bigot(ry)*, *burglar(y)*, *citizen(ry)*, *knave(ry)*, *machine(ry)*, *pageant(ry)*, *rock(ery)*, *rook(ery)*, *scene(ry)* and *weapon(ry)*. Exceptions include: *grain*, *granary*; *statue*, *statuary*.

-CY

This suffix is seldom applied to the basic noun, some modification usually being necessary. Examples are: *lunatic*, *lunacy*; *magistrate*, *magistracy*; *president*, *presidency*; *pirate*, *piracy*; *primate*, *primacy*; *resident*, *residence*, *residency* (three nouns); *tenant*, *tenancy*; *truant*, *truancy*. No modification is needed in the following examples, where the suffix is a straightforward addendum: *bankrupt(cy)*, *captain(cy)*, *chaplain(cy)*, *colonel(cy)*, *viscount(cy)*.

-HOOD

The suffix *-hood* has a limited application to collective humanity, and is added directly to the basic noun to form, for example, *boy(hood)*, *child(hood)*, *girl(hood)*, *man(hood)*, *priest(hood)*, and *woman(hood)*. We saw earlier that attached to an adjective it can form *falsehood*.

## -SHIP

Another suffix applied to nouns of humanity to form other nouns, usually to indicate a state or an office, is *-ship*, which is added to the basic noun directly, as in *friend*(*ship*), *head*(*ship*), *judge*(*ship*), *owner*(*ship*), *scholar*(*ship*) and *trustee*(*ship*).

## -ATE

An *emir* rules over an Arab *emirate*. The Roman *triumvirate* was composed of three *triumvirs*. An *opiate* was originally a drug prepared from *opium*, and the word is now applied to substances which have similar effects but not necessarily similar origins. A body of *electors* is an *electorate*. These are all examples of the use of the suffix in the conversion of basic nouns to other nouns, and although it has other uses (for example, in the conversion of nouns to verbs described on page 243), they do not concern us in this section. It should perhaps be mentioned, however, that the suffix is a useful indicative part of the names of some chemical compounds; for instance, the *sulphate* of an element is different from the sulphide and the *chlorate* from the chloride.

## -URE

Unless the basic noun ends in *e*, the suffix is a direct addition, as in *forfeit*(*ure*) and *portrait*(*ure*). (*Forfeit* used as a verb has already been referred to.) The *e* of *candidate* is dropped to give *candidature*. A papal ambassador at a foreign court is a *nuncio*, and he is a member of the *nunciature*. *Imposture* is the act of an *impostor*. *Nomenclature*, although not derived directly from an English noun, is based on the Latin word *nomen* (*name*).

The addition of the suffix to verbs to form nouns is discussed on page 208.

## -IC

The suffix *-ic* forms adjectives more readily than it forms nouns, as I have explained at some length. Although there are several nouns ending in *-ic*, few of them are derived directly from other nouns. One is *philippic*, and even here the basic word is a proper noun, **Philip**. The word was originally applied to orations of Demosthenes against Philip of Macedon, but now is applied to any acrimonious declamation.

Another proper noun is *Muse*, one of the nine from mythology, from which the noun *music* is derived. Rather obscurely, the Muses were also responsible for the noun *mosaic*, a design composed of small stones. Etymological connections are found in *logic* (a noun-noun connection from a Greek word meaning "speech or reason") and *rubric* (an adjective-noun from a Latin word meaning "red"). Rubrics are the instructions printed in red in some editions of the *Book of Common Prayer*, and this ecclesiastical connection prompts a reference to the noun-noun conversion *bishopric*, a word for a bishop's office or diocese.

## -STER

On page 227, writing about the word *youngster*, derived from the adjective *young*, it was said that the suffix *-ster* was usually applied to nouns to form other nouns. As a direct addition it forms words like *prankster*, *punster*, *rhymester*, *songster* and *trickster*. Sometimes such nouns are used facetiously, but the suffix has a few worthier applications. A maker of malt, for example, could be a "malter", but somehow *maltster* sounds far more interesting. The attachment of the suffix to the verb *spin* to form the hard-working *spinster* has already been dealt with.

## -DOM

Nouns ending with the suffix *-dom* are formed from basic nouns to denote power, jurisdiction, office or condition. There is no need for any alteration of the basic word in conversion to (for example) *duke(dom)*, *earl(dom)*, *king(dom)* or *official(dom)*. *Wisdom*, as noted elsewhere in this book, is derived from the adjective *wise*. "By my *halidom*" was an old oath now often quoted in historical novels, *hali* being Old English for *holy*.

## -ISM

The addition of the suffix *-ism* to adjectives to form nouns has been discussed (page 224), but there are cases in which it can be attached to nouns. Examples are *cannibal(ism)*, *journal(ism)*, *pauper(ism)* and *Quaker(ism)*. *Criticism* should perhaps be regarded as derived from the verb *criticise* rather than the noun *critic*. The noun *dogmatism* is related to the noun *dogma*, but *pragmatism* (as already pointed out) can be derived only from the adjective *pragmatic* as there is no English noun "pragma".

## -EE

The French origin of the suffix *-ee* in its relation to verbs was explained on page 211. The suffix also is applied in the conversion of nouns to other nouns *usually* to denote a recipient, examples being *grantee* from *grant* (used as a noun) and *legatee* from *legacy*. There is one case, however, where the suffix does *not* denote the recipient. On page 212 *mortgage* was used as a verb in the sense of mortgaging one's property, but it could equally be a noun, as the borrower (*mortgagor* or *mortgager*), by means of a *mortgage* (noun), borrows money from the *mortgagee*.

The suffix is used also to indicate some connection between the formed noun and the basic noun; thus, a *bargee* is concerned with a *barge* and a *devotee* feels *devotion* towards his hobby or interest.

## -EER

The suffix *-eer* denotes a person who is concerned with, or is responsible for, the thing forming the base of the word. Examples are *chariot(eer)*, *musket(eer)* and *pamphlet(eer)*.

# CONVERSION OF ADJECTIVES TO VERBS

When an adjective is applied to a noun the sense of application may be conveyed by means of a verb which is formed by the addition of a suffix or a prefix to the adjective.

A common suffix for the purpose is *-en* (or *-n*), which gives such direct conversions as: *black(en)*, *bright(en)*, *deep(en)*, *loose(n)*, *sweet(en)*, *tight(en)*, *white(n)*. Modification of the basic word is found in: *high, heighten; long, lengthen; strong, strengthen*. (These examples were discussed on page 242, "Conversion of Nouns to Verbs".)

With *fat* the *t* is doubled to make *fatten*, the archaic *fatted* (calf) being retained in the parable of the Prodigal Son. In adjectives ending in *d* the *d* is doubled, as in *gladden, madden, redden* and *sadden*.

Some adjectives, inexplicably, can be used as verbs without the addition of *-en*, examples being *blind, cool, dry, foul, free, lame* and *thin*. The refusal of some adjectives to accept the suffix is also inexplicable: thus we say *moisten* but not "wetten", *quicken* but not "slowen", *thicken* but not "thinnen", *sharpen* but not "blunten". The adjective *hot* gives the verb (and the noun) *heat*. The expression "hotted up" is a colloquialism frequently used.

The suffix *-ify* is more commonly attached to nouns, as we have seen, but in a few cases it can be attached to adjectives to form verbs, as in *falsify* from *false* and *uglify* from *ugly*. There is modification of the adjective in the conversion of *clear* to *clarify*. In the verb *rectify* the base is from a Latin word meaning "right".

Some adjectives are converted to verbs with the aid of prefixes. For example, the prefix *en-* produces *en(dear)*, *en(feeble)*, *en(large)*, *en(noble)* and *en(rich)*. *Encumber*, as mentioned elsewhere, is the verb from the adjective *cumbrous*. Rarer prefixes give us: *dense, condense; strange, estrange; new, renew; fine, refine*.

# ADVERBS

Most people know what an adverb is and what it does. As an adjective qualifies a noun (as discussed on page 21), an adverb qualifies a verb to describe the manner or circumstances in which the action is done, and the commonest way of forming an adverb is to add the suffix *-ly* to the appropriate adjective. Thus we get *curious(ly)*, *economical(ly)*, *faithful(ly)*, *occasional(ly)*, *pleasant(ly)*, *strong(ly)* and *slow(ly)*. An adverb can also be used to describe an adjective, as in "*tremendously* happy".

When the adjective ends in *y*, this is replaced by *i* before the *ly*, examples being: *gay*, *gaily*; *happy*, *happily*; *merry*, *merrily*. Confusion is sometimes caused when the adjective itself ends in *ly*, but the same rule applies, with such results as: *friendly*, *friendlily*; *jolly*, *jollily*; *lovely*, *lovelily*; *naughty*, *naughtily*; *wily*, *wilily*; *ugly*, *uglily*. It is true that some adjectives of this type do not readily lend themselves to adverbial construction. In such cases, for example, "He behaved in a cowardly way" is preferable to "He behaved cowardlily".

From the adjective *kind* an unusual extension *kindly* has been formed, which besides being an adverb is also an adjective and itself produces another adverb, *kindlily*. *Sickly* is a similar extension of *sick*, but never seen is an adverb "sicklily". A peculiar adjective is *likely* ("a likely story"), which very occasionally you may find as the base for an adverb *likelily*.

Adjectives ending in *e* do not all receive the same treatment. In most cases the *e* is retained and the suffix added normally as in: *active(ly)*, *brave(ly)*, *sincere(ly)*, *strange(ly)*. The *e* is dropped from adjectives ending in *le* after a consonant, to give the following: *ample*, *amply*; *forcible*, *forcibly*; *humble*, *humbly*; *simple*, *simply*; *single*, *singly*; *subtle*, *subtly*; *terrible*, *terribly*; *treacle*, *treacly*. When *le* comes after a vowel the *e* is usually retained, as in *docile(ly)*, *hale(ly)*, *sole(ly)* and *vile(ly)*. *Whole*, however, as an exception, makes not "wholely" but *wholly*.

Three words which are both adjective and adverb are *fast*, *hard* and *tight*. "Run fast", "Work hard" and "Hold tight" are legitimate commands, but you should say "Screw it tightly". There is no adverb "fastly" but there is a word *hardly*, the adverbial use of which should be confined to the meaning of *scarcely*, so that "hardly any money" is the same as "scarcely any money". Occasionally "hardly earned" may be seen, but, perhaps because the sense of this can be ambiguous, "hard-earned" with the linking hyphen is preferable.

A peculiarity of English is that although there is an adverb *badly* there is no adverb "goodly". The word for this, the direct opposite of *badly*, is *well*, as in "Do it well". *Goodly* is an archaic adjective which had various vague meanings connected with *good* ("a goodly sum", for example), but it is not an adverb.

There is a fairly common practice of adding *-ly* to past-tense or past-participle formations to produce adverbs like *admitted(ly)*, *alleged(ly)*, *hurried(ly)*, *supposed(ly)* and *undoubted(ly)*. Care should be taken, however, to avoid the practice if the result sounds unwieldy or unnatural. Some present participles also can take *ly* to form adverbs, as in *joking(ly)*, *laughing(ly)*, *loving(ly)* and *menacing(ly)*.

As we have discussed, the adjectives *quick* and *slow* are very often misused as adverbs, either through ignorance or lack of space. "Get rich quick" is as bad as the official warning seen on roads, "Go slow". As for "new laid eggs" – well, perhaps only a fussy pedant would insist on "newly-laid eggs".

# 9

# SPELLING RULES AND CONVENTIONS

In this chapter some spelling matters are examined in detail. To devise a logical sequence, however, would be futile as there is much in the subject of spelling that is illogical. The fact that one section of this chapter precedes another, therefore, does not necessarily mean that it is the more important.

## -ISE OR-IZE?

Etymologists have tended to add to the confusion that exists in the vexed question of choice, if any, between these two suffixes. Some have asserted that as most traditional English verbs are ultimately of Greek composition, in which the root contains the equivalent of *izo*, the *ize* spelling should be used for most verbs, *ise* being adopted for those verbs which are not of Greek origin. If this were to be a "rule" to be remembered it would be useless to most people, who have to write countless things every day.

The French changed the **z** into **s** long ago, and those French infinitives (mainly derived from Greek through Latin) which correspond with our own always end in *iser.* While nearly all *ize* words may be spelt *ise* the converse does not hold. In British English some words are now never spelt with **z**, such as *advertise*, *advise*, *chastise*, *comprise*, *compromise*, *devise* and *exercise*. In the eighteenth century many writers favoured *surprize* and *enterprize*.

If you use *ise* in nearly all cases you will be safe. *Recognise* can take *s,* though *recognize* is more common. The verb makes the noun *recognition*, or, much less commonly, *recognizance* (always with **z**) and *cognizance*. There is a slight difference in meaning between *cognition* (the act or faculty of perceiving) and *cognizance* (knowledge, notice, awareness).

It is interesting to observe that although the verb *criticise* can be spelt with either *s* or *z*, the noun *criticism* has no alternative, all *ism* nouns being spelt with *s*. In words in which there is a British choice between *s* and *z*, Americans normally use *z*. In words in which there is no choice, and are always spelt with *s*, America follows British practice. Although *analyse, catalyse, paralyse* and *synthesise* are spelt with *z* by Americans, our friends agree with our noun-spellings *analysis*, *catalysis*, *paralysis* and *synthesis*.

## EI AND IE

There are numerous words in which the letters *e* and *i* occur together, either as *ei* or *ie*. In some words the combination produces the sound *ee*, and it is these which are our immediate concern. The hundreds of others in which the two letters occur together but which are not pronounced with a definite *ee* sound have no part in our present discussion.

One of the most commonly-remembered spelling rules in English, which we were taught in our first schooling, is: "*i* before *e* except after *c*". This rule applies only to the words in which the combination produces the sound *ee*, as in *belief, chief, field, frieze, grief, niece, relief, retrieve, thief* and *tier*.

In none of these words is there a *c* before the *i*. Other words, in which the vowel sound *is* preceded by *c*, include *ceiling*, *conceive*, *deceive*, *perceive* and *receive*, in all of which *e* comes before *i*. The exceptions – all words with an *ee* sound – are so few that they can be easily remembered, and include *counterfeit*, *seize*, *weir* and *weird*. *Either* and *neither* can be pronounced as *ee* or *eye*, but if you prefer an *ee* sound these words, too, can be numbered with the exceptions.

## L OR LL?

Words ending in *l* or *ll* sometimes give rise to doubts when they have to be converted to other words or parts of speech. The rules and customs governing the spelling of such words have been simplified here by listing the various possible changes for selected words. This section is an extension of the notes on page 187.

| Basic verb | Past tense and past participle | Present participle | Related noun (if any) |
|---|---|---|---|
| ail | ailed | ailing | ailment |
| anneal | annealed | annealing | annealment |
| annul | annulled | annulling | annulment |
| appal | appalled | appalling | |
| apparel | apparelled | apparelling | apparel |
| appeal | appealed | appealing | appellant, appeal |
| befall | befell | befalling | |
| carol | carolled | carolling | carol |
| conceal | concealed | concealing | concealment |
| control | controlled | controlling | control, controller |
| distil | distilled | distilling | distillation, distiller |
| enthrall (enthral) | enthralled | enthralling | enthralment |
| equal | equalled | equalling | equality |
| excel | excelled | excelling | excellence |
| fall | fell, fallen | falling | fall |
| fell | felled | felling | feller (of trees) |
| fill | filled | filling | filler |
| fulfil | fulfilled | fulfilling | fulfilment |
| initial | initialled | initialling | initial |
| install | installed | installing | installation |
| instil | instilled | instilling | instillation |
| parallel | paralleled | paralleling | parallel |

| propel | propelled | propelling | propellant, propeller |
| repeal | repealed | repealing | repeal |
| repel | repelled | repelling | repellent |
| reveal | revealed | revealing | revelation |

Conversions of *–ll* adjectives to nouns include: *dull*, *dullness*; *full*, *fullness*; *ill*, *illness*; *small*, *smallness*. Although the adjectives *dull* and *full* make *dullness* and *fullness*, occasionally *dulness* and *fulness* are seen. *Dull* can also be a verb, making *dulled* and *dulling*. *Full*, too, can be a verb, in the sense of dressing cloth with fuller's earth.

The noun *instalment* has no connection with the verb *install*, instalments being periodic payments (by hire-purchase, for instance) or parts of a serial story.

The single *l* after the *e* in *paralleled* will be noted. As pointed out earlier, however, this past tense (and past participle used as an adjective) is seldom or never heard without its negative qualification, as in "unparalleled magnificence". Another interesting fact is that although the verb *propel* makes the noun *propellant*, *repel* makes *repellent*.

As a suffix for converting nouns to adjectives, *-ful*, meaning "full of", has only one *l*, and in *skilful* and *wilful* one *l* is dropped from the basic words *skill* and *will*.

There is the group of words prefixed by *al-* which is an abbreviation of *all*, as in *almighty*, *almost*, *already*, *altogether* and *always*. The fact that all these are "correct" does not mean that you can write "alright", which is all wrong. If you can remember to use *all right* you are showing your awareness of the written word.

*Wool* in British English makes the adjectives *woollen* and *woolly*. In America the first adjective is *woolen* and the second can be *wooly* or *woolly*. The dropping of one *l* where we use a double *l* is common practice in American English, to give such spellings as *equaled*, *leveled* and *traveler*, and *jewellery* is *jewelry*. More is said later about American spelling.

## -ECTION OR -EXION?

In certain nouns there is a choice between the endings *-ection* and *-exion*, some philologists defending *-exion* as being *sometimes* correct on etymological grounds. *Connection* is sometimes written *connexion*, yet "correxion" is never seen. *Inflexion* is the normal spelling, and *inflection* is acceptable. *Reflexion* is seldom seen, but *complexion* is standard. *Bisection*, *dissection* and *section* are never spelt with *x*.

## PLURALS

Most English nouns form plurals ending in *s* or *es*. There are, however, several other ways of indicating plurality, and representative lists of nouns and applicable plural endings are given below.

| Singular | Plural | Singular | Plural |
|---|---|---|---|
| *-um* | *-a* | *-a* | *-ae* |
| addendum | addenda | alga | algae |
| agendum | agenda | antenna | antennae |
| bacterium | bacteria | formula | formulae |
| corrigendum | corrigenda | lacuna | lacunae |
| datum | data | larva | larvae |
| dictum | dicta | nebula | nebulae |
| erratum | errata | | |
| gymnasium | gymnasia | *-is* | *-es* |
| medium | media | analysis | analyses |
| memorandum | memoranda | antithesis | antitheses |
| maximum | maxima | basis | bases |

| | | | |
|---|---|---|---|
| minimum | minima | crisis | crises |
| spectrum | spectra | emphasis | emphases |
| stratum | strata | metamorphosis | metamorphoses |
| | | neurosis | neuroses |
| *-on* | *-a* | synthesis | syntheses |
| criterion | criteria | thesis | theses |
| octahedron | octahedra | | |
| phenomenon | phenomena | *-us* | *-era* |
| | | corpus | corpera |
| *-us* | *-i* | genus opus | genera opera |
| bacillus cactus | bacilli cacti | | |
| focus | foci | *-a* | *-ata* |
| fungus | fungi | dogma | dogmata |
| gladiolus | gladioli | stigma | stigmata |
| locus | loci | | |
| narcissus | narcissi | *-en* | |
| nucleus | nuclei | brother | brethren |
| radius | radii | child | children |
| tumulus | tumuli | man | men |
| | | ox | oxen |
| | | woman | women |

Although the archaic **brethren** has been included in the list for illustration, the usual plural, of course, is **brothers**. Not included in the list are two *-im* plurals, **cherub(im)** and **seraph(im)**.

In the case of nouns ending in **y** after a consonant the **y** is replaced by *ies*, as in **beauties**, **cities**, **cries**, **ladies** and **skies**. After a vowel the **y** is retained and **s** added, as in **boys**, **keys**, **quays**, **trays** and **monkeys**.

Plurals of nouns ending in **o** vary in their treatment. **Cargoes**, **echoes**, **grottoes**, **heroes**, **potatoes**, **tomatoes**, **tornadoes**, **vetoes** and **volcanoes** all take **e** between **o** and **s**. Plurals omitting the **e** include **avocados**, **autos**, **dynamos**, **folios**, **radios**, and **ratios**.

Nouns of Italian origin are sometimes given their native plural form, as in *graffiti* (from *graffito*), *libretti* (from *libretto*) and *soli* (from *solo*), but the plural of *solo* is often expressed as *solos*. *Imbroglio* also is of Italian origin, but its English plural is usually *imbroglios*. French is well enough known in Britain to justify *bureaux* and *tableaux*.

Nouns ending in *f* (or *fe*) are inconsistent. Some take an ending *fs*, others *ves*, and others can take either, as shown in the following table.

| Singular | Plural | Singular | Plural | Singular | Plural |
|----------|--------|----------|--------|----------|--------|
| | *-fs* | | *-ves* | | *optional* |
| chef | chefs | calf | calves | dwarf | dwarfs |
| chief | chiefs | elf | elves | | dwarves |
| cliff | cliffs | half | halves | hand-kerchief | handkerchiefs |
| | | | | | handkerchieves |
| cuff | cuffs | hoof | hooves | | |
| gaff | gaffs | knife | knives | scarf | scarfs |
| gaffe | gaffes | leaf | leaves | | scarves |
| giraffe | giraffes | loaf | loaves | staff | staffs |
| proof | proofs | self | selves | | staves |
| puff | puffs | sheaf | sheaves | wharf | wharfs |
| roof | roofs | shelf | shelves | | wharves |
| serf | serfs | thief | thieves | | |
| tiff | tiffs | wife | wives | | |

Despite the plurals of *gladiolus* and *narcissus* – *gladioli* and *narcissi* – the plural of *crocus* is *crocuses*. Other *-us* nouns which take the *-es* plural are *circuses*, *lotuses*, *prospectuses*, *hiatuses*, *ignoramuses* and *octopuses*. For *hippotamus*, both *hippopotami* and *hippopotamuses* are acceptable, and for *rhinoceros* the plural is either the same singular word or *rhinoceroses*. *Iris* makes *irises*.

Nouns ending in *ch*, *sh*, *ss* or *x* take *es*, as in *churches*, *flushes*, *crosses* and *foxes*. (Already referred to is the exceptional *oxen*.) Nouns ending in *ix* or *ex* vary in treatment, giving, for example: *annex(e)*, *annexes*; *apex*, *apexes* or *apices*; *appendix*, *appendices*; *index*, *indexes* or *indices*; *matrix*, *matrices*. (*Annex* can be spelt with or without the final *e*.)

Three examples of nouns ending in *on* which take the plural *a* are *criteria*, *octahedra* and *phenomena*. Many other nouns ending in *on*, however, take *s*, as in *aeons*, *chameleons*, *lexicons*, *neutrons*, *polygons*, *pantechnicons* and *rhododendrons*.

Most nouns ending in *s* take *es* for the plural, even *lens* (*lenses*) and *summons* (*summonses*), which seem to puzzle many. In some cases the singular and the plural are the same word, examples being *corps*, *innings*, *mews*, *series* and *species*. Some nouns are naturally plural and cannot be given singular forms, such as *pincers*, *pliers*, *pyjamas*, *scissors*, *shears* and *trousers*.

Finally, there are those irregular and inconsistent plurals which infuriate many people but add to the rich diversity of English: *booth*, *booths*, but *tooth*, *teeth*; *house*, *houses*, but *louse*, *lice*, and *mouse*, *mice*, *noose*, *nooses*, but *goose*, *geese*, and *mongoose*, *mongooses*; *boot*, *boots*, but *foot*, *feet*.

Surnames ending in *s* can perplex people when plurals are required, but needlessly so. They should be treated as most other normal nouns ending in *s* and given *es*, so that "the Jones" is wrong and "the Joneses" is right, as also are "the Mosses" and "the Blisses". Where possessives are concerned people often get themselves into a muddle, but more is said about this in the section on the apostrophe.

One of the most serious mistakes, which is found regularly in the Press, on television and radio, is the treatment of plural nouns as singular, such as *criteria*, *data*, *media*, *phenomena* and *strata*.

## FEMININE FORMS

Where a noun is definitely masculine it can usually be converted to the feminine form by addition of the suffix *-ess*, or *-ss*, as in *authoress*, *mayoress*, *priestess*, *princess* and *shepherdess*. The basic noun is modified in the following examples: *abbott*, *abbess*; *actor*, *actress*; *ambassador*, *ambassadress*; *duke*, *duchess*; *emperor*, *empress*; *governor*, *governess*; *hunter*, *huntress*; *marquis* (*marquess*), *marchioness*; *master*, *mistress*.

It should be mentioned that although a mayoress is the wife of a mayor, and thus always feminine, a mayor need not be a man. The chief citizen not uncommonly is a woman, who is the mayor or even the lord mayor. Similarly a chairman can be a woman ("Madam Chairman"), the title applying to the office and not to the individual.

A *clerkess* is known only in Scotland, or among Scots abroad.

Besides the *ess* (or *ss*) ending there are the irregular endings shown in the following examples: *administrator*, *administratix*; *draughtsman*, *draughtswoman*; *executor*, *executrix*; *hero*, *heroine*; *rajah*, *ranee*; *testator*, *testatrix*; *tsar*, *tsarina*; *yachtsman*, *yachtswoman*.

Where there is no special feminine form of the noun, and it is *necessary* to signify the sex of the person concerned, it is usual to refer, for example, to a woman doctor, a woman painter, a woman teacher.

The femininity of some animals is denoted by *-ess*, as in *lioness* and *tigress*. Other females have special names, such as *bitch*, *mare* and *vixen*, but this is not the place for a comprehensive list.

## COMPARATIVE FORMS OF ADJECTIVES

A few adjectives have their special forms of comparatives, easy examples being *bad*, *worse*, *worst*, and *good*, *better*, *best*. The second and third words of the groups mean "more bad" and "most bad" and "more good" and "most good".

Some adjectives make their comparatives by the direct addition of *er* and *est*, as in: *hard, harder, hardest; quiet, quieter, quietest; slow, slower, slowest.*

Where the basic adjective ends in *y* treatment is variable. After a consonant the *y* is usually dropped to give, for example: *dry, drier, driest; gloomy, gloomier, gloomiest; happy, happier, happiest; ugly, uglier, ugliest. Gay,* where the *y* follows a vowel, makes *gayer* and *gayest. Shy* can follow two patterns, *shyer* and *shyest* and *shier and shiest.*

Where an adjective of one syllable ends in a single consonant after a "short" vowel the consonant is doubled to give, for example: *big, bigger, biggest; fat, fatter, fattest; hot, hotter, hottest.*

An example of a "long" vowel is provided by the adjective *far,* and here *th* is inserted for convenience of diction to make *farther* and *farthest.*

After other long vowels the final consonant stays single, as in: *clear, clearer, clearest; fair, fairer, fairest; poor, poorer, poorest.* When the long-vowel adjective ends in *e, r* or *st* is simply added, as in: *cute, cuter, cutest; large, larger, largest; rare, rarer, rarest.*

Many adjectives do not readily accept the *er* and *est* treatment, and for those it is necessary to use *more* and *most.* "The most beautiful woman" is obviously more pleasant to hear than "the beautifullest woman". Although *more pleasant* is written here, *pleasanter* would have been acceptable. *Some* adjectives, indeed, can take both *er-est* and *more-most* forms, the choice depending on euphony, rhythm and context.

Adjectives ending in *ous* refuse to accept *er* and *est*, and when Lewis Carroll makes Alice observe "curiouser and curiouser" the remark is confined to Wonderland.

## COMPARATIVE FORMS OF ADVERBS

In theory there is nothing wrong with the sentence, "James runs quicklier than John", but in practice "James runs more quickly" is smoother. The *-lier* form is archaic but may have poetic or deliberately unusual applications. Adverbs ending in *ly* almost invariably need the *more* and *most* formations.

The *-er* and *-est* formations are restricted to those adverbs *not* ending in *ly*. We should therefore say, "He runs faster" (or "fastest"), "She works harder" (or "hardest").

The independent adverb *soon* easily makes *sooner* and *soonest*; but *often* and *seldom* take *more* and *most*.

Although earlier, on the subject of adverbs, it was said that "Hold tight" was as legitimate as "Work hard" and "Run fast", "Screw it more tightly", is still preferable to "Screw it tighter". "Easier said than done" is an ungrammatical colloquialism, but trips off the tongue more smoothly than "More easily said . . ." or even "Easilier said . . .".

## NEGATIVE FORMS OF WORDS

Prefixes making negatives are applicable to verbs, adjectives, nouns and adverbs. Examples of their use are listed below, and it will be seen that in most cases (modification being noted where necessary) the prefix is simply added to the base. (Appropriate negative prefixes for *-able* and *-ible* adjectives are given in the list on page 267–8.)

| **Verbs with *-un*** | **Verbs with *-mis*** |
| --- | --- |
| unbend | misapply |
| undo | misbehave |
| undress | miscalculate |
| unfasten | misconstrue |
| unhinge | miscount |
| unlatch | misjudge |
| unmask | mislead |
| unquote | mismanage |
| unroll | misplace |
| unseat | misquote |
| | misspell |
| | misunderstand |

## Verbs with *dis-*
disagree
disarm
disarrange
discourage
disenchant
disjoint
dismount
disown
displease
disqualify
dissuade

## Verbs with *de-*
decipher
decompose
deconsecrate
decrease
defame
deform
degenerate
degrade
dehydrate

## Adjectives with *-un*
unattached
unattractive
unhappy
unnatural
unpopular
unreasonable
unremitting
unrepentant
unsteady
unwanted

## Adjectives with *-dis*
disadvantageous
disagreeable
discontinuous
disgraceful
dishonest
disillusioned
disloyal
disobedient
disorderly
displeased

## Adjectives with *-im*
immaculate
immaterial
immature
immoderate
immodest
immoral

## Adjectives with *ir-*
irredeemable
irreducible
irrefutable
irregular
irrelevant
irreligious

immovable
impermeable
impolite

irremediable
irreparable
irresistible
irreverent
irrevocable

## Adjectives with *mis*-
miscast
misled
misused

## Adjective with *-ig*
ignoble

## Adjectives with *il*-
illegal
illegible
illegitimate
illiberal
illimitable
illiterate
illogical

## Adjectives with *in*-
inaccessible
inactive
inaudible
incoherent
indecent
inefficient
inexperienced
inhuman
innocuous
insignificant

## Adjectives with *non*-
non-commissioned
non-ferrous
non-playing
non-returnable
non-static
non-stick

**Nouns with _dis-_**

disadvantage
disaffection
disagreement
disarmament
disarray
disbelief
discomfort
discontent
discredit
disgrace

**Nouns with _mis-_**

misadventure
misalliance
misconception
misdeed
misdemeanour
misfire
misfortune
misrule
misuse

**Nouns with _de-_**

decomposition
defoliation
deformation
dehydration
demerit

**Nouns with _non-_**

non-acceptance
non-aggression
nonconformist
non-delivery
non-payment
nonsense
non-starter

## ADVERBS

In the main, the same prefixes are used for negative forms of adverbs as for negative adjectives. Where possible, the suffix _-ly_ is a simple addendum, and where necessary slight changes are made to the basic forms. A final _e_ is dropped, and a final _y_ is replaced by _i_. Examples of negative adverbs (one for each prefix except _non-_) are: _**unsteadily**_, _**disloyally**_, _**misguidedly**_, _**improbably**_, _**illegally**_, _**irrevocably**_, _**inaudibly**_, _**ignobly**_.

## NOTES

In *discourage*, *dis-* replaces the *en-* of *encourage*. In *dissuade*, *dis-* replaces the *per-* of *persuade*. *Unquote* (verb) is "to close the quotation". *Misquote* is "to quote inaccurately".

Adjectives include adjectival participles. Adjectives with the prefix *de-* are excluded from the lists as they are derived from verbs which already carry the negative *de-* prefix, such as *deform(ed)* and *dehydrated(d)*.

Most *non-* adjectives at present take the hyphen, exceptions being made in the case of established words like *nonsensical*. *Non-stick* is an adjective made from the verb *stick*. *Non-* nouns taking the hyphen are of comparatively recent origin, unlike established nouns like *nonconformist* and *nonsense*. Some of the *dis-* and *mis-* nouns are also verbs.

## -ABLE AND -IBLE ADJECTIVES

As many adjectives ending in the suffixes *-able* and *-ible* can cause doubts as to which suffix to use, you will find here a selection divided into fifty of each of the two categories. The appropriate negative prefixes also are shown.

*-able*

| | | |
|---|---|---|
| in alienable | un alterable | in appreciable |
| un believable | in calculable | in capable |
| in conceivable | un consolable | un creditable |
| in curable | un debatable | in definable |
| un demonstrable | in dispensable | un eatable |
| in estimable | in excusable | in explicable |
| in hospitable | in imitable | un justifiable |
| un likeable | il limitable | un manageable |
| im measurable | im movable | in numerable |
| un obtainable | im passable | un payable |

267

im penetrable
im probable
ir redeemable
ir reparable
un serviceable
un touchable
in vulnerable

im permeable
un questionable
ir refutable
ir revocable
in sufferable
un usable
un wearable

im practicable
ir reconcilable
ir remediable
in separable
in supportable
un viable

## -ible

in accessible
in combustible
in compressible
in corrigible
in defensible
in digestible
in divertible
in eligible
in expressible
in flexible
in gullible
il legible
im passible
im plausible
ir repressible
ir reversible
in tangible

in admissible
in compatible
in controvertible
in corruptible
in delible
in discernible
in divisible
in exhaustible
in extensible
in frangible
un impressible
in miscible
im perceptible
ir reducible
ir responsible
in sensible
in visible

in audible
in comprehensible
in convertible
in credible
in destructible
in distensible
in edible
in expensible
in fallible
in fusible
un intelligible
in omissible
im permissible
ir remissible
ir resistible
in susceptible

## NOTES

*Passible* (as distinct from *passable*) means "capable of feeling or suffering". *Incorrigible* is commonly used, but its base, *corrigible* ("capable of being corrected") is seldom used.

*Invaluable* is not the negative form of *valuable*; it means "above valuation, of inestimable value".

The noun *force* leads to two verbs, *force* and *enforce*. The verb *force* leads to two adjectives, *forcible* and *forceful* – negatives *inforcible* and *unforceful*. The adjective from the verb *enforce* is *enforceable* – negative *unenforceable*.

For notes on *inflammable*, see page 213.

# PUNCTUATION

Punctuation being a matter for only written language, like the use of capital letters, it should be considered with spelling. Remarks here are confined to two punctuation marks which are intimately connected with spelling – the hyphen and the apostrophe.

## THE HYPHEN

For more details see pages 110–114.

Hyphens should generally be avoided in favour of one word or two and a modern dictionary consulted in case of doubt.

Spelled out numbers between 21 and 99, excluding multiples of ten take hyphens:

"The number is six hundred and twenty-five."

"The reaction lasted thirty-one six-hundredths of a second."

Military ranks and family relationships are generally hyphenated:

"Brigadier-General Bellingham-Smythe is visiting the barracks today."

"My daughter-in-law has her great-grandmother's name."

Hyphens are customary in some verb-based noun compounds such as: *do-gooder*, *cure-all*, *make-believe*, *runner-up*, *go-between* and *passer-by*. But others are spelled solid: *rundown*, *shutdown*, *breakthrough*, *flypast*.

Adjectives like *air-cooled*, *devil-may-care*, *far-flung*, *life-giving*, *never-ending* and *quick-acting* are always hyphenated.

Examples of fixed phrases that always have hyphens are the following:

"Joan and Bernard are having a heart-to-heart."

"We're having a get-together at my house on Friday."

"The forget-me-nots look lovely in the spring."

Such phrasal nouns as *go-as-you-please*, *give-and-take*, and the old-fashioned *n'eer-do-well* also have hyphens.

Two awkward words are *cooperate* and *coordinate*, with their derivatives *cooperation*, *cooperative* and *coordination*. The hyphen is no more justified here than in other *co-* words such as *coagulate* and *coincidence*; it may be used to avoid any suggestion of an *oo* sound, but it also produces anomalies like *unco-ordinated* and *unco-operative*. There is nothing wrong in simply writing *cooperate* and *coordinate*.

## THE APOSTROPHE

The apostrophe has two functions – to indicate possession, and to take the place, for the sake of abbreviation, of omitted letters, and for a full explanation see page 19 and pages 120–122 in Chapter 5.

# THE USE OF CAPITAL LETTERS

Spelling is entirely a matter for the written language. The use of capital letters (or upper-case in printers' parlance) is also a matter for the written language. Any study of spelling, therefore, would be incomplete without an examination of the use of capitals, about which there seems to be some confusion. Some people sprinkle capitals indiscriminately over their writing without realising how irritating the practice is to the reader. Some omit capitals when their use is justified. Some apparently think that all nouns require capitals. Some limit the use of capitals to nouns they regard as important.

For the correct use of capital letters see page 124 in Chapter 5.

# DIPHTHONGS AND DIAERESES

The definition of a diphthong has been gradually altered over the past few centuries. Even as late as the nineteenth century it was applied to a sound like *ou* in *sound* and *mouse*, which is produced by a rapid contraction of two vowel sounds *ah* and *oo*. Today, however, a diphthong (*not* "dipthong") is understood to be defined as a combination of two vowels to produce a *single* sound, which is not the same as a rapid contraction of sounds. There are now only two diphthongs in English, *ae* and *oe*, two combinations which are both pronounced *ee*. It need hardly be said that these combinations occur without the *ee* sound in numerous words, but these cases are not diphthongs and do not concern us now.

Words containing the diphthong *ae* include the following – *aegis*, *aeon*, *aesthetic*, *anaemia*, *archaeology*, *diaeresis*, (*en*)*cyclopaedia*, *haematite*, *haemoglobin*, *mediaeval* – as well as the proper names *Aegean*, *Caesar* and *Mycenae*. In *Aegean* the *Ae* is the diphthong, the *ea* after the *g* being two separate syllables.

Words containing the diphthong *oe* are less common, and seem to be largely confined to the vocabularies of science, medicine and classical mythology. They include *coelacanth*, *diarrhoea*, *foetid*, *foetus*, *oenophile*, *oesophagus*, *oestrogen*, and the names *Oedipus* and *Oenone*. It is interesting that the word *people* contains the diphthong in reverse but with the same effect. *Manoeuvre* (not an *ee* sound) is an outsider (American *maneuver*).

The Americans have discarded the diphthong *ae* in favour of a single *e* in most instances except proper names such as *Aegean* and *Caesar*, although they have retained *oe*. In both British and American English the *a* has entirely disappeared from *aether* and the *o* from *oecumenical*.

Printers sometimes use a character called a ligature which combines two letters, and among the ligatures in use are the diphthongs *æ* and *œ*.

A diaeresis (plural *diaereses*) is a mark, consisting of two dots, placed over the second vowel of a pair of adjacent vowels to indicate that it is sounded separately. The diaeresis should be used only where otherwise there may be some doubt about pronunciation. Its use in *aërate*, for example, is to be encouraged if only to act as a brake on those innumerable people who want to mispronounce the word "areate". Its use seems justified in *daïs* and *naïve*, but one could reasonably argue that *chaos* is equally deserving. Incidentally, it is curious that the feminine form of *naïve* (masculine *naif*) persists in English to cover both sexes. The noun, *naïveté*, is sometimes expressed in the anglicised form of *naïvety*.

Some proper names usually take the diaeresis where two adjacent vowels appear, as in *Aïda*, *Chloë* and *Thaïs*, but the *Brontë* family's insistence on it in the single final *e* seems to have been hardly justified when an acute accent (*é*) would have had the same effect. Sir Noël Coward used the mark only in his later years.

## AMERICAN SPELLING

The following is a list of the commoner words in which American spelling differs from British spelling.

| British | American | British | American |
|---------|----------|---------|----------|
| anaemia | anemia | analyse | analyze |
| armour | armor | axe | ax |
| behaviour | behavior | calibre | caliber |
| cancelled | canceled | candour | candor |
| carburettor | carburetor | catalogue | catalog |
| centre | center | cheque | check |
| colour | color | councillor | councilor |
| counsellor | counselor | defence | defense |
| disc | disk | dived | dove |

| | | | |
|---|---|---|---|
| encyclopaedia | encyclopedia | enrol | enroll |
| enthralment | enthrallment | equalled | equaled |
| favour | favor | foetus | fetus |
| fulfil | fulfill | gaol | jail |
| glycerine | glycerin | goodbye | goodby |
| grey | gray | haematite | hematite |
| haemoglobin | hemoglobin | honour | honor |
| humour | humor | jewellery | jewelry |
| kerb | curb | labour | labor |
| levelled | leveled | libelled | libeled |
| licence *(noun)* | license | litre | liter |
| manoeuvre | maneuver | meagre | meager |
| mollusc | mollusk | mould | mold |
| moult | molt | neighbour | neighbor |
| odour | odor | offence | offense |
| omelette | omelet | paralyse | paralyze |
| parlour | parlor | plough | plow |
| practise *(verb)* | practice | pretence | pretense |
| | *also* practise | | |
| programme | program | pyjamas | pajamas |
| quarrelled | quarreled | sceptic | skeptic |
| sceptre | scepter | skilful | skillful |
| smoulder | smolder | sombre | somber |
| storey | story | succour | succor |
| sulphur | sulfur | theatre | theater |
| traveller | traveler | travelling | travelling |
| tyre | tire | vice | vise |
| woollen | woolen | | |

As a general rule, all nouns which in British English end in *our* (such as *candour* and *humour* in the above list) end in *or* in American English. However, the following words are the same in both: *glamorous*, *meter* (instrument), *coloration*, *honorific*, *humorist*, *humorous*, *laborious*, *license* (verb), *Saviour* (in the Christian sense), *stupor* and *tremor*. In British English *pavior* (page 210) is found more often than *paviour*. The Americans use both *practice* and *practise* for the verb.

The differences between *aluminium* (British) and *aluminum*, and between *speciality* and *specialty* (American) are differences not in spelling as much as differences in the words themselves.

It may be useful here to give a list of words of which the spelling can vary in both British and American English: *cider*, *cyder*; *cipher*, *cypher*; *fantasy*, *phantasy*; *fuse*, *fuze*; *lichgate*, *lychgate*; *mortice*, *mortise*; *pygmy*, *pigmy*; *silvan*, *sylvan*; *siphon*, *syphon*; *siren*, *syren*; *sty*, *stye* (on the eyelid); *wych-elm*, *witch-elm*.

# 10

# NOTES ON SELECTED WORDS

This section of the book is a list of words intended mainly, but not wholly, as a spelling guide. There are hundreds of words, however, which, instead of condemnation to mere inclusion in a cold list, deserve comment, observation and discursive treatment. In the following pages there is a selection of such words. It is intended that this section is used with a good dictionary to hand. If you are not quite sure of the meaning of a word it is suggested you consult your dictionary. In this way you will build up your vocabulary as well as your spelling.

**abjure** The infrequency with which this word is used may perhaps be attributed to the rather horrific finality of its meaning, "to renounce, recant, retreat, or abrogate anything upon oath". It is sometimes misused in a sense of command or appeal, as in: "I abjure you to . . .", when the word to be used is not *abjure* but *adjure*.

**accept**, **except** To many people these sound alike, with the unfortunate result that "Present company accepted" is sometimes heard (instead of *excepted*).

**accessary**, **accessory** Few people seem to be aware that the legal term *accessary* (as in "accessary after the fact") is different from the word *accessory*, which is applied to a piece of equipment or a contribution.

**adapt**, **adopt** The noun from the first verb is *adaptation.* The noun from the second is *adoption*.

"We shall adopt, as our motto, 'Nil desperandum'."

"At last they decided to adopt a child."

"The play is adapted from the German."

"We could adapt the curtains to fit the windows of the new house."

Hardly anyone finds any trouble in the use of the verbs *adopt* and *adapt*. There is evidence of confusion, however, in the derived nouns *adoption* and *adaptation*. It is not uncommon to see or hear "adaption", the only fault in the use of which seems to be a lack of observation.

**adjure** See *abjure*.

**adopted**, **adoptive** When a child is *adopted* his new parents become *adoptive* parents.

**advice**, **advise**, **adviser**, **advisory** To *advise* is to give *advice*. A person who gives advice is an *adviser* (occasionally spelt *advisor*), and he serves in an *advisory* function.

**affect**, **effect** The confusion between these is not diminished by the fact that although the first is *always* a verb the second can be verb or noun. Something which has an *effect* on you *affects* you. When you achieve something, or bring something about, you *effect* it.

*Affect* is a verb, and *only* a verb. When used transitively it means "have an effect on".

"The only matter now affecting the issue is the legal right of the lessee to enter the land."

"Onions do not affect my eyes as they do other people's."

"She was visibly affected by the sad proceedings."

*Affect* can also be used intransitively to mean "pretend", but in this sense it is always followed by "to", as in:

"He affects to be a wealthy man."

"She affects to be a woman of no importance."

This meaning of *affect* gives the noun *affectation* (pretence).

*Effect* can be both a noun and a verb. Here it is as a noun:

"The effect of the speech was to electrify the audience." "Certain drugs have a soporific effect."

"Independence may have the effect of arrogance."

Here is *effect* as a verb, meaning "bring about":

"The judge said he hoped the arrangement would effect a reconciliation between the parties."

"After much heated discussion the disputants appealed to the chairman, who recommended that a compromise be effected without delay."

"Effecting the right degree of temperature in the furnace is a matter of great skill."

It should be noted that the verb *effect* is always transitive.

**affection, affectation** The first is a word for fondness, emotional attachment; the second signifies pretence, artificiality.

**albumen, albumin** The first is the white of an egg, the second a class of protein.

**align** The derivation is French (*aligner*, arrange in line), and unaccountably this form is used nearly always in preference to the acceptable *aline*. (See *gn* words.)

**all right** Always two words. See page 149.

**ambidextrous** See *dextrous*.

**amend, emend** These are not quite the same in meaning. To *amend* is to correct errors or make improvements. To *emend* is to remove errors from a book or manuscript.

**amok** You can run *amok* but not "amuck", which is a corruption. *Amok* is one of the several Malayan words in English.

**analyst, annalist** These two sound alike. An *analyst* is one who *analyses.* An *annalist* is one who compiles *annals*, or records of historical events.

**animus, animosity** The first, though literally an animated spirit, is often wrongly given the same interpretation as *animosity*, a feeling of enmity.

**ante-,anti-** The prefix *ante-* means *before*, as in *antedate*, *antediluvian* (before the flood), *antechamber*, and *antecede* (precede). The prefix *anti-* shows opposition, as in *anticlimax*, *anticyclone*, *antidote*. *Antipathy* is the opposite of *sympathy*. An *antimacassar* was placed over the back of an armchair to shield it from the effects of macassar oil with which hair was dressed.

**apogee** It is remarkable how certain scientific words have crept into everyday speech, one example being the astronomical word *apogee* – the highest point of an orbit in its relation to the earth – which is popularly used for a culmination or the highest attainment.

**apophthegm** This word is included in this section as it is such a tongue-twister. It means a terse or witty saying, a maxim. (See *gm* words.)

**aposiopesis** You may never use this word or have even heard it. It is a rhetorical term meaning a sudden breaking-off in speech for dramatic effect, a device favoured by some politicians.

**apposite, opposite** In a sense these two adjectives are antonyms (words of opposite meanings). *Apposite* means fit, apt, appropriate, so that if it is misread or misprinted as **opposite** a meaning contrary to the writer's may be given.

**archiepiscopal** Of the many words starting with *arch* this is probably the one most likely to be misspelt. The conjunction of the two vowels *i* and *e* can be confusing, and either is liable to be omitted.

**artefact**, **artifact** Archaeologists use both spellings.

**artiste** The use of the French word to describe, for example, a professional singer or dancer was an English affectation. At least it distinguishes a performer from an *artist*, a word which is properly applied to one who practises one of the fine arts.

**asphalt** This material is often miscalled "ashfalt" or even, strangely, "ashfelt". It has nothing to do with ash, and careless spellers and talkers must take careful note of the word.

**assurance** This has two connected meanings: (1) guarantee that something is true, certainty, self-confidence; (2) in a commercial sense, insurance, so that an insurance company may call itself the X Assurance Company.

**auger**, **augur** Liable to be confused. An *auger* as a noun is a drill, or as a verb the word describes the act of drilling with an auger. An *augur* is an omen, or as a verb it means to prognosticate from signs and omens.

**aural**, **oral** These two sound almost alike. *Aural* pertains to the ear, *oral* to the mouth or speech.

**balmy**, **barmy** These are very often confused. The spelling of the first should be remembered by its association with *balm*, a soothing ointment, so that it has come to mean "soft, soothing, fragrant", as in "a balmy evening". *Barm* is yeast formed in fermentation, and as its vapour is said to induce lightheadedness *barmy* has come to mean "crazy, volatile"

The correct usages are shown in the following sentences: "You must be barmy to believe everything he tells you."

"Isn't it a wonderfully balmy evening!"

(The second sentence, although couched as a question, is meant as an exclamation, and therefore receives the exclamation mark rather than the question mark.)

**bark**, **barque** I refer here to the floating kind of bark, neither the bark of a tree nor the bark of a dog. *Bark* is usually a poetic word for any ship or boat. *Barque* is a technical term for a ship of special rig.

**behest** "The darkness falls at thy behest." The lovely line of John Ellerton calls attention to a word which is now seldom used in the harsh world of commands, orders and requests.

**biannual**, **biennial** The first means "twice a year", the second "every two years".

**billion** Traditionally, a billion in the United Kingdom and many other parts of the world was a million million. In the United States and France it was only a thousand million. A few years ago it was decided, mainly by international financial interests, that henceforth a billion should be interpreted as a thousand million. Obviously, to such organisations as the oil industry and other huge businesses continental barriers do not exist, and consistency now seems highly essential.

**bonanza** A mining term for a rich ore-deposit, first used in Nevada after the Spanish word for prosperity or fair weather.

It is now applied indiscriminately to any piece of good fortune.

**boycott** In 1880 Captain C. C. Boycott made himself unpopular by evicting many of the tenants of his employer, Lord Erne, in County Mayo. In retaliation his neighbours and the other tenantry thenceforth avoided all contact with him and his family, or agreed to *boycott* them.

**broadcast** It is occasionally forgotten that the *-cast* ending in this and similar words is past tense and past participle. We hear dreadful solecisms like "broadcasted", "forecasted", but 'The sky is overcast' never presents problems.

**bucolic** In the minds of many this fine old word is associated with good cheer, hearty drinking. As an adjective, however, all it means is pastoral, rustic, and as a noun it is a pastoral poem.

**bunkum** Students of history will know that this is a corruption of *Buncombe*, a county in North Carolina, the representative of which made a speech in Congress in 1820 merely to please his constituents. His speech was so worthless that the word has clung, albeit in a different form, and has even led to the modern verb *debunk*.

**by-law**, **by-product** These are often misspelt "bye-law" and "bye-product".

**cadaver** You may not often today come across this word for a corpse, but it still has its uses and is not yet due for abolition. The adjective *cadaverous* means not only "corpse-like" but also "deathly pale".

**cannon**, **canon** Though sounding exactly the same the two are very different. A *cannon* is a big firearm. A *canon* is (1) a Church decree; (2) a general law or principle; (3) a list of works by a particular author; (4) part of a mass; (5) a member of a cathedral chapter.

**canter** Pilgrims to Canterbury rode their horses at a gentle pace called the *Canterbury*, gradually shortened to *canter*.

**canvas**, **canvass** The coarse material which is used for innumerable purposes, and on which artists paint, has one *s*, the plural being *canvases*. The verb describing a search for support (in elections, for example) has a double *s*, its other formations being *canvasses*, *canvassed* and *canvassing*.

**carat** Two meanings: (1) a unit of weight for precious stones, equal to 200 milligrammes; (2) a 24th part, so that 22-carat gold is 22/24ths pure.

**carcase**, **carcass** Alternative spellings of the same word. The plural forms are *carcases* and *carcasses*.

**carillon** Because this is a French word with a liquid *l* many people want to insert an *i* and mispronounce it "carillion".

**carnelian** Although there is an alternative spelling *cornelian,* the mineralogist spells the name of this semi-precious stone with an *a*. This spelling is more logical as the Latin derivation, *carnea*, means flesh-coloured. Another word for the same mineral is *sard*, from Sardis in Lydia, one of its ancient sources.

**causal** Often misprinted or misread as *casual*, with which it has no connection. It is an awkward adjective formed from the noun *cause*. A person addicted to its use might say: "Inflation and high wages are causal one with the other". There is an even more awkward extended noun, *causality*.

**censer**, **censor**, **censure** A *censer* is a vessel for burning incense. A *censor* is an official who examines documents in search of objectional material. *Censure* as a noun means "disapproval"; as a verb it means "to disapprove, reprimand, blame".

**charisma** One of the most abused words of modern times. It means "a divinely conferred power or talent, a capacity to inspire followers with devotion and enthusiasm". The noun, and its adjective *charismatic*, are now applied to persons whose qualifications are dubious.

**chauvinism** Napoleon's faithful soldier Nicolas Chauvin little knew how his name would be perpetuated. In his unquestioning devotion to his emperor he was accused of excessive patriotism, a sentiment which came to be called *chauvinism* in a derisory manner. The meaning has shifted somewhat to imply male supremacy, and today *chauvinism* and *chauvinist* are clichés flung about by people who know nothing about their origin.

**choir**, **quire** The pronunciation of both is *quire*, although the spelling is now nearly always *choir*. The archaism is preserved in the 1662 edition of the *Book of Common Prayer*, "In Quires and Places where they sing" (rubric after the third collect, Morning Prayer). (See also *quire*.)

**climax**, **anticlimax** The true meaning of *climax* – progression to the top rather than the top itself – is seldom appreciated, but the Greek word for ladder, *klimax*, makes it obvious. The associated adjectives are *climactic* (not to be read as *climatic*) *anti-climactic*.

**comment** As a noun this calls for no discussion. Its extended form *commentary*, however, has led to the establishment of *commentator*, the person who delivers the commentary. This has led to a verb "commentate", which is a far cry from the simple verb *comment*.

**compass** The magnetic needle indicating magnetic north is a *compass*. The instrument used for drawing circles or arcs is a *pair of compasses*.

**complacent**, **complaisant** These two words, which sound almost alike, can be confused. *Complacent* means self-satisfied, too willing to let things take their course or stay as they are. *Complaisant* means excessively courteous, obsequious.

**complement**, **compliment** It is quite common for *compliment* to be written instead of *complement*; the reverse is less common. *Complement* means the completion of something, a quantity required to make up an existing quantity to a given total. Figuratively, a well-chosen wine can be said to *complement* a good dinner. A *compliment*, as everyone knows, is an expression of courtesy, of approbation.

**comprise** This, a transitive verb, is *not* the same as *compose* or *consist*, and it is ill-treated every day. You can say "composed of" or "consist of" but *never* "comprised of". Correct use lies in the following example: "The United Kingdom comprises England, Scotland, Wales and Northern Ireland". You must *not* say: "The United Kingdom is comprised of. . ."

**contumely, contumaceous** To treat someone with *contumely* is to treat him in an insolent and reproachful manner. It is an unusual sort of noun because of its *-ely* ending, and deserves an occasional airing. The ending of the adjective is one of the standard adjectival suffixes, giving the word – despite its unpleasant association – a rich poetical sound.

**council, councillor, counsel, counsellor** A *councillor* serves on a *council*. A *counsellor* gives advice, or *counsel*. As a barrister representing a client he is called *counsel* (as in "counsel for defence"). In the United States the lawyer representing a client is a *counselor*. *Counsel* is also a verb, meaning "advise".

**credible, creditable** *Credible* means "believable" and is the opposite of *incredible*. *Creditable* means "worthy of credit".

**crevasse, crevice** A *crevasse* is a deep fissure in the ice of a glacier, or a fissure in the embankment of a river. A *crevice* is any fissure or narrow opening.

**criteria** This, though the plural of *criterion*, is sometimes misused as a singular noun, in the same way as careless people misuse *media* and *phenomena*.

**currant, current** The fruit is the *currant*. The flow of electricity, water or anything else that flows is the *current*. There is also the adjective *current* (meaning present, prevailing, as in "current prices"), from which is derived the adverb *currently*.

**cygnet, signet** These two words which sound alike refer, of course, to (first) a young swan, and (second) a seal (not the aquatic kind).

**dalmatian** The dog, originally native to Dalmatia, is not a "dalmation".

**data** It must be remembered that this is the plural form of the noun *datum*, so that you must say "these data".

**decimate** Originally this meant to kill one in ten, but corruption has led to its present association with general massacre.

**dependant**, **dependent** These words are often confused, the greater tendency being to use *dependant* for *dependent*. *Dependant* is a noun, being someone or something dependent on someone or something else. *A dependant* is a person who depends on another for support.

"As a married man and a father I have several dependants who look to me for support."

*Dependent* is an adjective meaning "depending on something or someone".

"He is dependent on me."

"The *Daily Reflection* is independent of party, creed and sectional interests."

"The prisoner was described as of independent means."

**deprecate**, **depreciate** Literally, to *deprecate* is to try to avert by prayer, but it has come to mean "to express disapproval of something, to plead earnestly against, to regret". *Depreciate* means "to fall in value", but this meaning has been stretched somewhat to include "disparagement". As expression of disapproval can be equated with disparagement there are senses in which the two verbs can be interchanged, and they are often confused because they can be very similar in meaning. Consider this sentence:

"The City Architect deprecated the tendency of the Works Department to allow famous buildings to get into bad states of neglect."

2

The City Architect could have been either praying against the tendency – that is, wishing that the tendency was absent – or disparaging it. In this case, therefore, either *deprecated* or *depreciated* could be used with similar effect.

If, instead of praying for our enemies (as morally we should), we pray against them we *deprecate* them, just as we deprecate all the things we should not pray for – war, disease, famine, suffering. Yet often *deprecate* (or one of its derivatives) is used instead of *depreciate* (or one of its derivatives), as in the following two examples:

"Self-deprecation is a virtue of the humble-minded."

"The chairman, publicly deprecating the committee's rash action, rose and left the room."

Ask yourself the meaning of each sentence.

Does the first mean that the humble-minded pray against themselves or disparage themselves? They are not likely to pray against themselves, and the obvious meaning is that they disparage themselves. The correct expression, then, is "self-depreciation".

In the second sentence, is the chairman praying against the committee's action or disparaging it? He is certainly disparaging it, so that the word should be "depreciating".

*Depreciate*, in one sense, means disparage. In another sense, of course, it means decline in value, but then it is used intransitively, as in: "The value of the machine depreciates by 20 per cent, each year, and will thus be written off in five years."

**depute** The noun *deputy* is well enough known, and so is the verb *depute* ("appoint as deputy"). This word is included here in recognition of its Scottish use as a synonym for *deputy*, as in "depute treasurer", with the emphasis on the first syllable.

**derring-do** "Deeds of derring-do". What a strange expression! The original form of this, *dorrying don*, "daring to do", is attributed to Chaucer, but apparently it was interpreted by Spenser as a noun,

***derring doe*** (without the hyphen), and in this form it has been assimilated into the language as an expression for desparate courage.

**desiccate** It is tempting to misspell this as "dessicate".

**dextrous**, **dexterous** These are variants of the same word, the first (the commoner) form being a contraction of the second. ***Dexter*** means "pertaining to or situated on the right-hand side", and in heraldry it signifies a position on the right of the shield (the viewer's left). ***Dexterous*** originally meant "right-handed", but now means "skilful with one's hands, adroit, clever". The associated noun is ***dexterity***, and a person who can use both hands with equal facility is ***ambidextrous***.

**didactic** If you are lecturing someone, perhaps unconsciously, you are being didactic. The word is no longer applied to true teaching, and many people resent didacticism in others.

**dietician**, **dietitian** Both spellings are accepted.

**digit**, **digital** The Latin ***digitus*** has come a long way from its original meaning of ***finger***. Because people counted on their fingers ***digit*** was applied to numbers under ten. When the new mathematics first appeared the word was impounded and then adopted by the computer wizards. Now we have digital computers, digital clocks and digital watches.

**dilapidate** Usually encountered in the adjective ***dilapidated*** and the noun ***dilapidation***, which are often misspelt "delapidated" and "delapidation".

**dilettante** This word, of Italian origin (the final ***e*** pronounced with an accute accent), refers to a lover of the arts but more particularly an amateur who toys with several interests.

**diphtheria** Common mispronunciation usually makes this "diptheria". Remember that the *p* is followed by *h*.

**diphthong** *Not* "dipthong".

**discomfit**, **discomfort** These two are very often confused. *Discomfit* is a verb, meaning "to defeat, put to rout, frustrate, thwart" (see *rout*). Its noun is *discomfiture*. *Discomfort* as a noun (its usual form) is the opposite of *comfort*; as a verb it means "to deprive of comfort, cause uneasiness".

**discompose** Not to be confused with *decompose*. Meaning "to disturb the composure of", it is the opposite of *compose*, so that you could say: "Don't discompose yourself".

**discreet**, **discrete** These adjectives are explained on page 222. *Discreet* means "circumspect in speech or action; tactful and trustworthy" or "unobtrusive". Its associated noun is *discretion*. Discrete means "distinct, discontinuous, detached, separate". Its associated noun is *discreteness*.

**disinterested**, **uninterested** There is some misunderstanding about these two, which do *not* mean the same. *Disinterested* means "neutral, without prejudice, unbiased, impartial, unselfish, not caring one way or the other". *Uninterested*, the direct opposite of *interested*, is more vehement than *disinterested* and implies the holding not of an impartial view but of a definitely negative view.

**dissect** Remember the double *s* here. With a single *s* the word would be *disect*, an obsolete form of *bisect*.

**disassociate**, **dissociate** As these two verbs mean the same, the second and shorter one is preferable. It is easy, however, to flounder over the spellings, and the positions of the letter *s* must be noted.

**draconian** Adjective originally applied to harsh punitive measures directed against the Athenians by the legislator Dracon about 620 BC. Now used generally for any severe imposition.

**egoist**, **egotist** These are not quite the same, although in effect they can be. An *egoist* is a self-centred person, while an *egotist* (a word which appeared after *egoist*) is one who talks about himself excessively.

**elicit**, **illicit** These two similar-sounding words can trap the unwary. *Elicit* is a verb meaning "extract", as in: "You must elicit the information". *Illicit* means "unlawful, not permitted".

**eligible**, **illegible** These are easily confused. *Eligible* means "suitable, fit or deserving to be chosen, qualified to apply" (perhaps for an appointment). *Illegible* means "unreadable".

**embarrass** This is sometimes misspelt with a single *r* on the analogy of *harass*.

**emend** See *amend*, *emend*.

**emigrant**, **emigrate**, **immigrant**, **immigrate** An *emigrant* is a person who leaves his country to *emigrate* to another country. An *immigrant* is the opposite, a person who *arrives* in a country, or *immigrates*, with the object of settling there.

**enquire**, **inquire** See *inquire*, *enquire*.

**ensure**, **insure** These are not the same. *Ensure* means "to make sure" of something. *Insure* means "to pay a premium against the possibility of misfortune", and leads to the nouns *insurance* and *assurance*. See *assurance*.

**entrepreneur** This is given several shades of meaning by the French, who apply it even to a funeral undertaker. In English an entrepreneur is a middleman, an agent, a contractor, one who undertakes an *enterprise* (note the similarity) in the hope of making a profit.

**envelop, envelope** The verb is *envelop*, the noun *envelope*.

**epicure** The trouble about words coined from people's names is that the people themselves are often forgotten. Epicurus, an Athenian philosopher who died in 270 BC, taught the virtues of perfection, of the highest taste in one's choice of pleasure, especially the pleasure of food. Hence someone who is extremely particular and delicate in his eating habits is an epicurean.

**erupt, irrupt** These can understandably be confused. To *erupt* is to break through violently, as in a volcanic eruption, or burst out. To *irrupt* is the opposite, to burst *inwards*, so that an *irruption* is an invasion from outside, perhaps by the enemy.

**esoteric** If this adjective is seldom used it may be because it is just what it is – esoteric. The word means "restricted to the initiated, not generally intelligible".

**etiolate** An attractive verb with unattractive associations. It means "to blanch", and is applied to plants which turn white if kept in the dark and to people who become unhealthily pale.

**eupeptic** Despite its esoteric appearance this adjective has quite an earthy meaning – pertaining to, or having, a good digestion.

**euphemism, euphuism** Each of these can be misused for the other. A *euphemism* is a delicate expression for something that could be offensive, or a polite way of saying something. A *euphuism* is a pedantic affectation of elegant, high-flown and would-be witty language.

**euphoria** One of those words which sleep for a long time and are then suddenly rediscovered and overworked. Generally it is used partly in its proper sense of a feeling of well-being, but the fact that the feeling has to be based on over-optimism is often overlooked.

**except**, **accept** See *accept*, *except*.

**exculpate** This verb, meaning "to free from blame", has been largely superseded by *exonerate*.

**exiguous** A pleasant adjective (meaning small, slender) which deserves to be more popular.

**exotic** Simply this means "foreign, attractively strange or unusual, introduced from abroad". It does not necessarily have any romantic associations, but it has been known to be confused with *erotic*.

**factitious** Although a different word from *fictitious* this bears some resemblance to it in appearance and in meaning ("artificial, not genuine, contrived").

**farther**, **further** In general there is little distinction between these, although a choice may lie in the context. *Further* is exemplified in "At the further end of the room" and "A further reason exists". *Further* is also a verb, as in "To further his own ends". *Farther* is more suitable in the sentences: "Manchester is farther from London than Bristol" and "The sound went farther and farther away".

**ferment**, **foment** These are often confused. *Ferment* is the verb to describe the chemical process known as *fermentation*. To *foment* is (1) to apply a hot poultice or dressing – a *fomentation* – and (2) to encourage, to promote, as in "foment a revolution".

**filibuster** Originally a noun of Dutch and Spanish origin meaning "freebooter", or one who engages in unauthorised warfare against a foreign state, this is now applied to one who tries to obstruct legislative proceedings by prolonged speaking. It is also used for the act itself ("a filibuster on the part of Mr X"), and has given rise to a verb *to filibuster*.

**forbear**, **forebear** People often confuse these two similar words. **Forbear** (verb, accent on the second syllable) means "to abstain or refrain from doing something, to be patient". A *forebear* (noun, accent on the first syllable) is an ancestor.

**forgo**, **forego** These are confused far too often. *Forgo* means "to deny oneself, to abstain, to decline" ("I decided to forgo the pleasure of her company."). It has a past tense *forwent*, a present participle *forgoing*, and a past participle *forgone*. *Forego* means "precede" ("go before"). It has a past tense *forewent*, a present participle *foregoing*, and a past participle used as an adjective in (for example) "*foregone* conclusion".

Very frequently *forego* is wrongly used instead *of forgo*, as in: "Will you promise to forego your half-holiday if I grant you this favour?" Here, *forego* should be *forgo*.

Perhaps the reason for the error is the fact that *forego* in its correct sense has fallen into disuse. There are so many other *fore-* words that people may forget that *for-* words exist as well. *Forget* is one of them.

**former**, **latter** If you *must* use these words remember that they can refer to *only* one of two items. If you are listing more than two items, the correct and logical expressions are *the first* and *the last*.

**fuchsia** Any doubt as to the spelling of the noun describing this flowering shrub should be dispelled by the realisation that it was called after the sixteenth-century German botanist L. Fuchs.

**furore** Many people seem to be rediscovering this old Italian word without, however, giving it the full value of its three syllables, *fur-or-ay*. If it is limited to two syllables it loses much of the force of its meaning of "great excitement or enthusiasm".

**further**, **farther** See *farther*, *further*.

**gamble**, **gambol** These have a similar sound, except for the slight emphasis of the *o* in *gambol*. The first is understood; the second is associated with spring lambs.

**gipsy**, **gypsy** Alternative spellings. The second is preferable as these wandering people are believed to have originated in *Egypt*.

**gm words** There are no English words starting with *gm*, but there are several containing the combination. *Paradigm* (listed later) is one of those in which the *gm* occurs at the end, in which case the *g* is silent. It is silent in *phlegm*, but sounded in *phlegmatic*. It is silent in *apophthegm* (listed earlier), but sounded in *apophthegmatic*. In *dogma*, where the combination does not fall at the end, the *g* is sounded, as it is also in *dogmatic*. The same construction is seen in *enigma (enigmatic)* and *magma (magmatic)*.

**gn words** There are several words starting with *gn* (such as *gneiss*, *gnomon*, *gnu*) in which the *g* is silent. Where the *gn* falls within a word the *g* is usually sounded, as in *bigness*, *cygnet*, *malignant*, *signatory*, *signet*, but an exception is *physiognomy*, where the *g* is silent. Where the *gn* falls at the end of a word it is silent, as in *align*, *deign*, *feign*, *impugn*, *malign*, *reign* and *sign*.

**griffin**, **gryphon**, **griffon** A *griffin* is the same as a *gryphon*, a fabulous creature with an eagle's head and wings and a lion's body. A *griffon* is (1) a kind of vulture, and (2) a coarse-haired breed of dog.

**grisly**, **gristly**, **grizzly** Three adjectives liable to be confused: (1) causing horror or dread; (2) applicable to meat; (3) grizzly bear.

**gubernatorial** A curious adjective meaning "of a governor". As the two words are from the same Latin word for *governor*, *gubernator*, there is no reason why we do not say "governatorial" or "gubernor".

**harass** Unlike *embarrass*, this has only one *r*.

**haywire** "It's all haywire", we say. Apparently the wire for baling hay was often used in attempted makeshift repairs to various kinds of farm equipment, but sometimes the result was a confused tangle of wire – hence our idiom.

**hers** This possessive pronoun does not carry the apostrophe.

**hoard, horde** The first is applied to things, as in "hoard of gold". Originally a *horde* was a tribe of Turkish clansmen, and the noun has come to be applied in a derogatory sense to a multitude of people, as in "hordes of tourists".

**homogeneous** This is sometimes misspelt and mispronounced as "homogenous", perhaps on the basis of "homogenised milk".

**hubris** A word used by some writers, ignored by others, and possibly skipped by readers who have no time to think about it. It is a Greek word for insolent pride or presumption, and in Greek tragedy its indulgence inevitably led to an unfortunate fate.

**hypercritical, hypocritical** To be *hypercritical* is to be excessively critical of something. To be *hypocritical* is to exhibit *hypocrisy*, a pretence of virtue.

**illegible, eligible** See *eligible, illegible*.

**illicit, elicit** See *elicit, illicit*.

**immanent, imminent** Two distinct words. *Immanent* means "inherent, in-dwelling". If an event is *imminent*, it will happen very soon.

**immigrant** See *emigrant, emigrate, immigrant, immigrate*.

**inflammable** See page 213.

**influenza** This common word is included merely because of its interesting derivation from Latin through Italian and Spanish. Its first recorded appearance in Europe was apparently in 1510, when the disease was attributed to the *influence* of the stars.

**ingenious**, **ingenuous** These two words, often confused, have no etymological connection. *Ingenious*, associated with the noun *ingenuity* and with *engineer*, means "inventive, good at organising, or specially skilful". As a "switched" adjective it can be applied to something which is the *result* of ingenuity, such as "an ingenious device" or "an ingenious explanation". *Ingenuous* means "open, frank, innocent, artless", and its noun is *ingenuousness*.

**innocuous** A trap for spellers. Note the double *n* and the single *c*.

**inoculate** On the strength of *innocuous* it is tempting to double the *n*, but the temptation must be resisted.

**inquire**, **enquire** These are broadly alike in meaning, but *enquire* usually conveys a meaning of simply asking. Which to use is a matter of personal choice, but *inquire* is the more common, just as *inquiry* seems to be more favoured than *enquiry*, especially in the case of an investigation.

**insure**, **ensure** See *ensure*, *insure*.

**interregnum** Literally this is a period between two reigns, and the double *r* would be more obvious if the two parts of the word were separated by a hyphen. Besides periods between reigns of monarchs the word is applied to intervals between service periods of two governments or two functionaries. It has now come to be used, not always strictly correctly, for a suspension of operations, a pause.

**invalid** As sometimes occurs in English, the two meanings of this word have different pronunciations – "*in*valid" (noun) for the unwell person, and "in*val*id" (adjective) describing something of no weight, force or cogency, the opposite of *valid*.

**invidious** This is a word used by people who may not know its meaning and use it in the wrong sense. Literally it means "envious", but it has two other interpretations – (1) tending to provoke envy or ill-will, and (2) offending through real or apparent injustice. In short, it is rather a vague word and is better left alone. Anyone who says "My position was invidious" probably could not explain what he meant.

**invite** This is a verb. Those people who use it as a noun instead of the musical *invitation* have no defence.

**isthmus** This is hard to pronounce and awkward to spell.

**its**, **it's** The instructions relating to these two little words cannot be repeated too often. The possessive *its* never has an apostrophe. The abbreviation *it's* for *it is* needs the apostrophe.

**jejune** This is included here because of the unconscious wish of some people to connect it with the French *jeune*. It has nothing to do with youth, its meaning being (1) "meagre, scanty", and (2) "devoid of interest in life, depressed".

**latter**, **former**. See *former*, *latter*.

**lay**, **lie**, **laid**, **lain** (See page 45.) The common misuse of these words makes grammarians prematurely grey. You can *lay* something down, and a hen *lays* an egg. In the past tense, you *laid* it down and the hen *laid* an egg. You **lie** on the bed (present) and you *lay* on the bed (past). You must never say "I *laid* down" but you can say "I *laid it* down". You must never say "I was *laying* down" but you can say "I was *lying* down" and "I was *laying it* down". You must never say "I went for a *lay*-down" but you can say "for a *lie*-down". If A lies under or over B, B is *overlain* or *underlain* by A – *not* "overlaid" or "underlaid". *Overlay* and *underlay* are nouns – thus a coverlet or a veneer is an *overlay* – and as verbs can be used in the past tense as in "The carpet overlay the floor".

**liaison** There is a tendency to omit the second *i* in the spelling. It is regrettable that the noun has led to a colloquial back-formation verb *liaise* (make liaison) (followed by *with*), the use of which, though sometimes convenient, is not to be encouraged.

**licence, license** In British English *licence* is the noun and *license* the verb. A *licensed* house can have a seven-day *licence*. The landlord is the *licensee*. In American English both noun and verb are *license*.

**lineal, linear** These two demand to be confused. *Lineal*, an adjective, means "to be in the direct line of descent or ancestry", and gives the noun *lineage*. *Linear*, also an adjective, means "to be in line or on line", giving such expression as "linear perspective", "linear extent". It is applied also to two related forms of ancient writing in Crete and Greece, Linear A and Linear B.

**loath, loathe, loth** Three similar words often presenting doubt. *Loathe* is a verb, so that you can detest or hate something. *Loath* is an adjective, meaning "unwilling or reluctant". *Loth* is another form of *loath*, and is used mainly in the strange idiom, "nothing loth". "When asked if he would like a holiday, Jim, nothing loth, accepted the offer."

It is quite common to find *loathe* and *loath* confused:

"I loath travelling by train" (instead of *loathe*).

"Though loathe to leave home, he went abroad to seek work" (instead of *loath*).

*Loathing* is a present participle often used as a noun, as in: "He viewed the scene with loathing".

**magniloquent** A splendid word combining "magnificent" and "eloquent", defined as "lofty in expression". Used in an oratorical sense it may convey a suggestion of boastfulness.

**marquess, marquis** These are the same, spelling being dependent on the personal preference of the holder of the title. His wife is a *marchioness*.

**mat, matt** One of our illogicalities is that while we now favour *net* instead of *nett profit* we cling to a *matt surface* despite the legitimacy of *mat*.

**media** Readers must never be guilty of the common error of treating this noun as singular. It is, of course, the plural form of the noun *medium*.

**miscible** There is nothing wrong with the adjective *mixable* from the verb *mix*, but as it is a back-formation from the older *miscible* (itself from a Latin root) the second is rather more acceptable and, in science, is the standard word. The negative form is *immiscible* and the noun *miscibility*.

**moot point** It is a mystery that so many people say "mute point" when the two words *moot* and *mute* are utterly different. A *moot point*, something to be debated, discussed and pondered over, derives its name from the Anglo-Saxon town assembly, or court of justice, which was a *moot* or *mote*, while the meeting-place was the *moot hall*. There should be no doubt about *mute*, which simply means "silent".

**mortice, mortise** Applied to a lock, a joint or a chisel, either spelling is acceptable but the second (with *s*) is more common.

**nadir** An astronomical word (opposite of *apogee*) which has passed into normal speech. It is the point of the heavens directly opposite the zenith, and the word is used popularly for the lowest possible attainment, the place or time of greatest depression.

**naphtha** Common mispronunciation and misspelling often turn this word into "naptha". Remember that the *p* is followed by *h*.

**naught, nought** Both mean "nothing". *Nought* is the numerical expression of the figure 0, while *naught* is used mostly in an archaic or poetic way, as in "set at naught", "bring to naught".

**net** As an alternative to *nett*, this has become the standard spelling in Britain as it is in America.

**news** This is now singular, although in many nineteenth-century writings you will find it used as a plural, as it is in French (*les nouvelles*).

**noisome** Unless it is realised that this adjective has nothing to do with noise doubtful spellers may want to insert an *e*. The word means "hurtful, noxious, offensive, disgusting", the essential point being that the thing *annoys* (from Middle English *noy*).

**nought, naught** See *naught, nought*.

**onomatopoeia** This is a favourite trap in spelling games, a tendency being to misspell the final syllable as "-aeia" or "-eia".

**oral, aural** See *aural, oral*.

**orient** As noun, *Orient* means, geographically and with a capital O, The East. Oriental means "eastern or pertaining to The East". As a verb, *orient* means (1) to place something in a known relation to the cardinal points, and (2) to determine one's position in such relation. The noun from the verb is *orientation*, and this has unfortunately led to a back-formation verb "orientate" which is a modern and clumsy form of the verb *orient*.

**ours** This possessive pronoun does not carry an apostrophe.

**outwith** A Scottish form of *outside*.

**overlook** This can be an ambiguous verb. Your house can overlook the sea, you can overlook mistakes, you can overlook instructions, and as a superintendent you can overlook (oversee) somebody's work.

**overly** One of the less pleasant American words which should be avoided; an unnecessary extension of *over*, as in *overly anxious*, *overly luxurious*.

**paean** A cheerful noun from the Greek, originally meaning "a choral song addressed to Apollo" (one of whose names was Paian), but now given wider application to include any triumphant song ("a paean of praise").

**paradigm** A word sometimes used irritatingly by people who delight in superior mystification. It means a pattern, an example, a model, and, in grammar, a table of different forms taken by a particular word. (See *gm* words.)

**parameter** One of those scientific words which have wandered into the ordinary speech of people who misuse them. In mathematics a parameter is described as "a quantity remaining constant for a particular case". In popular usage it seems to have various vague applications, one being to describe a framework on which to hang ideas, another a prescription of limits surrounding a set of conditions.

**peninsula** This is the noun. The adjective is *peninsular*, which some people think is the noun.

**perpendicular** To many this means "vertical", and to architects it represents a style of architecture. Geometrically, any line at right-angles to any other line, or any plane at right-angles to any other plane, is *perpendicular* to it, though it need not be vertical.

**phenomena** You often hear "this phenomena", but this word is the plural form of the singular noun *phenomenon*.

**phlegm**, **phlegmatic** See *gm* words.

**phosphorus** Some people seem to have a compulsion to spell this noun *phosphorous*. There *is* such a word, but it is an adjective. (See page 233.)

**piteous**, **pitiable**, **pitiful** The person who *pities* is full of pity and therefore *pitiful*. The object of his pity, or the condition of the object, is *piteous* or *pitiable*. "A pitiful sight" is therefore nonsense.

**pn words** In words like *pneumatic* and *pneumonia* that begin with *pn* the *p* is silent.

**portentous** This adjective (from the noun *portent* and the verb *portend*) is often misspelt and mispronounced as "portentious", perhaps in the mistaken belief that it should rhyme with *contentious* and *pretentious*.

**potation**, **potion** There is some similarity between these. A *potation* is a draught, a beverage, the act of drinking. A *potion* is also a draught, but is usually medicinal.

**practicable**, **practical** Although the meanings are not quite the same the difference is sometimes negligible, and if you use one where the other would be more suitable nobody will be shocked. *Practicable* means "capable of being effected". *Practical* has several associated meanings, but the best are perhaps "efficient" and "suited to conditions". The solution to a problem or course of action can be practicable. A person, method or tool can be practical. An idea can be either.

**practice**, **practise** In British English *practice* is the noun and *practise* the verb. In American English *practice* is both, but *practise* also is occasionally used as a verb. It is odd that the verb is applied not only to training, or learning, or trying one's skill, but also to the carrying-out of a profession. The noun has two meanings corresponding with those of the verb; thus, a doctor conducts a *practice,* and acquisition of a skill needs *practice*.

**practitioner** As everyone knows, this noun is applied to a person who practises a profession, or who conducts a professional practice. The ending probably developed when it was realised that the word *practiser* did not cover a wide enough field; thus, anyone constantly practising upon a musical instrument would be a *practiser*, not a *practitioner*.

**pragmatic** One of those words which are constantly on some people's lips – especially politicians' lips – whether or not they understand it. It has several associated applications, the commonest being to the learning of practical lessons from history and to the judging of matters according to their practical significance. A *pragmatic* approach to a problem is one which should yield the most practical result. Its associated noun is *pragmatism*.

**premise, premiss** The words, pronounced similarly, both refer to a proposition laid down, assumed, or proved, from which another is inferred. The plurals are *premises* and *premisses*, the first of which is applied to buildings and adjoining land.

**prescribe, proscribe** To *prescribe* is to lay down or impose authoritatively, or, in a medical sense, to advise on a course of treatment or medicine. To *proscribe* is to prohibit, to reject, to publish the name of something as doomed or condemned, to outlaw, to banish, to forbid or to denounce as dangerous. Thus, an organisation or a publication can be proscribed by a government, an authority or anyone else who considers it is dangerous, subversive or seditious. By modern general usage, however, there is no implication that the proscribed organisation or publication must cease to exist.

**prestidigitator** This, a favourite word for spelling-bees (literally "one who is quick-fingered"), is merely a long and pretentious word for a conjuror and has nothing to recommend it.

**principal, principle** These two words have been responsible for countless erasures and alterations. If you want to use the *adjective* remember that the right word is that containing *a*: *principal*. Unhappily the same word is applied as a noun to the head of a college, a leading actor, a capital sum creating interest, and an authority who gives orders. *Principle* is always a noun, and refers (for example) to a fundamental philosophy, a doctrine, a rule of action or law, and a code of behaviour.

**prophecy, prophesy** The noun is *prophecy*, as in "He makes a prophecy", or, in the case of the plural, "He makes prophecies". The verb is *prophesy*, as in "He will prophesy" or "He prophesies". The related adjective is *prophetic*.

**proven** This form of the past participle of the verb *prove* is an alternative to *proved*. It is no longer commonly used, but is still applied, for example, to wills. In Scottish law a verdict of "not proven" in a criminal trial is permissible.

**ps words** There are many words in English starting with *ps* but with an *s* sound. All are of Greek origin, and some examples are: *pseudonym*, *psoriasis*, *psychiatry*, *psychic* and *psychology*.

**pt words** Some *pt* words (silent *p*) are: *ptarmigan*, *pterodactyl*, *Ptolemy* and *ptomaine*.

**pusillanimous** An alternative adjective for faint-hearted, cowardly, lacking strength of purpose.

**putative** You may not hear or see this very often, but it is a good adjective meaning "reputed, supposed, commonly regarded as".

**quash** An abstract verb meaning "to annul, make void, suppress", often confused with the verb of physical action, *squash*.

**quasi-** This prefix is growing relatively popular. Meaning "seemingly, not really, almost", it finds application in such expressions as *quasi-cultural*, *quasi-international*, *quasiscientific*.

**quire**, **choir** See *choir*, *quire*. Apart from its choral association, a *quire* is a quantitative paper measure (twenty-four sheets, *or* a set of four sheets folded into eight leaves).

**rarefy** This verb, meaning "to make rare, less dense", is not "rarify". It makes two nouns, *rarefaction* and *rarefication*.

**receipt** Besides its usual sense of acknowledgment of payment, this is an old-fashioned term for a culinary *recipe*. Dr Samuel Johnson introduced the *p* into *receipt* in his *Dictionary* of 1755, but strangely kept to *conceit* and *deceit*.

**recipe** See *receipt*.

**refuse** The two senses of this word have nothing in common except the spelling. Even the pronunciations differ.

**remonstrance** Noun from the verb *remonstrate*, but much more. The Grand Remonstrance was the statement of grievances presented by Parliament to Charles I in 1641, and subsequently the word *remonstrance* by itself has been sometimes applied to any set of public grievances.

**renege**, **renegue** Alternative spellings of the same word. Although it is the verb associated with the noun *renegade*, the noun is heard far more often.

**reset** This frequently appears in reports of Scottish legal proceedings. It is both verb and noun, meaning "to receive stolen goods" and "the act of receiving".

**resin**, **rosin** Two nouns meaning almost the same, except that *rosin* is usually applied to the solid form of the tree secretion *resin*.

**reverend**, **reverent** The first means "worthy of veneration", and when used as a title for clergymen is usually abbreviated to "The Revd". It should never be used for the surname alone, as in "The Revd Jones", but with a Christian name or some other title as in "The Revd Silas Jones" or "The Revd Dr Jones". Without the title a clergyman should be addressed as "Mr Jones". *Reverent* means "feeling or showing reverence", the opposite being *irreverent*.

**rh words** In words starting with *rh*, such as *rhapsody*, *rheostat*, *rhetoric*, *rheumatic* and *rhombus*, the *h* plays no part in the pronunciation.

**rhododendron** The ending of this Greek word is *-on*, not (as many people mispronounce it) "-um".

**rhyme**, **rime** *Rime* is an archaic, almost obsolete, form of *rhyme,* and is also a word for hoar-frost.

**rout**, **route** A *rout* in the eighteenth century was an evening party, or assemblage. It is also applied to the disorderly defeat of an army, as in "put to rout". As a verb, meaning "to dig out", it is used in gardening and in woodwork, a *router* being a special groove-cutting tool. A *route* is a course taken to arrive at a destination.

**scrumptious** Originally applied to anything which was considered to be first-class, stylish or excellent, this adjective now seems to be confined in its use to the description of delicious food.

**semantics** The study of the meanings of words. The late entrance of the noun into the common vocabulary may be due to its absence from some older reputable dictionaries. It is one of those words which enjoy phases of popularity; some politicians (who have adopted it almost as their own), when confronted by something not to their liking, are apt to dismiss it with: "It's just a matter of semantics".

**sentient** Worth inclusion in this section as it is an expressive word seen occasionally, meaning "having a sense of feeling". A sentient person should thus be a sympathetic person.

**separate** It is a common mistake to write "seperate", "seperating" and "seperation", perhaps because the *a* in the middle is usually an indistinguishable sound.

**sequacious** It is a pity that this archaic word is seldom seen, for it is truly expressive, meaning "lacking independence or originality, showing inclination to follow in a servile way".

**sergeant, serjeant** *Sergeant* is the military or police rank. *Serjeant* is applied to official functionaries such as Common Serjeant, Serjeant-at-Arms.

**series** Both singular and plural.

**sheriff** Despite the frequency with which this word has been used in the past and is still used, in surroundings as far apart as ancient British cities, Sherwood Forest and the American West, some people want to give it a double *r* and a single *f*.

**signet, cygnet** See *cygnet, signet*.

**sinister** This, the opposite of *dexter*, originally meant *left* as opposed to right, so that in heraldry anything on the left of the shield (the viewer's right) is *sinister*. The ancient association of the word with evil has no obvious explanation.

**sovereign, sovran** Alternative spellings of the same word, but the second is practically obsolete.

**species** Both singular and plural.

**spoil, spoliation** *Spoliation* (wartime plundering, robbery or destruction) is the noun of the verb "to spoil" or "to despoil". Some people imagine that it is a corrupt form of "spoilation", but this is not so. **Spoil** is the word at fault, as the Latin verb is ***spoliare***.

**stile, style** A *stile* is (1) part of a door-frame, and (2) the device that helps you to cross a fence. A *style* is (1) a manner, collective characteristics, and (2) an ancient writing instrument.

**subtle** There is no satisfactory explanation for the *b*-less pronunciation. Sometimes you hear a pronunciation *subtile*, and although it is meant to be facetious there is, oddly enough, an archaic word of this spelling which means the same as *subtle*.

**sumptuary** Though connected with *sumptuous* in derivation this adjective has only a remote connection with it in meaning. It pertains to the regulation of expenditure, particularly state or official expenditure, so that a "sumptuary law" should have restrained anyone's desire for a sumptuous feast, for example.

**sumptuous** Originally, anything sumptuous was not only costly but it showed evidence of extravagance. Now, of course, it is applied mainly to feasting, as in "a sumptuous repast". It is often confused in spelling and pronunciation with *scrumptious*.

**supererogation** A difficult word to pronounce, meaning "doing more than duty requires". The adjective is even more difficult – *supererogatory*.

**supersede** There is no logical reason why this should not be spelt with a *c* to make it conform with *concede*, *intercede* and *recede*, but this is one of the delightful inconsistencies of English spelling. The related noun is *supersession*.

**surrogate** A noun for a deputy or substitute, especially in an ecclesiastical sense. For example, a parish vicar or rector, as a *surrogate* of his bishop, is authorised to grant marriage licences without the reading of banns.

**swingeing** Present participle of the verb *swinge*, which is seldom heard. It is etymologically connected with *swing*, as the verb originally meant "to beat or strike with a swinging motion". It is now used in such senses as "swingeing taxation", "swingeing cuts", meaning taxation or cuts having the effect of a heavy blow. To distinguish it from *swinging* it is pronounced with a soft *g*.

**symposium** This interesting word may not be generally appreciated as the equivalent of the Greek word for *banquet*. The philosophers of ancient Greece observed the friendly custom of preceding a debate or a learned discussion by a convivial party, but in more mundane centuries the word has come to be applied, rather regrettably, to the discussion itself.

**tawdry** This common word has had such a bizarre history that it deserves inclusion in this section. The foundress of Ely Cathedral in the seventh century (according to the Venerable Bede writing in the eighth century) was Etheldreda, wife of King Egrid, whose name was corrupted to Audrey, later St Audrey. The inhabitants of the Isle of Ely instituted an annual fair, known as St Audrey's Fair, where cheap jewellery, gaudy trinkets and showy lace – St Audrey's lace – were sold. Apparently the lace was so terrible that its adjective was applied to anything in bad taste and of little value, and the description *St Audrey's* was corrupted to *tawdry*. In *The Winter's Tale* Mopsa says to Clown: "Come, you promised me a tawdry-lace and a pair of sweet gloves."

**tenterhooks** A tenter is a frame on which cloth is stretched to dry. A tenterhook is a hook for attaching the cloth to the frame. By obscure association to be *on tenterhooks* is to be in a state of suspense.

**tenuity** This delicate word conveys a suggestion of slimness, slenderness, and its adjective – used more often – is *tenuous*, as in "The tenuous relationship between the two sciences..."

**terminology** Noun applied to the correct use of terms, or words, giving the adjective *terminological*. Mr (later Sir) Winston Churchill in a speech in 1906 said: "It cannot in the opinion of His Majesty's Government be classified as slavery . . . without some risk of terminological inexactitude".

**terrestrial** Dozens of people asked to spell this word would spell it "terrestial".

**theirs** This possessive pronoun does not carry an apostrophe.

**their**, **there**, **they're** Of these three, which sound alike, only the first two are liable to be confused in spelling. The third (a contraction of *they are*) is usually understood.

**threshold** A single *h*. Contrast *withhold*.

**tinker's cuss** This *cuss* is probably different from the colloquial corruption of *curse.* It was probably the metal patch with which the tinker repaired pots and pans. "Not worth a tinker's cuss" means "almost worthless", and if his *cuss* was a curse why should *his* curse be different from the curse of any other honourable tradesman?

**tortuous**, **torturous** The first, meaning "twisted, winding, crooked", is sometimes confused with the second, which means "causing torture, cruel".

**trauma** One of those words which somebody discovers, others pick up and use too often, other people misuse, and eventually, from fatigue, retires into oblivion. It is a medical noun signifying a wound or external injury, and now its meaning can include severe shock. In popular speech, however, it is used as a noun for anything unpleasant, the adjective being *traumatic*, as in "traumatic experience".

**uninterested**, **disinterested** See *disinterested*, *uninterested*.

**verisimilitude** The length of this word may account for the fa that it is seldom used. The nearest approaches to its meaning are "probability" and "likelihood", but its actual meaning is "the *appearance* of truth" or "resemblance to reality". Sir W. S. Gilbert's lines in *The Mikado* are famous: "Merely corroborative detail, intended to give verisimilitude to an otherwise bald and unconvincing narrative."

**vicar, vicarious** The close connection between these two words has been forgotten. *Vicarius* in Latin means "a substitute", and, very briefly, the vicar of a parish was a substituted incumbent, or one who performed his ecclesiastical duties on behalf of somebody else, perhaps a religious house or an individual. The adjective *vicarious* thus means "substituted"; for example, a parent can vicariously enjoy his son's success, or anyone watching a lunar film can be a vicarious astronaut.

**victuals, victualler** *Victuals* are provisions, and the *victualler* is the person who supplies them. The accepted pronunciations – "vittles" and "vitteler" – may owe something to the Old French *vitailles*, although this word is obsolete.

**vilify** The adjective *vile* makes the verb *vilify* (with the *e* replaced by *i*) and the noun *vilification*.

**waive, wave** Although these sound alike, *waive* (forgo, relinquish, not insist on) is used much less frequently than *wave*.

**while** This word is used in parts of the north of England, especially Yorkshire, to mean *until*. This use can lead not only to ambiguity but also to danger. Somebody might instruct a child: "Do not cross the road while the light is green".

**who's, whose** The first is an abbreviation of *who is* or *who has*, as in "Who's the best man?" and "Who's got the job?" The second is the possessive form of *who*, as in "Whose is that hat?" and "The guards, whose duty it was to protect them . . ." The similar pronunciation leads to confusion and misspelling. Incidentally, **whose** is often used instead of **of which the**, despite the fact that **who** is a **personal** pronoun.

**wistaria**, **wisteria** Gardeners and gardening books differ about the spelling, but it does not matter as the American scientist after whom the climbing plant is named spelled his name in two ways, **Wistar** and **Wister**, before he died in 1818.

**withhold** It is easy to forget the second *h*, but the pronunciation should aid memory. Contrast **threshold**.

**wont**, **won't** "According to his wont" means "According to his custom or habit". **Won't** is a contraction of **will not**. It should be "willn't" (like **didn't**), but has been corrupted to its accepted form perhaps because it rhymes with **don't**.

**your**, **you're** Occasionally these are wrongly interchanged. **Your** is the possessive form of **you**, and **you're** is a contraction of **you are**. **You've** as a contraction of **you have** cannot be confused with anything.

**yours** This possessive pronoun does not carry an apostrophe.

# INDEX

**A**

Abbreviations 84–5, 122, 168
Adjectives 21–2, 80, 93, 111–12,
    134–5, 166
    , verbal 37
Adverbs 22–3, 134–5, 251–2
"All" 56, 64
    right" 149
"Also" 77
American spelling 272–4
"An" 142
"And/or" 168–9
Apostrophe 19–20, 63, 66, 120–2
Articles 22, 141
"As" 28–9
    from" 167–8
    regards" 163–4
    to" 163–4
"Assuming" 151–2
"At about" 142
"Attain" 145
"Averse from" 149

**B**

Brackets 74, 109–10, 118–20
"Build, to" 170
"But" 24–5, 26–8, 147

**C**

Capital letters 22, 124–6
"Centred" 160
"Christmas" 149
Circumlocution 26, 80
"Circumstances" 141
"Chart"/"Charter" 138
Clause 23

Clichés 161–2
Colon 97–9, 108
Comma 74, 85 et seq., 106–8
Commercial English 162–3
"Compare" 143–4
Complement 48
Compound adjectives 80, 114–15
    sentence 71 et seq.
    subject 49
    verb 18
    words 110–11
Conditional 33, 42–3, 135
Conjunctions 23–9, 73
"Convince" 160
"Could" 40, 42–43

**D**

Dash 74, 115–18
Definite article 22
Diaereses 271–2
"Different from" 145
Digressions 81
Diphthongs 271–2
"Disinterested" 160
"Due to" 138–40

**E**

"Each" 129–32
"Either" 54–5, 63, 64, 133–4
Ellipsis 35, 49–50, 166
Enumeration 87–9, 93
"Every" 64, 129
Exclamation mark, 101–3, 109
Exclamations 32, 101–3
"Extended tour" 146–7

**F**
"For" 28
"Former, the" 164–6
Full stop 83–5, 106–8
Future tense 33, 39–42

**G**
"Great Britain" 175

**H**
H, silent 22, 142
Hyphen 80–1, 110–14, 118, 269–70

**I**
Idiom 17
Imperative 33, 44
Imperfect 36
"Include"/"Including" 137–8
Indefinite article 22, 142
Infinitive 33–4
    , split 34–5
Interjections 32, 101–3
Intransitive 45, 70, 71
Inverted commas 103
"It" 65
Italics 126

**J**
"Judging" 152

**K**
"Kind, those" 141–2

**L**
Latin abbreviations 168
"Latter, the" 164–6
"Lay" 45–7
"Learn" 147–8
"Lend" 147
"Lie" 45–7
"Little" 169

"Loan" 147
"Lost to" 167

**M**
"Messrs" 172
Moods, verb 33
"Moot point" 149

**N**
"Neither" 54–5, 63, 64, 133–4
"None" 54, 64
Nouns 18–20
    , collective 48, 121
    , proper 18, 121
Numerals 82, 93

**O**
Object 45, 70–1, 127–8
Omission marks 123–4
"Only" 76
"Open" punctuation 84
"Ought to" 145

**P**
Padding 81
Paragraphs 77–82
"Parallel with" 143
Parenthesis 74, 81, 89–91, 116–18
Participles 36–9, 150 *et seq.*
Parts of speech 17–18
Past tense 33, 36
"Persuade" 160
Phrase 23
Plurals 19, 48–9, 54, 132–3, 170–2, 257–60
Possessives 19–20, 62–3, 66, 121–2, 170
Predicate 69–70
Prefixes 112–13
Prepositions 29–31, 142–3
Present tense 33, 35–6

"Promise" 144
Pronouns 51 *et seq.*
  , demonstrative 52–7
  , indefinite 64–6
  , interrogative 61–2
  , objective 71
  , personal 51–2
  , possessive 62–3
  , relative 57–61
  , subjective 71
Punctuation 83 *et seq.*

**Q**

Question mark 99–101, 108–9
Quotation marks 103 *et seq.*
Quotations 93–4, 98–9, 103 *et seq.*
  , interrupted 109–10, 123

**R**

"Reason" 140–1
"Right here" 148–9

**S**

"Scotch"/"Scottish"/"Scots" 172–3
Scottish usage 173–4
Semicolon 94–7, 108
Sentences 67 *et seq.*, 136–7
  , compound 71 *et seq.*
  , simple 25, 33
  , starting 24–5
"Shall" 39–42
"Should" 40, 41, 42–43
"Since" 28
Singular 48–9, 132–3
"Some" 56–7, 64
Subject 45, 67, 69–70, 127–8
  , compound 49
Subjunctive 33, 43–44
Syntax 75–6

**T**

"Teach" 147–8
Tenses 33
"That" 41, 52, 58–61, 148
"Times greater than" 146
"To be" 48–50
Transitive 45, 70, 71
"Try and" 145–6

**U**

"Uninterested" 160
"Used to" 144

**V**

"Verbal agreement" 160
Verbs 20, 33 *et seq.*, 67, 142–3

**W**

"What" 61, 62
"Which" 58–61
"Who" 57–8, 61, 128–9
"Whom" 57–8, 128–9
"Whose" 57, 58, 129
"Will" 39–42
"With regard to" 163–4
"Would" 40